A-Rafting on the Mississip'

The Fesler-Lampert *Minnesota Heritage* Book Series

This series is published with the generous assistance of the John K. and Elsie Lampert Fesler Fund and David R. and Elizabeth P. Fesler. Its mission is to republish significant out-of-print books that contribute to our understanding and appreciation of Minnesota and the Upper Midwest.

The series features works by the following authors:

Clifford and Isabel Ahlgren

J. Arnold Bolz

Helen Hoover

Florence Page Jaques

Evan Jones

Meridel Le Sueur

George Byron Merrick

Grace Lee Nute

Sigurd F. Olson

Charles Edward Russell

Calvin Rutstrum

Robert Treuer

CHARLES EDWARD RUSSELL

A-Rafting on the Mississip'

University of Minnesota Press

MINNEAPOLIS • LONDON

First University of Minnesota Press edition, 2001

Every effort was made to obtain permission to reproduce
copyrighted material used in this book. If any proper
acknowledgment has not been made, we encourage
copyright holders to notify us

Published by the University of Minnesota Press
111 Third Avenue South, Suite 290
Minneapolis, MN 55401-2520
http://www.upress.umn.edu

A Cataloging-in-Publication record for this book is available from
the Library of Congress.

Printed in the United States of America on acid-free paper

The University of Minnesota is an equal-opportunity
educator and employer.

11 10 09 08 07 06 05 04 03 02 01   10 9 8 7 6 5 4 3 2 1

PREFATORY NOTE

MEMORIES of a boyhood on the Mississippi have been liberally reinforced for this attempt to chronicle an odd chapter in the history of American development and the rise of a gigantic American industry.

The great period of the lumber business and of the raft, which nearly coincided with the great period of the Mississippi steamboat, was inscribed in memorials that were competent and well ordered even if little heeded by the generality of mankind. Often those that saw this vivid epoch were moved to write of it and to write well.

First among them was George Byron Merrick, who for many years kept a card index of all the steamboats on the upper river and brought to their recording a mind insatiable of detail and an almost singular appreciation of the dramatics of commerce. He was not only a notable historian himself but the cause of much history writing by others. A cloud of witnesses confirmed and supplemented him before it was too late. Under his inspiration, or because of his appeals, many old-time river men were jotting their reminiscences. To all of them as to him I am indebted.

Loyalty to their early love is the badge of all their tribe. Even when he had pitched his home so far away as Alabama, Mr. A. D. Summers, who used to go with the rest of us down to the old mill to swim from a raft, dwelt in his soul by the waterside. Year in and year out he collected material about this queen of all the streams

v

of all the earth, about her wayward career, about the men that had served her, and this he most generously made available for the present venture.

One of the master chroniclers of the great old times is Captain Fred A. Bill of St. Paul, long an executive officer of the Diamond Jo Packet Company and before that of varied experiences on the river. With care and unflagging interest he has garnered information from all sources about life and doings in the vanished heyday. It was he that collated and gave to the world the diary of Stephen Hanks, invaluable to every inquirer about the settlement of the upper Mississippi basin, and it was he that induced William Cairncross to write his strange and adventurous career on three rivers. He it was also that wrote the best description extant of the scenery of this Ganges of the New World, dealing with it as an understanding devotee, a student, and an artist.

All of these resources might have more or less failed me but for one other great gift of fortune. For more than forty years one man, Mr. J. W. Murphy, has published at Burlington, Iowa, a remarkable weekly newspaper. "The Burlington Post" is its name, and worth remembering. It has been printed to uphold good causes and sanely to impart knowledge, but incidentally to gather and to preserve all current notes of permanent value concerning the great river. It was in the "Post" that for three years Captain Merrick published his "Steamboats and Steamboat Men," the mine inexhaustible of treasure for all that wish to know what navigation really was in the days when the inland rivers fed the national life. It was in the "Post" that Captain Bill printed Hanks's diary and many other vital matters, and it was to the "Post" that the old river men, scattered over the world, contributed from the full stores of their memoirs. For many months I

Prefatory Note

was a burrower in the files of this useful publication, and now that my work is done I find myself parting from it with regret but also with a sense of grateful obligation as to a good friend.

But in a different way, whosoever has sailed on the Mississippi and known in his heart the witchery and joy of it, has stores of his own that he does not derive from and could not well share with another. Of all things connected with or suggesting the river, whether these be logs or lumber or rafts or Renwick's Pier or Cat Tail Slough, of all news about the river and all experiences and adventures along and around the river, he will hear or read always with avidity, but his own incommunicable glorying is in the sights and sounds that come back to him whenever he will let them. For then he will hear played at him from the limestone cliffs the deep melodious music of the old *Minnesota's* whistle, and then he will see again Frontenac in the earliest morning or Trempealeau sleeping in the red sunset, and so maybe with profit to his soul brood the more upon the river of his memories, dreams, and love that is so like to an epitome of his own existence, flowing out of the mystery above into the mystery below.

C. E. R.

NEW YORK, May, 1928.

vii

AFTER A SMASH

*Raft boat "James Fisk, Jr.," reassembling the fragments of a raft
that had hit an island*

CONTENTS

ix

ILLUSTRATIONS

Illustrations

A-Rafting on the
Mississip'

Chapter I

THE BAD MEN FROM BLACK RIVER

THAT hot, sun-flooded, breathless afternoon, when the Mississippi below us was all polished gold and blue and the town was mostly asleep, the women folks of our house had gone in a skiff bargain-hunting to Port Byron and my grandfather and I were left alone. Down in his den on the riverside he was silently at work, but whether concreting his next sermon or mending West Rambo's best trousers, I was to guess. Either would have been within the lines of his habitual endeavors, for on Sundays he was the preacher of the Baptist church of Le Claire and on week-days the town tailor. The preaching he did chiefly for the love and joy of it. At times we had reason to think that the tailoring proceeded upon a like basis of economics.

I had that afternoon an engagement elsewhere and one of importance; but for a singular reason I was not keeping it. With Stump McKane, Butch Tinker, Art Dawley, Bill Hillbourne, and Happy Day I had signed up to play scrub on the bottom of the old stone quarry; instead of which here I was, close prisoner, mewed in a stuffy house on one of the best afternoons for scrub that a boy ever saw. Not that I was laid by the heels for misdeeds. The truth is, I was afraid to go abroad and equally afraid to let anybody know I was afraid.

3

A - Rafting on the Mississip'

A Black River raft was tied up just below my grandfather's house.

The explanation will seem now lame and impotent, but to me in those days it was as good as the law. True enough, a raft moored below my grandfather's house was no novelty. Many rafts found harborage there; rafts from the Chippewa River, from the St. Croix, from the far regions of the Mississippi, from the Wisconsin,[1] from many places with names unknown—and doubted if they had any. Let it hail from whatsoever port, a raft made fast to our peaceful shores would stir sober citizens to uneasiness and fill us children with vague alarms. Experience had somewhat overtutored the world of the law-abiding in the ingenious deviltries of raft crews; yet were there gradations in guilt. Raftsmen from the Chippewa, the Wisconsin, from any other stream might be violent, crapulous, reckless, and boisterous; by common consent they were not without a human substratum. Only raftsmen from the Black were known to be always the true sons of perdition of the rip-roaring branch of the family tree. With them, according to general belief, rafting was but a diversion; the real business of their souls was battle, murder, and sudden death.

"A Black River man would as soon stab you as look at you," said old Deacon Conduit, who kept the hotel and had been three times to St. Louis.

Everybody agreed that this was sound judgment, and it was of record that when a Black River raft was signaled the Widow Fowler invariably hid her spoons.

Thus Black River had become for all that part of the West a kind of Bitter Creek. All the men from Black River were bad men; the farther up the river you went the worse they were. Those that visited Le Claire were believed to be from the headwaters. No doubt

[1] In local speech at that time always "Wisconse."

4

they had of this ill name more than they earned. I remember that when the general store at Rapids City was entered and robbed all the country-side needed not to be told that a crew of Black River men were the villains, although it was afterward proved that the robbers were only imitators of those "banditti of the prairies" once historic in the Middle West. A daring hold-up one night on the Davenport Road came near to bring Black River to its lowest repute until a local journalist discovered that it was only a joke played by drunken soldiers from Camp McClellan. Simple computation would have shown that if the Black River raftsmen had really done all the evil laid to their charge they would have had no time to work rafts or attend to other business, but it can hardly have escaped notice that arithmetic and hysteria are no bedfellows. A slight reaction was started for a time by the Larkins incident. Old Man Larkins had long and notoriously mistreated his pretty young wife. When she eloped and Larkins went about ascribing her dereliction to Black River the town laughed behind its hand. I forget what new outrage returned us to low pressure. I think it was the burning of Judge Cook's barn, which was well-known to be Black River and no mistake.

It will be seen that at the age of nine, and with the weird imaginings of childhood assailing me, the Black River raftsmen that rode the nightmare through my troubled dreams galloped apace upon a pavement of substance, particularly after that man's body, full of stab wounds, came ashore below the old lime-kiln. By some mischance, I was playing mumble-peg back of Dave Carr's fence and not twenty feet away when they took it up, naked and blue and horrible. Black River again. No, I thought I would not play scrub that afternoon. To reach the old stone quarry I must pass the length of the Black River raft tied up there, and the belief was unanimous in my gang that raftsmen, making war upon all mankind, had a special grudge against boys. As witness the case of Johnny Gordon, fresh in my mind.

But the reason I was afraid to let any one know I was afraid was of another color. My grandfather was as fearless a man as ever stood in shoe leather. Nothing on the face of the earth or in the waters under could daunt him. In a region rather ill-reputed for violent weather, he would climb upon the porch in the midst of the most terrifying thunder-storm that he might have a better view of the lightning; and as for men, he feared nothing that walked, drunk or sober. In some way he had discovered or divined my terror about raftsmen and applied to it the medicament of ridicule, in which he had a pretty gift. Thereafter, I communed alone with my fears.

The unwonted stillness of the empty place hung weights upon my spirits; the blue fly sang in the pane that afternoon, if ever. There was an abominable old clock over the fireplace, a clock with a red moon looking down upon a green sea. It ticked more loudly than any other clock I have known and seemed to have more ticking to do. I do not know if the fact in nature has been generally noticed, but nothing else makes so much noise as a ticking clock in an otherwise silent house. An electric riveter on a steel beam construction is by comparison soothing and restful. In these conditions I was rapidly accumulating a case of fidgets. For relief I got down the first volume of my grandfather's "Cassell's Illustrated History of England" to look at the pictures, and had gone as far as the spirited portrayal of Boadicea leading a charge upon the detested Romans, when I was aware that some one was knocking at the back door, and there popped back into my mind the case of Johnny Gordon.

6

The Bad Men From Black River

Johnny was older than the rest of us, but still counted as one of our gang. He worked summers for Waldo Parkhurst, the grocer, and only the afternoon of the very day before he had gone aboard that Black River raft to deliver purchases. A man was lying behind one of the raft shanties, and Johnny, never noticing because of the things he was carrying, stepped on his foot. The man jumped up with a yell, and then Johnny was scared, for he saw that the man was crazy drunk. So he dropped his baskets and ran, and the man ran after him with a long-handled boat-hook. Johnny was making the better time and likely to get clear, when the man threw the boat-hook and the point hit the fugitive in the leg. So he jumped overboard and made to shore and hobbled up to our house crying, and there was an ugly gash in his leg that my grandmother tied up. And that was a Black River raftsman.

So now with somebody knocking on the back door, the whole of that story fell upon me and I judged that the man with the boat-hook had come to take revenge on us because we had harbored Johnny and fixed up his leg. Of course, it might be only Stump McKane to see about that scrub game (although Stump's usual approach was no farther than the back alley and signified by yells), or it might be Mis' Corey, come to return the six fresh eggs she borrowed the last time she had company up from Keithsburg; but with the resolute pessimism of the fearful, I argued for the worst. Now, the back door was bolted that afternoon. I happened to know, because I had bolted it myself, not being quite sure that even so the place was safe from possible assault; and what might come if I unbarred it I shivered to think of. On the other hand, I knew that if I called my grandfather he would scorn me for a coward and then discover about the bolted door, which was against his wishes. This, on the whole, seemed the overweighing

7

terror, and the pounding on the portal growing louder, with a trembling hand I pulled the bolt and nearly fainted. There stood a group of raftsmen and of course they were from that Black River raft.

I think I started to run and the first man called me back.

He was tall and spare, I remember, with long dark mustaches and a red face. All his companions ran to bone and angles and were notably tall, or seemed so to my morbid fancy. Also, the first man had a prominent Adam's apple, and for years afterward I never saw a man with that style of throat architecture that did not start in me a sense of dismay. All the band had big black slouch hats which they held in their hands (as a sign of amity, I think) while they mopped their foreheads with red handkerchiefs. Some had red handkerchiefs tied around their necks.

I have no doubt I registered the extremity of terror, for I remember the leader softened his 4 A.M. voice and plainly essayed to look pleasant.

"Sonny," he said, or something like that, "kin you get us a sight of the elder? We need him right bad—an' we ain't goin' to hurt nobody."

" 'Deed we ain't," said the others.

I managed to steer my quaking legs to a place whence I could make my grandfather hear.

He came at once, probably noticing something unusual in the husky and quavering noises I made with my dry larynx. At a glance he seemed to size up the situation, had the cutthroats into the living-room, and asked them to sit down. Then he fetched out the buttermilk and asked what he could do for them. I remember distinctly that they sat forward upon the edges of their chairs, and the first aid to my shaking soul came in the queer discovery that they were as uneasy as I was. It appeared that there was a man on the raft that had

8

been taken powerful bad and wanted a parson, and it looked as if he was going to slip his lines right soon, and would the elder come and say a prayer or something?

The elder arose with alacrity, took his Bible in one hand and me, voluble with protests, by the other, and started for the Black River raft, sink of iniquity.

A plank ran from the up-river end to the shore. We teetered across, I being still far from confident that we were not walking to our deaths. Two or three shanties stood in the middle of the raft. The sick man lay in one of these on a pile of blankets. He was dying of a stab wound.

My grandfather opened his Bible and read a chapter, the chapter that contains the passage about "Come unto me all ye that labor and are heavy laden"; I remember that well. The men stood about with their hats off and their heads down. At the end, he knelt to pray, and, what seemed to me incredible, some of the men knelt too. I saw them do it—saw them, no doubt, with bulging eyes. He prayed aloud, and when he finished and said "Amen" the raftsmen said "Amen" after him. I heard them say it. When we started homeward one of the men walked along with us and talked with my grandfather. I remember hearing him say that the sick man was his partner and I wondered what kind of business the two were engaged in. Just before we reached the plank this man asked if he might give me something. He asked it in a way that puzzled me, because it was as if he were afraid of my grandfather. Then he took from his trousers pocket a knife and gave it to me; not a common jack-knife, as one might expect, but, curiously enough, a small pearl-handled knife such as a woman might use about her needle work. My grandmother always insisted that he had stolen it. Then he reached down and gently patted my

hair and smoothed it. He had a great black beard and it
was all smelly with tobacco and whisky. When we were
on shore I looked back and the man had gone out to
the end of the raft and was sitting alone on one of the
big oars. I nudged my grandfather and he saw him too,
and then turned about and did not look any more.

After that I was not afraid of Black River raftsmen
nor of any others. When a raft tied up in front of my
grandfather's, instead of moving toward the cellar, I
went down to the shore and sat on the rocks to watch
the raftsmen and listen to their singing. Next to dancing, and ahead of quarreling, singing was their choice
for joy. They had a wide répertoire, too; all of it, with
one exception, their own, I think, for I have never met
with it since. It appears that the edge of the general
criticism of raftsmen was softened with an admission
that they sang well.

To be without fear of raftsmen was to win distinction in the eyes of all my fellows; even Stump McKane
was afraid of the Black River breed. But having by
this crude schooling learned that they were not to be
feared, I was slowly drawn to them as the strangest
and most interesting human beings I had ever seen, and
from that queer threshold went by the back door into
a great and still uncelebrated chapter of the American
development and the story of a marvelous industry.

A million volumes on our library shelves celebrate
the romance of war or of adventure. Often the romance
of business seems to be as exciting, always it is more
reasonable and human, and yet it remains largely un-
heralded. In all of its variations in all this wide world,
there could hardly have been another phase of it like
to this. There could hardly have been another instance
where a commerce grew so swiftly to such colossal pro-
portions, where it was carried on among so many vicissitudes and hazards, or where it played so important a

part in determinative history. For it was this business
that built the true American Empire, that enabled a
desert to be transformed into a vast park, and made the
change so quickly that now the mind can hardly keep
pace with its magic. How a part of the Great West
was wrested from the British, a part from the Indians; how it was settled in a desperate conflict with
savage men and savage conditions—these things have
been fully told. What has not been recorded, so far as
I know, is that the agencies of the settlement, more
important than guns or fighters, were the raft and the
raftsman.

Besides, and what comes home to the main purpose, it
was a business carried on in regions and ways that produced types of men, good men, bad men, different from
any others on this continent and well worth a place in
the human record.

It is strange to reflect now that for centuries a great
part of the flat plain outstretched from the western
slope of the Alleghany Mountains to the eastern slope
of the Rockies had been undergoing a chemical process
that perfectly fitted its soil to be the world's granary.
With exceptions to be noted hereafter, it was, from
what is now the western line of Indiana to the bases
of the Rockies, prairie land. Grass, the universal and
indomitable grass, covered it thickly, summer after summer; grass and bewildering flowers. Every few years,
when the frost had killed and the sun had dried this
riot of lush herbage, fire swept the plains; fire started
by the Indians in their hunts, fires started carelessly
from their camps, or otherwise; but fires. The annual
growth of grass amassed a thick, rich, greasy black soil
upon the original yellow clay left after the glaciers had
departed; the fires impregnated the black soil with the
salts needed for perfect grain-growing.

A large part of this almost inconceivable domain of

riches we acquired from France by the Louisiana Purchase, and traces still remain of the bold beginnings of settlement made by the French in their tenure. As early as 1788, Julian Dubuque and ten of his compatriots had a village on the site of what is now the city that bears his name, and French trading-posts had been pushed up the Mississippi, the Minnesota, and other streams right into the heart of the region populated by what we are told were the most savage and perilous of Indians; hob-a-nob with the fierce Winnebagos and fiercer Sioux. Even then the French had that marvelous *savoir-faire* that has since made them the most successful colonizers in the world. Even then they could live among red as among black, brown, or yellow men without shooting them, and it is to be noted without enthusiasm that in all the wars between Whites and Reds on the North American Continent, the Whites were of our own speech. The French traded with the Indians but did not bring war upon them.

The first consequential American explorer of the purchased region was Captain Pike, Zebulon Montgomery Pike, a name that seems scantly hung with the historic laurels it deserves. He was of the stock of the Revolution, in which his father had been one of the heroes; he himself was a brevet lieutenant-colonel in the United States army when he was only twenty years old. In 1806 he was sent to discover the sources of the Mississippi, and led an expedition of keel-boats that in eight months and twenty days, through adventures that pass imagination, penetrated to the headwaters and returned to St. Louis. His report on his labors is the classic of American exploration.

After the War of 1812 had determined the nationality and redeemed the independence of the United States, the Government established three military posts on the upper Mississippi—Fort Snelling, near what

is now the city of St. Paul; Fort Crawford, near what
is now the city of La Crosse; Fort Armstrong, on what
is now the great arsenal station of Rock Island. The
first steamboat that ascended the upper Mississippi, the
celebrated *Virginia*, in 1823, went to carry supplies
to Fort Snelling.

From 1816 on, American pioneers pushed into the
new country to trade with the Indians for furs and
lead, but it was not until the treaty with the Sacs and
Foxes and the end of the Blackhawk War that the
gates swung open to this illimitable garden.

As a means to obtain other people's lands, the Blackhawk War was one of the most perfect devices ever
known to man. Some of its other aspects may be differently esteemed. In the history of national morals
it is not to be forgotten, since it was the first notable
triumph of American imperialism and the example
upon which other successes in that line have been more
or less patterned. As it is also basic to the present narrative, pardon me if I run over its outlines.

The Sacs and Foxes were allied and related tribes
that lived in the basin of the Rock River but also
held lands on both sides of the Mississippi from the
Wisconsin to the Missouri. It appears from the records
that they were peaceable and had (for Indians) a
rather unusual tolerance for agriculture, so to call it.
In 1804 the United States made with them a treaty
that came subsequently under a liberal bombardment
and was fashioned with a certain skill for which before
long we became justly famous. It provided that the
Indians should give up their lands in the Rock River
basin and move to the west side of the Mississippi.

The validity of this covenant was always doubtful.
According to the version of the settlers and the War
Department, certain chiefs of the Sacs and Foxes, au-
thorized to do so, assented to the bargain and bound

13

their people to it. According to the version of Black-hawk, a white man had been killed by a Fox Indian and the slayer had been arrested and was imprisoned at St. Louis. The Indians had a custom by which blood guilt could be compounded by heavy payments, and were unenlightened about an eye for an eye and the rest of the white man's refinements. Certain chiefs went to St. Louis, sought the American commandant, and offered their remission payments for the offense of their friend. The commandant told them that what he wanted was land. They agreed to give him tracts on both sides of the Mississippi. On this composition the Indian slayer was released—and then shot dead as he left his prison.

Blackhawk said that the chiefs that signed the treaty had first been made drunk.

If precedent be any indication, Blackhawk's account seems the truer to form, at least. On all sides the title must have been regarded as fly-blown, because in 1815 a new treaty was negotiated with some of the Sac and Fox chiefs, which aimed to ratify the compact of St. Louis. For a year Blackhawk and all his band refused to sign or be bound by it. In 1816 they were brought into it, reluctantly and with many misgivings. It appears from Blackhawk's own account that his untutored mind had now acquired an impression that the white man was lacking in scrupulous rectitude.

Whichever version of the treaty incident may be right, and nobody is now likely to find that out, one thing is plain enough. In both of the bargains it was stipulated that the Indians were to remain in possession of their lands until those lands should have been sold to actual settlers.

Chief Blackhawk and his band lived in a village at the junction of the Rock and Mississippi rivers, a village that had existed on that spot for 150 years. The

The Bad Men From Black River

Indians had an almost passionate, and doubtless foolish, attachment to a dwelling-place that they had long occupied. Their fathers were buried on that spot, and all that kind of thing—so absurd to our better intelligence. In 1826, while Blackhawk and the able-bodied men of his band were away on a hunting expedition, a party of whites appeared in the village, seized and fenced in the Indians' corn-field, and took possession of Blackhawk's lodge.

When the Indians returned, the white settlers refused to heed Blackhawk's indignant protests and held to the lands they had taken. This condition lasted until the next year, the whites holding and tilling the Indian lands. In the following winter, the Indians being again gone hunting, the whites burned all the Indian lodges, forty in number. When the hunters returned and protested this action, the angry whites kicked them off the premises.

The Indians seem to have shown rather more patience than was to be expected of mere savages. They now planted new ground and tried to resume their usual ways of life. The next spring, when they returned from the winter's hunt, they were met by government agents, who notified them firmly that they must abandon their new-made homes and trek to the west side of the Mississippi. The barbarous red men asked for a reason. They were told that their lands had been posted for sale. For sixty miles around there was excellent and unoccupied land. None of this had been offered for sale; only the exact site of the Indian village had been placed on the market.

Article Seven of the treaty contained this provision:

"As long as the lands which are now ceded to the United States remain their property, the Indians belonging to said tribes shall enjoy the privileges of living and hunting upon them."

None of this land had been sold: it had only been offered for sale.

Blackhawk declined to abandon his claim until he had consulted with white men that he felt he could trust. He went to Detroit and saw General Cass and others. They told him that until he should sell his land he had an undoubted right to remain upon it and advised him to return and hold quietly to his possession and his rights.

The braves went hunting as usual that winter, and before they returned in the spring the squaws had planted the corn crop. When the hunters arrived the government agent at Fort Armstrong notified them to move across the Mississippi or troops would be sent to deport them.

Meanwhile the whites plowed up the corn that the squaws had planted. When the squaws protested the whites beat them.

This seems to have been about all the Fox blood would stand, and Blackhawk notified the white settlers to get off the land they had seized or he would drive them off.

The old adage about the bully must have grown out of inter-racial clashings. A meeting of the settlers drew up a memorial picturing their fearful state, about to be murdered in their beds by hordes of bloodthirsty, marauding savages. This they sent post-haste to the governor of Illinois, assuring him that a great Indian uprising was at hand and they must have help or perish.

The governor responded by calling out seven hundred militiamen.

These, with ten companies of regular troops, overawed Blackhawk and carried him and his people across the Mississippi.

A promise had been extorted from him that he would remain where he was put. The next year, with his band,

16

he left his camp, which was near the present city of Fort Madison, paddled up the Mississippi to the Rock, and was proceeding up the Rock, when General Atkinson, the commandant at Fort Armstrong, ordered him to return. He replied that he and his people were on a peaceful mission and wanted only a place to plant corn, which the Winnebagos had offered at a spot some distance up the river. It is quite possible he lied about this and the assertion of the excited whites was true that he intended to arouse all the Indians to a general warfare. In any event, he had broken his promise not to leave the west bank of the Mississippi. He said afterward that he understood this to mean the leaving of it upon a warlike errand. The whites replied that in view of the many examples of probity with which he had been advantaged by the Christian and the civilized, this plea showed again the incurable native duplicity.

General Atkinson sent an expedition of six hundred militia to capture him and bring him back. When Blackhawk learned that the white soldiers were approaching, he sent three young men with a flag of truce to conduct the troops to his camp. The bearers of the flag of truce were taken prisoners and one of them was shot. Five other Indians having been sent after the first, two of these were killed.

The troops continued to advance. Blackhawk marshaled fifty warriors and selected his battle-ground on the sloping side of a small stream. Fifty [2] against six hundred—but the attack was so swift and vehement that the superior race broke and fled. Many of the terrified militiamen did not abate their speed when the pursuit had ceased, and some never stopped until they were safe at home.

This is known in history as the Battle of Stillman's

[2] Thwaites, in his "Historic Waterways" (p. 87), says that Blackhawk's warriors in this fight numbered only forty.

17

Run. It appears, however, that more ran there than Stillman.

It was the actual beginning of the Blackhawk War. The Government, aroused by the defeat, sent General Scott himself to the scene of conflict. The Indians were driven north, and worsted in many battles. After one reverse the desperate Blackhawk tried to send away some of the women and children by placing them on rafts and despatching them down the river. Troops stationed along the shore shot them as they floated by. When Blackhawk and his fugitives tried to cross the Mississippi near the present town of Genoa, the steamboat *Warrior*, chartered by the army and armed with a six-pound cannon, came along and headed them off. The Indians, seeing they were hopelessly trapped, showed a white flag of surrender. Whereupon the *Warrior* let fly with its six-pounder into the midst of them.

The next day more troops arrived and shot about all that were left of the tribe, mostly women and children, who were trying to escape by way of the river. This is called in the records the Battle of Bad Axe. Blackhawk was captured soon afterward and taken to Rock Island. On September 21, 1832, he signed a new treaty by which the United States secured six million acres of Indian land lying west of the Mississippi. Sacs and Foxes that had survived the sharpshooters and the six-pounder were to receive twenty thousand dollars a year for thirty years. This ended the Blackhawk War and opened the West to settlement.

They allowed Blackhawk to come back the next year, 1833, long enough to see once more and weep over the site of his old village on Rock River. He died in 1838. He did not succeed in saving his lands or his people, but I think we have built a nice monument to him somewhere.

The Bad Men From Black River

In 1844 we pushed the remnants of his tribe across the Missouri and were done with them.

All fears of disaster at the hands of the murdering, treacherous, and wicked savages being now removed by these gallant deeds, the great tide of emigrants began to appear.

The earliest settlers landed from the sea at New Orleans and came up the Mississippi in keel-boats. Then others came over the Alleghany Mountains, down the Ohio to what is now Cairo, and so up the Mississippi; at first only a few, then more and more as the nature of that unequaled soil began to dawn upon the world, until they were moving in covered wagons, in ox-carts, on horse, on foot, in every way of travel known to man. But the rivers were the main highways.

As they arrived in the new domain they were to till they must be sheltered, and in the prairie region there was no timber of which to build. From Indiana to the Rocky Mountains, thirteen hundred miles, was one unbroken plain, virtually treeless—"leagues on leagues on leagues without a change." The fires that had fertilized it had kept it bare of trees. A few grew thinly along the streams, by which they had been protected, and here and there was a slender grove that for some reason had escaped the flames; but what were these for the hordes that were now appearing? Year after year the tide of westward-steering folk increased; soon it became a migration far beyond that of the Tartars or of the Cimbrians, and by comparison unequipped; for these moving millions were not for tents. It is eloquent of the situation that hundreds of newly arriving families resorted to huts built of strips of prairie sod piled like an Eskimo's igloo; not from poverty but because there was nothing else. Even important towns like Davenport and Dubuque, when they had emerged

19

from the log-cabin chrysalis, must be built of lumber
brought by water with difficulty and cost all the way
from Cincinnati; lumber from the woods of the Alle-
ghanies!

But all of northern Wisconsin and northern Minnesota was covered with the noblest growth of white-
pine trees that ever stood; a wonderful vast forest, an
unimaginable kingdom of pine. East to west, it started
by Lake Huron in Michigan and swept to the farther
limit of Minnesota; northward it went from the parallel
of the Wisconsin River into unknown fastnesses of Can-
ada. Need and supply were never more aptly simul-
taneous. The pine was soft, easily cut, rapidly worked,
easily floatable. Only one obstacle intervened. The supply was far away from the settler whose imminent need
demanded it. That long distance the raft and raftsmen,
Black River and all, came to bridge with the help, as
so often happens, of means unpromising.

Chapter II

HERE COMES THE STEAMBOAT

AS if at a touch, the rivers became the arterial system of this wonderful new empire; they were to its people then what railroads are to us now. Transportation, communication, supplies, trade, news, and knowledge must go along these highways. Say that a man in New York was impelled by business or other dire need to venture far away into the pathless wilds, perhaps as far even as Dubuque. His natural route would be to Pittsburgh or Cincinnati as best he could, thence by Ohio River steamboat to Cairo, and so up the Mississippi, being perhaps three weeks on the way. My grandfather did the lap from Philadelphia to Pittsburgh by canal-boat. Even when the railroad began to drive westward it halted long at Chicago. Thence one might go by stage or wagon to the Illinois or the Rock River and there be happy in a steamboat's crowded cabin. But the Rock River—what is the Rock River now?

The steamboat, the steamboat—everything depended upon the steamboat! The Government sent its mails by steamboat and had steamboat mail-clerks as now it has similar clerks on the railroads. At first, man being still an imitative ape, the western river vessel was patterned after the lake steamer or after the river keel-boat, when it looked like an open skiff, overgrown and gallumph-

21

ing. Even so, call it nothing but Noah's ark with an unsure engine and a pair of wheels, and it represented an immeasurable advance; for there may have been means of navigation more toilsome and dreary than keel-boating, but I have not encountered them. When the wind was up-stream a keel-boat might make headway with a sail. But in a river so crooked as the Mississippi and with winds so fitful as those that blow in the western country, this seems to have been more an aggravation than a cure of trouble. Most of the time a keel-boat was poled against the stiff current, or men would go ashore and haul on a line. Thus, favored by fortune and the weather, they might make from eight to twelve miles a day, if the day were not too short. Yet keel-boats were used as late as 1832 and a great commerce was carried upon them. In 1828 George Davenport was running a line of them between St. Louis and the mouth of the Rock River and serving his times, taking furs and lead and then grain downward and bringing gingham and sugar and powder and rum the other way.

Keel-boats traversed not only the main streams, the Mississippi and later the Missouri, but many tributary rivers as well; and the tributaries, as you are to see, were pivots of the industry we are dealing with.

If you will look at a good map of the upper Mississippi basin it will appear like two herring backbones, placed at an angle, the spines being the Mississippi and Missouri and the ribs the smaller streams joining the main columns. It was by these that the settlers found their way to their new homes. Rivers were then navigated regularly that seem now no more than meadow creeks. Steamboats traversed the Des Moines clear to the forks of the Raccoon, where a trading-post had been established on the site of what is now the capital city of Des Moines. They traveled by schedule on streams like the Iowa, the Cedar, and even the Maquoketa. This seems incredible now, because you would not think that anything heavier than a dead oak leaf could navigate the Maquoketa, but it is a fact of record, nevertheless. In 1862 a steamer called the *Enterprise* was running there tri-weekly, and Captain Merritt found an entry of one called the *Maquoketa Belle* that seems to have been built for service on that pretty but immature streamlet. Iowa City was the first capital of Iowa, and pioneering citizens used to reach it by steamboat on the Iowa River. The state house was an architectural gem (unaccountable for the times that built it), rare and joyous as a water spring in a dry and thirsty land. To-day it is the assembly hall of the state university and in its corridors the echo of a steamboat whistle would startle like the clap of doom.

Steamboats went 150 miles up the Rock River.[1] I once remarked this to a resident of Dixon, Illinois, and he inquired in an insulting manner if the steamboats of my prehistoric era customarily moved upon skids. Steamboats ran on the Black, the Wisconsin, and the Chippewa. The St. Croix was a main traveled road as far as Taylor's Falls. Navigators then used to do things that seemed inexplicable except as legerdemain. In 1861 another steamboat called the *Enterprise*, twenty-six tons burden, was built at Wausau, Wisconsin, and navigated the Wisconsin River from Wausau to the Mississippi. She had to pass down a considerable waterfall at Stevens Point and negotiate many rapids and innumerable shoals, so that to this day the trip is a mystery even to river men; but she did it, and the *Enterprise* lived to run for years on the St. Croix.

[1] It was a townsman of mine, Captain W. H. Gabbert, that held the distance record on this wayward stream. One of his contemporaries, coming along unexpectedly through the rich meadows, was presented with a town lot in each of the budding communities that his adventurous vessel visited.

A-Rafting on the Mississip'

The Falls of St. Anthony, now in the city of Minneapolis the Beautiful, were supposed to be the head of navigation on the Mississippi; but steamboats ran regularly above the falls to Grand Rapids, 319 miles, and even to Bemidji, and for years carried a great commerce. Regular lines of packets and freight boats navigated the Minnesota as far as Mankato and sometimes even to Granite Falls, where, only a few years ago, the vestiges of the wreck of one of them still protruded as a kind of melancholy fossil from a lost geological epoch.

The Missouri carried an enormous traffic, greater than ever after the discovery of gold in California. Then the mucky old stream became part of a transcontinental route for the gold hunters and others. In 1866 the steamer *Peter Balen* ran from Pittsburg, Ohio, to Fort Benton, Montana, and cleared $66,000 on the single trip, said to be three times the value of the vessel. Fort Benton was the last stop on the Missouri. Thence the transcontinental travelers moved by stage or wagon, or stuck fast.

Steamboats even ascended the Yellowstone and Big Horn.

All these rivers were physically alike. They were shallow, they had soft alluvial bottoms, they shifted and twisted about, they had more different moods and tempers than any woman. The difficulties of navigating them were great and complicated. Because they were so shallow, steamboats built for use on them (after builders had passed out of the imitative stage) must be flat-bottomed and constructed with a care that pondered every ounce of weight. Considering their burden, they were in their prime the lightest-draft steam vessels that ever floated. The hackneyed old phrase about the western steamboat that could run over a field after a heavy dew was not so wild an exaggeration after all.

Here Comes the Steamboat

The packet *Iowa City*, on which I once traveled, drew but twenty inches, and the *Chippewa Falls*, when light, but twelve. If I remember correctly, the largest steamers ever constructed for use on the upper Mississippi had no more than five feet of hold; most of them had three and a half feet or four.

The hull was only a platform on which to place machinery and freight. Seldom was anything carried in it; everything was carried upon it. Necessarily the upper works, cabin, and structure for state-rooms and the like must be of the flimsiest construction. And yet with all these limitations, many a Mississippi River steamer was beautifully designed, beautifully built, and adorned into a floating palace. Often the skill and sometimes the good taste of the builders went beyond praise.

Lordly creations of their art, traversing the main streams, might be of a truly impressive grandeur, but for the small tributaries ingenuity was most taxed to provide something that would carry engine, freight, and passengers and still get over the sand-bars.

One of the celebrated packets on the Des Moines River was the *Little Morgan*, of which its captain and owner, Granville W. Hill, was justly proud because he usually succeeded in going through to destination when other boats were balked by low water, high water, bars, snags, or temporary dams of débris. The head of navigation on the Des Moines was that post at the fork of the Raccoon, by this time become Fort Des Moines. Mr. Tacitus Hussey has written an interesting history of navigation on the Des Moines and has this note about Captain Hill and his boat:

On April 5, 1862, the *Little Morgan* arrived at Fort Des Moines with a cargo of goods for several merchants on the west side of the river and a consignment also for Isaac Brandt, who had a store at that time in the old Griffith Block on Locust street, northeast of the place where the Chicago &

Northwestern Railway depot now stands. As there was no communication by wagon on account of high water at the time it was a problem with the captain as to how the heavy consignment of queensware and glassware sent direct from St. Louis was to be delivered to Mr. Brandt. The saucy *Little Morgan* was equal to it, however. She cruised down the river a little way, and striking just the right place in the overflowed bottoms, nosed her way up to the store, which stood on the second ledge, or bank, tied up almost at the door, threw out her gangplank and unloaded the goods as if it were an everyday occurrence. A large crowd collected to see the sight which so far as known was never seen before or since. It was an excellent advertisement for Mr. Brandt, and also for the enterprising steamboat captain. When the goods were unloaded there being not enough room to turn around, the boat backed gracefully out, found the channel a mile or two below, and soon was on her way to the lower ports.

Mr. Hussey hunted up the manifest of the *Little Morgan* for this trip, finding it in the file of an old newspaper. It is worth quoting because it shows how far civilization had gone in 1862. Even in that year Fort Des Moines must have been a place of importance for the distribution of goods to the settlers.

Latshaw & Woodwell, 6 cases of hardware, 50 kegs nails, 20 boxes castings.

Keys & Crawford, 30 cases dry goods, 12 cases hats, 4 hogsheads sugar.

Rollins & Harmony, 4 barrels of dried fruit.

W. W. Moore, 13 cases of dry goods.

John McWilliams, 2 hogsheads of sugar, 6 kits of mackerel.

H. M. McAllister, 12 cases of boots and shoes, 6 cases dry goods.

Laird Brothers, 10 sacks coffee, 30 boxes soap, 4 cases dried fruit, 14 boxes candles, 20 crates wooden ware.

Isaac Brandt, 8 casks glassware, 14 cases dry goods, 2 boxes boots and shoes, 10 barrels salt, 2 hogsheads sugar, 4 crates crockery.

Here Comes the Steamboat

As factors in any real transportation service some of the boats of those days would seem to us merely facetious. The *Michigan*, a side-wheel packet on the bosky Des Moines, was about the size of a steamship's yawl. Yet she was supplied with all the appurtenances of a full-sized steamboat, made regular trips, and handled an astonishing cargo and passenger list. Even the natives thought she was small, but her captain was proud of her record and sensitive about her size. Once when she landed at Keosaqua a crowd of townspeople came aboard and asked if they could see her. With delight Captain Johnson showed them from keelson to pilot-house. When he was done, the spokesman said:

"Captain, how long will your boat be lying here?"

"About two hours," said the captain.

"Well, now, look here," said Lusty Juventus, "my wife has never seen a steamboat and she's sick in bed. Can't you let me put your boat on my wagon and take it up to my house and show it to her? I promise to take good care of it and be back with it in two hours."

The crowd guffawed, for this was what it had come to hear; but Captain Johnson is said to have been cruelly mortified and left speechless. With some reason, for as long as the *Michigan* survived, the jest was fastened upon her, that being the river way.

Mr. Hussey illuminates with an incident showing the vital importance of the steamboat to the social machinery of that day. He says that once the steamer *John B. Gordon* arrived at Fort Des Moines just at "early candle lighting" of a Sunday evening when the worshippers had assembled in the churches for evening service. When the *Gordon's* whistle was heard the entire congregation in each church, including the sexton, slipped out of doors and made for the landing, leaving the ministers to put out the lights and follow in more dignified fashion.

27

A-Rafting on the Mississip'

Humorists said that if at a wedding the clergyman had proceeded as far as "Wilt thou have this woman—" and a steamboat-whistle should sound, he would be obliged to say, "the remainder of the service will be held at the steamboat-landing."

The Chippewa was another shallow stream that required light-draft vessels. One of the most successful that ever stemmed its fidgety current was called the *Monitor*. One day in 1863 while bound up she ran into the bank above Rumsey's Landing and went aground broadside on. In a few moments she was observed to be floating again and proceeding upon her way. The accepted version of the incident was that she grounded on the starboard side while the pilot was on that side of the wheel. He moved over to the other side and the boat floated free. He himself stated that all he shifted was his quid of tobacco, but this seems improbable. I have heard it said in pilot-houses that when the *Monitor* struck a bar head-on, two deck-hands would get out, seize her one on each side, walk over the bar with her, and deposit her on the other side; whereupon she would resume the journey. This may be deemed doubtful, because it appears from the registry list that she was of nearly twelve tons burden, and it seems unlikely that two deck-hands could carry so heavy a weight unless they were persons of unusual muscular development.

Sometimes even the lightest-draft vessels would come to grief. It will be remembered, maybe, that the Minnesota River flows out of one end of Big Stone Lake and the Red River of the North from the other, one making for the Gulf of Mexico and the other for the North Pole. When the Red River region began to attract settlers, John B. Davis, a Mississippi captain, conceived the notion of taking his boat up the Minnesota as far as he could, and then going across the land to Big Stone Lake, perhaps to see what there really was

ST. PAUL'S LEVEE IN THE OLD DAYS

*The famous steamers "Time and Tide," "Jeanette Robert," "Frank
Steele," and "Grey Eagle," at the foot of Jackson Street, 1859*

PACKET "MINNEAPOLIS" IN 1869 AT LANDING IN MINNE-
APOLIS WHERE WASHINGTON AVENUE BRIDGE IS NOW

in this theory about the heavy dew. He had proceeded well upon his way and the project seemed not impossible, when his boat got into a hopeless position, was wrecked, and had to be abandoned on the prairie. Then the Indians took out of her whatever pleased their fancy, but thoughtfully left the boiler.

The emigrants that joined the tide moving westward by steamboat must have found the journey long and circuitous, but it was picturesque and to the imaginative could hardly have been boresome. Lively chances of being blown up, wrecked, or sunk must have alleviated any tendency to a tired feeling. Steam navigation was new; steam itself was a young giant of unguessed ways and testy temper. Let a passenger have nerves and an aversion to violent and sudden death, and the habit the western steamboats had of exploding their boilers must have alone added a vivid interest to every voyage. The early history of steamboating is grisly with such disasters. Captain J. W. Darragh, an upper river pilot of distinction and studious ways, having a singular fancy for statistics, kept for fifty years a record of all accidents on the inland water highways. Casting up the items he entered, it appears that in the half century covered, 141 steamboats were destroyed by boiler explosions, and twenty more were burned following similar mishaps. He gives the names of fifteen that were sunk by Confederate fire in the Civil War and records but one case of collision having fatal consequences—a remarkable record that shows the pilot-house to have been more advanced in navigation than the engine-room.

But the blame hardly lodged against the engineers of that period. For a long time after the introduction of steam machinery, all of it was crude, unscientific, and largely experimental. The boilers were of iron, the water-gage protection was faulty; of the vast, accurate, and truly admirable volume of knowledge of steam and its ways that now enables us to travel so far and so fast in safety, almost nothing was collected. Sometimes it was possible after the event to learn why the boilers exploded: sometimes no human ingenuity could cope with that problem. Sometimes the boilers exploded while the boat was soberly and dutifully making its way along, sometimes they blew up while the boat was lying peacefully at the levee, and both varieties seemed for a long time equally mysterious.

A few examples will be enough to remind us of the risks the pioneers took when they started forth to redeem the wilderness. I will not dwell upon the unforgetable tragedy of the *Sultana,* April 26, 1865, when 1228 persons lost their lives, the worst of all accidents on the Mississippi, for that is familiar in history and explicable by reason of the boat's leaky boilers. But what shall we say of the explosion on the beautiful *Princess* on a Sunday morning in February, 1858? She was twelve miles below Baton Rouge, proceeding steadily and well, Andrew Sweeney, noted as one of the most careful and competent chief engineers on the river, being on watch, and without a moment's warning all of her boilers exploded, blowing the stately fabric to pieces.

The first vessel to come with help to the scene was the packet *R. W. McRae,* of which John E. Rowland, afterward a familiar figure on the upper river, was clerk. Fifty years later the horror of it was still strong upon him. I submit three of his pregnant sentences.

I can never forget the agonizing sight that met my gaze at the little cottage filled with the suffering and dying officers and passengers. Only the year before I had been associated with the officers on the beautiful *Princess,* the men I now saw lying on the floor and in beds, suffering untold agony.

He names the captain, the two clerks, and the pilot as among those he saw.

Here Comes the Steamboat

We ministered to their needs in every possible way, with sweet oil, mattresses and medicines, and the cabin floor of the *McRae* was full of the unfortunates, our boat taking them to the different points at which they had embarked such a short time before this dreadful calamity overtook them.

Engineer Sweeney was among the lost. His body was never recovered.

On December 2, 1852, the packet *Geneva* stopped at a wood-yard four miles below Alton, Illinois. She had been but a few minutes at her moorings when her three boilers exploded—simultaneously, it is said. Cause never known. The loss of life among passengers and crew was heavy.

On May 13, 1867, while the packet *Lansing* was lying at the landing, Hampton, Illinois, both boilers exploded and wrecked all the upper part of the vessel. Among the killed were Robert Smith the pilot, who was in the pilot-house, and Van Dyke the clerk, who was in his office. Van Dyke's body was blown clear across the Mississippi and was found on the Iowa shore. Smith's body was blown in the other direction, across the town. A woman passenger, who happened to be dozing on a sofa in the rear of the cabin, escaped unhurt.

Even as late as 1872 unexplained explosions were recorded. Thus the *James Malbon* on July 30 of that year blew up with the loss of fifteen lives while steaming at her regular gait above McGregor, Iowa. She was a new boat; this was her first season. Captain Malbon, for whom she was named, was at the wheel. His body was blown across the river and fell upon an island. A spoke of the wheel he was handling had been driven through his neck.

Foaming water in the boilers was often deemed to be the cause of these disasters. After a few more years they came to be rare. It is strange to reflect that seventy years of navigation were required to teach us the primer of safety.

Snags, of which we shall have more to say when we come to the towboat, were a perennial and persistent source of danger, their favorite hunting ground being always the Missouri. Up to 1894, records showed 294 steamboats lost on its turbulent waters, of which 193 had been wrecked on snags. The one consolation about the snag peril was that when a steamer was pierced by a snag she was necessarily in shoal water and the passengers had a fair chance to escape; in their night-clothes, maybe, or with the water chasing them to the roof, but still a chance. In a boiler explosion, or often in a fire, the odds were against them.

Steamboats took fire, bumped into one another, hit rocks and sank, hit sandbars and stuck for hours or maybe days, were liable to be tied up by low water or carried into the woods by high, ran into logs, wrecks, and keel-boats, and withal prospered, multiplied, transported the moving millions, and performed an indispensable function to society and civilization.

About 1852 the annual arrivals of steamboats at St. Louis exceeded 3,000. Ten years later, 1,015 steamboats arrived at St. Paul, then become the great entrepôt for all the undeveloped Northwest behind it. In 1856 the total steam tonnage employed on the Mississippi and its forty-four navigable tributaries was said to exceed the total steam tonnage of Great Britain. On May 7, 1857, twenty-four steamboats were counted lying at the St. Paul levee,[2] and in those years it was customary to see sixteen or eighteen vessels in a row tied up there.

[2] A few words about upper Mississippi nomenclature. "Levee" (pronounced levy) is landing-place. "Slough" is the body of water back of an island and separate from the main channel; what on

Here Comes the Steamboat

Even habitual steamboat travelers usually found the trip embroidered with novelties. The rivers shifted their courses so often and easily that boats seldom traversed twice exactly the same channel. In 1840 the steamboat *Fortune* passed up what is now Fifth Avenue in the city of Rock Island, turned where is now a great building, discharged her freight at the corner of Fifth Avenue and Thirtieth Street and left by way of Sylvan Water, a slough or chute that has not seen a steamboat in sixty years. Since 1842 the mouth of the Missouri River has moved to the northward all of eighteen miles, and where was formerly rushing water are woods and farm-land. The town of Guttenberg, after subsisting for years upon river traffic, found itself shut off and left at one side by a shifting bar. All boats once called at Harper's Ferry, Iowa. Another shifting bar, and all Harper's Ferry knew of steamboats was an occasional echo of a far-away whistle.

At first, the woods along the shores and on the islands abounded in game. In springtime and fall, the sloughs and bays were covered with wild ducks and geese. One Golden, who kept a wood-yard near Bellevue, used to hunt ducks with a cannon. He had a small howitzer fixed in the bow of his boat, slew a hundred birds at a single discharge, and sold them to passing vessels.

the lower river was called a "chute." "Boat ways" are the wooden structures on which steamboats were hauled out to be repaired; answerable to an Atlantic dry-dock, though not looking like it. "Roof" is the uppermost deck of a steamboat. "Chimneys" are the funnels. "Texas" is the deck-house on the roof, containing the captain's and a few other state-rooms. "Old Man" is the captain. "Jackstaff" is the flagstaff at the bow, "verge staff" at the stern. "Larboard" or "labboard" is port. "Tow head" is an island with a low bluff point at the up-river end. "Roustabouts" or "roosters" are deck-hands. "Floater" is a hand on a floating raft. "Reef" is a long sand-bar with an abrupt side down-stream. "Crossing" is a place where the steamboat channel shifts from one side of the river to the other. Finally, and most important here, "towing" is pushing, not pulling.

It will be deemed in some quarters but poetic justice that the discharge of his field-piece made him deaf.

Indians, or signs of them, were to be seen most of the way from St. Louis to Stillwater—and beyond. Popular captains used to bring aboard the tamer sort to astonish the tourists and enable the winter fireside down East to be enlivened with the tale fantastic. Sometimes there were other diversions. In 1840 the packet *Indian Queen*, making a trip from St. Louis to St. Croix River points, ran out of fuel when she was above La Crosse. As there was no wood-yard handy, the captain tied to the shore and sent the passengers into the forest with axes to cut a supply. They cut it and killed several blue racers and other creatures of the wild, pleasant and unpleasant. When a steamer went on a bar, all hands would go fishing. What were known as channel catfish sometimes grew to about the size of small sharks. A passenger on the *Charlie Cheever* is said to have caught one that weighed 180 pounds.

Seldom were any of these rivers of a convenient stage; their habitude was for either floods or shoals. In 1864, for some unexplained reason, the upper Mississippi nearly went out of business, recording the lowest water ever known. Passengers bound for St. Paul had an interesting time. At Dubuque they must transfer to a light-draft steamer (if any) that took them as far as La Crosse. Thereafter they fared as chance offered, land or water. A Dubuque newspaper said that above La Crosse the river was not navigable except for shingles and light skiffs, and suggested wading. "The St. Paul Pioneer" responded with fiery indignation. Most persons believed that the end had come of river navigation. Two years later the whole region was flooded.

Besides its manifold perils, steamboat transportation had an incurable defect. It was helpless before the seasons. Six months of it was all the people could reasonably expect on the northern rivers; eight months as far south as St. Louis, if the winter were not too awful; for sometimes the ice would jam unexpectedly even at St. Louis and smash a dozen or twenty boats. Anywhere north of Davenport it was the common belief that in winter the river froze solid to its bottom. The boats ran as late in the fall as they dared—or later. The climate was as tricky as the river itself. All might be serene upon a lovely day in the far-famed Indian summer, say November, and the next day the river be impassable with ice.

This reminds me of an adventure of the favorite packet *Julia Dean.*

The winter of 1855-56 was at first unusually mild, and the *Dean,* which was a stern-wheeler with a record on the Des Moines River, was running between Keokuk and St. Louis. The fine, warm, balmy weather tempted her owner to continue after prudence would have laid the boat up. She left Keokuk on the evening of January 22, the weather warm and pleasant, with not a sign of winter. Soon after dark a biting cold wind set in, by midnight a thick snow-storm began, and as the pilots could see neither shore the *Dean* had to stop. The next morning she attempted to make Quincy, where she could find a harbor and land her passengers. By this time the river was filled with ice and it was soon evident that she could not proceed. She was run to shore in a spot far from habitation, where her two hundred passengers, including many women and children, looked out upon an arctic waste. The snow continued to fall in incredible volume; what had really arrived was a blizzard. Naples, a railroad station on the Illinois River, was the nearest help. The *Dean's* captain got a man to Naples and sleighs were sent over. Then the roads became all impassable. Several days went by before the storm abated and roads could be broken through. Then the passengers took a train to Springfield, Illinois, thence one to Alton, and finally landed in St. Louis. As for the *Dean*, where she had come to land, there she lay the rest of the winter, frozen in as Peary with his ship.

When winter descended, the river towns were for the most part *incomunicado*, or something like that, until spring. Not always; for enterprising citizens would run sleighs over the ice now and then, and try at some more favored spot to catch up with the whirling world. When Captain Russell Blakely, whose name we shall meet again, quitted steamboating, he organized fast express sleighs that gave winter-bound towns on the upper Mississippi an occasional contact with St. Paul and so through newspapers with the human orbit.

The rush of emigrants westward was so great that sometimes there were not men enough to operate the boats, and sometimes what there were exacted difficult conditions before they would ship.

In 1853 Captain Louis Robert was master of the *Greek Slave*, a celebrated packet of her day, and was operating her between St. Louis, Stillwater, and St. Paul, calling at Galena. Late in the autumn he was about to make his last trip for the season, planning to lay his boat up for the winter at St. Paul. He had a heavy cargo of freight and a full passenger list, when, as the time arrived to start, the crew struck. Not for higher wages; for something else. Most of them lived in Galena; they did not want to be stranded in St. Paul for the winter and they demanded a guarantee that they should be brought home. Everybody struck except the chief engineer, the pilots, the mate, one chambermaid, and one cabin-boy. Captain Robert thought that with a scratch crew he could manage to get the boat under way, but a scratch crew could not feed the passengers, and that was the hinge of the difficulty; there was no steward.

At this juncture came the chambermaid to the rescue. She said to the cabin-boy:

"Here, you—run up-town and tell my beau Mike to come down here and be steward of this boat or the next time I see him I will cut his throat from ear to ear."

Mike came and the *Greek Slave* put into the stream. It was not yet out of its troubles. Captain Robert was suddenly stricken ill and unable to move from his bed, and the first morning out the boat managed to run upon a sand-bar five miles below Winona, hard and fast. Ordinarily a steamboat on a sand-bar, if it did not go on too far, could get itself off by setting spars like the legs of a grasshopper on each side, and then with the capstan and lines pulling herself up and off. The scratch crew could not work the spars, the boat never budged, the captain was sick, the winter close at hand, the thermometer falling ominously, and the two hundred passengers viewed with horror the prospect of staying where they were until they should be frozen in.

It happened that there was on board a landsman of prestige and ready wit, A. L. Larpenteur, a pioneer, the first wholesale grocer in St. Paul. He sized up the situation, went to the captain, whom he knew well, and proposed nothing less than to take charge of the boat.

Ordinarily the deck would have rocked at any such suggestion, but Captain Robert knew his man and consented. Mr. Larpenteur came out, in the captain's overcoat and hat, announced that he was in charge, and issued his instructions in a voice of authority. He knew enough about boats to know how the spars should be worked. The *Greek Slave* happened to be the first steamboat on the Mississippi that carried a steam capstan. Mr. Larpenteur had also a general notion of this implement. With its aid, with the spars, and with the starboard wheel backing, he worked the boat off the bar and proceeded. The next morning the pilots steered it and he captained it safely into Stillwater.

If nothing else fell in to give flavor to the journey, the Indians, being ungrateful wards of a benevolent government, might take pot-shots at the steamer when it was in a difficult position, or in lonely and remote places try to capture it. The Minnesota and Missouri rivers were the commonest scenes of these attentions. More than one steamer on the Missouri was stopped and turned back by the furious fire of the Indians on shore. In 1857 the *Kate Kearney* was bound up for Fort Benton with a valuable load of freight and many passengers. Much of the freight was machinery for the mines. She fought her way to a point a short distance above Fort Union, where the Indians, being more than ever aggressive and manifestly increasing in numbers, Captain John La Barge believed he should be no better than massacring his passengers if he should try to proceed, so he stopped.

News of his repulse reached St. Louis, where were the men that had shipped the mining machinery, and the same day they began suit against the owner of the boat, claiming heavy damages.

This was John S. McCune, an old steamboat man and ready of resource. He sent a pony express overland to Helena, Montana, where was Joseph La Barge, a brother of John. Joseph got the steamboat *Effie Deans*, the pilot of which he knew to be of the indomitable nerve required for the times and the task. The *Deans* started after the *Kearney*, met her, took off her cargo, and stood up the river, Indians or no Indians. She ran through their hostile fire and got within fifty miles of Fort Benton, but could go no farther because of the low water. The captain sent off a rider to the fort to report what had happened and to get teams. Joseph

La Barge was there and sent down thirty ox-teams of five oxen each. With these he transported all of the freight and passengers safely to Fort Benton. The passengers arrived at their destination not more than three weeks late. It would be interesting to know what they thought of the performance.

The suits were withdrawn as soon as it was known that the freight had arrived at the fort. If they had been won they would have crushed McCune.

But the steamboats still multiplied as the tide of migration rose, and the problem of housing its vast numbers caused the lumber industry to spring up like a magician's mango-tree. With so great and so insistent a demand and with the supply assured it could hardly fail to be profitable, and the rapidity with which the lumber fortunes were made had not been equaled in the country except in a few instances of overnight riches in the mines or the melon industry of Wall Street. For a time it seemed as if to touch lumber was to touch gold, and to this day along the Mississippi arise the unblushful foreheads of the architectural wonders that celebrated this wealth coming on winged heels.

Chapter III

THE PINE-TREE ELDORADO

WITH amusement or with concern, as the case may be, the philosopher is now to note that as the tide of this great business mounted, the two extremes of crime met in the pine-woods to work for it side by side.

Half-savage vagrant men cut down the trees and occasionally fought, robbed, maimed, or murdered one another in a region without law or other restraint. Cultured and respectable business men sat in carpeted offices and directed what was in cold truth a gigantic plunder of their fellow-citizens. To picture the uncouth lumberjack of the woods and the suave dweller in some city mansion as *arcades ambo* would have jarred in those days even the man in the street, but historically would have been no more than a statement of fact.

When the lumber trade of the Mississippi began, most of the land that stored all this dazzling wealth and most of the wealth upon it belonged to the people of the United States. Deemed among the most intelligent of earth's inhabitants, they daundered by, blank-eyed as so many seal or sheep, and saw themselves despoiled.

An area of their land larger than the whole of New England, with New York, New Jersey, Pennsylvania, Maryland, Delaware, and Virginia added, being in all 242,614 square miles, was filched from them by tricks to which the wiles of the card-sharp and the bunco-steerer seem blameless. The country needed a railroad to the Pacific coast. Adroit fortune-hunters induced a Simon-at-the-fair government to accept the policy of giving away the people's lands to help the building of such a railroad. With that the door of the public domain flew open and in trooped the thieves.

Their plan was simple. They organized a company, an alleged railroad company, that had the word "Pacific" in its title—Jayville & Pacific, Painted Post & Pacific, Baraboo & Pacific—and filed a map. Then the good, kind government bestowed upon the company the people's land at the sweetly generous rate of twenty square miles of land for each mile of track—or near-track.

In the beginning the lumbering interests had gone into the woods and helped themselves to the people's trees. This might have continued indefinitely, for the robbed people did not mind, but the trouble was that the timber cutters began to tell on one another. When it looked as if gentlemen that wanted logs might have to pay for them, happy relief appeared in the railroad land grant. Organize the Podunk Pacific Railroad and get a kingdom for a couple of marks on a map.

This grand good thing did not last long. The Government began to require something in the way of construction before it bestowed the people's land upon this form of banditry. When, therefore, aspiring exploiters in the lumber way could no longer get good timber land by making a noise like a railroad, they were driven to preëmpt what they wanted, or else to purchase it, purchase railroad grant land, purchase land granted for school purposes, or purchase from those that had secured land by preëmption.

The railroad land lay in alternate sections; every other section for twenty miles on each side of the line.

41

A - Rafting on the Mississip'

A section is a square mile. When the timber had been cut from a square mile that had been purchased, preempted, seized, grabbed, or otherwise obtained, there was nothing to hinder the cutting of it likewise from the adjoining square miles that had not been preempted, purchased, seized, grabbed, or otherwise obtained and therefore still belonged to the people. By securing one square mile it was easily possible to get the timber upon two square miles—always upon two and maybe (if no one was looking) upon four, five, or ten.

The whole region was wilderness, without organization or observation. Land from which timber had been lawlessly cut might be the property of the people of the United States, dully indifferent to what was going on; or of the people of Wisconsin or Minnesota, equally in the trance state; or of a school district that would not function for twenty years, and then find itself drained flaccid. In any case, once the timber had been cut, the land was for the most part worthless. But the timber, carried away, made into rafts and floated down to the sawmills, was worth a mint; in quick money-making it was the mint's only rival.

As the multiplex grabbing processes went on, the fortune-builders learned to use a singular agency called the "timber cruiser," whose vital part in this story comes next.

It is much the fashion to regard the human mind as an empty crate into which schools and the schoolmen obligingly tumble not only the broken meats of their own gained wisdom but everything else, including capacity, faculties, and wit. This satisfying notion receives a jar when we contemplate the work of the men that took rafts down the Mississippi and the hardly less astonishing achievements of the timber cruiser. The

42

business of this superman was to go through a forest
and, by looking at the trees as they stood, estimate
the number of feet of sawed boards that a given area
of woods would yield. One would say offhand that this
was mere guesswork. It was not. As the buying price
of a tract might depend upon the cruiser's report,
guesswork was cut out and the report based upon sure
perception. In the eyes of the exploiters a good timber
cruiser was the noblest work of God and to other persons a creature of almost miraculous gifts. The commonest remark in the timber region was that a real
cruiser was born to his job. A man without the afflatus,
or whatever the peculiar endowment is to be called,
could never come by it. After all the years, still linger
around these precincts the fame and exploits of great
cruisers, whose deeds unjustly missed an epic setting
but helped to make history.

In the forests the pines were mixed with other trees,
and so irregularly that one section might have three
times as many as another. Value hung upon their number and as much upon their size; a hundred young
trees were worth nothing; ten large trees might be
worth much. Except for the pines the land was deemed
as so much Sahara desert.

Unobserved and untrammeled, the cruiser went his
way. To send with him any one but another cruiser
would be a wasted precaution; only another cruiser
could understand the cruising process, and if two con-
flicting reports were turned in, which should go as true?
Besides, there was something else. "Why, yes," replied
a noted lumberman one day to his bright young clerk,
"I can send a man to check the cruiser, but who's going
to check the checker?" As to an outsider, let him be
as alert as a hawk, he could only stand and blink. The
cruiser would cast one glance at a great round trunk

of a standing pine in the woods and enter in his book that it would scale so many thousand feet of board. What could an outsider make of that?

No, the cruiser was the axis of the timber industry when there were no more granted lands to be skinned of their trees and the fortune-builders must needs resort to vulgar and costly purchase, to taking the trees from unbought land, or maybe to a process of false entries not altogether safe. When the cruiser said that a certain area would yield one million feet of lumber, the entry or purchase was arranged upon that basis. If subsequently it was found that the true yield was ten million feet, the purchaser was the better off and the Government or the seller could go whistle. There were honest cruisers that took too much pride in their calling to betray anybody through it; but there were also flabby men, as there are in every line of human effort, whose reports could be had by the highest bidder. As the fortune-builder had means and the Government was ineptly or crookedly represented, great areas of the richest timber-land were sold for a contemptible fraction of their real worth. The cruiser might report that there was no pine on a tract, whereupon it might be sold for $1.25 an acre or something like that, when the actual value of the tract would be a quarter of a million dollars or more.

It might be thought that in the happy state of the trade with a great and rapidly growing demand for lumber and a supply that could be had and forwarded without dishonor, men would be content with gains that went far beyond the horizon of formulated business. It was not so here, certainly. The times were feverish. Men's imaginations were fired with tales of the gold hunters, of gigantic wealth made in an hour in Wall Street, of fabulous profits in real estate deals in the new western country. The old notion of amassing a fortune by a life of patient endeavor went out before the dream of getting it between Monday morning and Saturday night, and the people's empire was plucked from their hands.

I hardly have need here to underline the fact that the plucking had no possible relation to the lumber industry as carried on to-day nor that even in the wild times of license there were honest lumbermen, and many of them. There are honest men everywhere, glory be. Money was made in the lumber business without stealing it, much money. But a man content to get his timber by paying its worth counted nothing against the horde that reduced the public domain to scrub oak and sand.

If direct action to this end were undesirable through visions of the prison door, the false entry in the public land office was open always to the simplest practitioner. The purpose of the Government about the public lands, if any, was to foster their occupation by actual settlers. To this end the Homestead Act was fatuously devised, with a name that came in some regions to have only a sardonic meaning. The frauds committed against it, if revealed naked and unashamed, would shake optimism; hence I omit them. A division of the paternal government's paternal floundering about the public domain was called the Stone and Timber Act, which provided that a person discovering timber on the public lands could file a claim for forty acres and no more, whereupon the timber became his, after some formalities about betterments or the like.

To prevent the grabbing of large tracts by individuals or corporations, it was provided that no man could file in his own name on more than forty acres, but eight men could file on 160, provided none took more than twenty acres for himself.

So far, good. But the loophole for fraud lay in the

fact that claims could be filed by power of attorney. In
the grand rush to seize the timber land Golconda, powers of attorney were filed and entries made in the names
of lumberjacks that knew nothing of the matter,
valets, clerks, butlers, dead men, horses, cows, cats, and
dogs. A story that went the rounds of the Northwest
was typical. It related that the daughter of one of the
lumber magnates, having a pet monkey that became the
owner of much good timber under the name of Simian
Wynwood, a clerk in the land office was at pains to
correct the apparent error in the spelling of his Christian name.

At all times and in all ways, the filing on the forty-
acre allotments allowed a generous leeway to the agile
and the unscrupulous. The first person that got to the
land office with a claim and a description of the forty
acres captured the prize. When the land had been sur-
veyed, the sections were numbered and the numbers
accurately blazoned upon trees or stakes; hence to the
initiated the description was easy. Explorers and timber cruisers became more than ever invaluable in the
rush to grab the steadily diminishing tracts of rich
timber. Often when a choice area had been filed on by
one interest, another with stronger forces would jump
the claim and hold it. Having secured one forty for
the sake of appearances, it was as easy to cut the timber from the adjacent forties as it had been from adjacent sections. Upon forties as upon sections it still belonged to the people. What of it? Nobody cared a hang
for the right of the matter. Get the timber—as in im-
perial Rome men got privilege, land, and slaves.

George Henry Warren, a native of Detroit, went into
the woods in 1870 to explore and to locate timber lands,
and spent many years in these occupations, which he
carried on without losing his head or his moral standards. Long afterward, when he was an honored citizen

of Minneapolis, he wrote a book,[3] unluckily a book for
private circulation only, in which with scarifying comments he bared a mine of information about these conditions. He says that once he discovered that land he
had filed on had been seized in the manner of brigand-
age by other interests, he was foolish enough to think
of appealing to the law and engaged Attorney Gust
Wilson of Wausau, one of the best lawyers in the state.

"Now, don't try that," said Mr. Wilson as soon as
the case had been stated to him. "All of those fellows
have had 'some of them hams' and you can't get a jury
in all that county that will bring you in a verdict of
guilty, no matter how great or strong your evidence
may be."

It was like a shooting affair in the early mining
days of California. No juryman would vote to convict,
because he did not know how soon he might be in the
same situation himself.

Chance and luck, often pendent upon slender threads,
had much to do with successful timber-getting. Warren says that once when he was wandering alone in the
forest his eye fell upon the dead body of a wood-pigeon.
A wood-pigeon was no great matter, and negligently he
picked it up. It was still warm. Instantly the thought

[3] "The Pioneer Woodsman as He Is Related to Lumbering in the
Northwest," by George Henry Warren, Minneapolis, 1914. Chapter
IX is largely devoted to "Tracing Gentlemen Timber Thieves." At
one place he says:
"Many logging jobbers having formed this habit of helping themselves to government timber, found it difficult, after the government
lands had been entered by private purchase of others than themselves, to discontinue their practice of taking timber that was not
their own."—Pp. 56-57.
And again:
"It was a country where the custom had grown among lumbermen
to enter a few forties of government land, sufficient at least to make
a show of owning a tract of timber on which to conduct a winter's
operation of logging and then to cut the timber from adjacent or
near-by forty-acre tracts of land yet belonging to the government."—P. 56.

flashed upon him that there were other scouts on that
trail. He went about with caution and silently, watching and listening, until he came upon the footprint of a
man. Then he considered with himself, and started to
beat it for the land office. He had to creep through the
woods, concealing his presence, until he came to a lake,
which he crossed in a canoe. Then he walked on, at his
best pace and without stopping, to a settlement where
he hired a conveyance. All night he drove through the
woods and across the open country and the next afternoon he reached the land office.

Then he filed on the land where he had picked up the
pigeon. Two hours afterward the other party arrived
and cheerfully started to file on the same land. It was
already Warren's. If he had encountered those men in
the woods there might have been a grimmer story, for
he tells of a resort to cave-man tactics that occurred
in the upper Mississippi woods over such a disputed
claim.[4]

Some persons of a thoughtful turn of mind con-
temned the cruiser and his works, deeming him a needless burden. All their preference was for the public
auction of land, so that everything might be fair and
square and above suspicion. When a parcel of good timber-land was to be sold at auction they merely sent to
the spot a squad of trusty strong-arm lads from the
logging camp.

"How much is offered for this valuable land?" says
the auctioneer, the preliminaries being over.

"One dollar and twenty-five cents an acre," says the
agent of the lumber magnate.

"One dollar and fifty cents," says some one else.

Immediately the strong-arm lads, in wedge formation, place this intruder at their head and march him

[4] *Ibid.,* pp. 80-82.

at double quick to the outside world and far away from troublesome scenes.

"Sold for one dollar and twenty-five cents an acre," says the auctioneer.

The advantages were apparent. No trouble, no chance of unpleasant remark, no expensive cruisers, and the land safely acquired.

Captain E. E. Heerman, who became one of the noted pilots of the upper Mississippi, saw in his youth one of these well-managed performances and wrote a vivid description of it.

Warren says that the scandalous proceedings of different species about the pine lands became so notorious that the public land office at Eau Claire was closed by the National Government. But he could not find that any of the thieves were prosecuted. He records the significant fact that after 1882, when there was a genuine auction of lands at which free bidding was allowed, the prices realized always bore some relation to the actual value of the land.

Suppose the tract to have been acquired, by whatsoever means, and the penitentiary to have been eluded, the next task was to cut down the trees and get them into rafts for the sawmills, at which point enters the other side of this grimy drama. The pine country was threaded with rivers that were tributary to the Mississippi and with creeks that flowed into these tributaries. At first the trees to be cut were handy to the streams and the work easy; fell the trees, trim off the branches, roll the trunk to the side of the river or creek; in the spring float it with the others down to a place where rafts were made up for the tributary. But every year the cutting went farther from the streams and into the heart of the forest. Then camps were erected in a remote, isolated region where the woodsmen spent the

49

winter in a state that was the renaissance of the jungle and nothing else.

Some were aliens of questionable history. Some were fugitives from justice, and nearly all were fit to show man in the primitive. Say one had committed a crime anywhere in the more orderly East; here was his safety. No sleuth could track him into this wilderness where was not a vestige of law, and the appearance of a sheriff's officer would have been the sign for another riot. Results can easily be imagined. The northern pine woods became an American Alsatia.

They had not been so at first, and here is a fact worth your heeding. At first, the men that went into the woods were of straight old American stock, hardy wanderers from Maine or elsewhere in northern New England, avid to make their way in the world but straight, clean, and quaintly religious after the school of Jonathan Edwards. Many of them began with nothing but an ax and their two hands and rose by hard work and merit. John Martin and Dorillus Morrison, afterward among the most respected citizens of Minneapolis, were of this order and beginning. But the Yankees soon graduated from the ax-handle and in their places came a different order of being.

What was called the camp that sheltered these toilers was a long, rude shack of logs. Sometimes one roof covered kitchen and sleeping quarters; sometimes, in later years, kitchen and dining-room were in a separate structure. A typical camp of my time had but the one building—and poor at that. In its center was an open fireplace; near-by the tables where the men were fed, and where they sat and smoked in the evening. From this extended the two wings, lined with rough bunks in tiers, one above the other. There were no mattresses; sometimes the bunks were filled with hay or straw, sometimes with cedar or hemlock boughs, and covered with blankets. For pillows the men used their coats, doubled up; sheets were unknown and the men usually slept in their clothes.

The camp was built with its one door facing the south, if that were possible, so as to get the full sun, when it happened to shine; the only window being opposite this door. Daylight was not really important in the place, for usually the sleepers were ousted from their beds and sent forth to work before dawn and did not return until after the dark had come.

The fireplace in the center was such as red Indians might have made. It was a pavement of stone and sand in a wooden box about eight feet square and a foot high, bu'lt on the floor of the shack. Over it was a funnel of slabs leading to a hole in the roof for the smoke, or part of it, to escape. Hooks and wires were arranged about it for the drying of wet clothes.

About sixty men constituted the population of one camp. The pay was wretched, all things considered, and I was never done wondering that even the ablest "labor recruiter" could induce men to undergo such drudgery on such terms. Experienced and skilful woodsmen received $40 a month; others $30 to $35. But the pay included board and lodging, and I think this was always held out as enticement of power. Adroit recruiters, busy in the slums of the cities, were wont to curl glib tongues about the advantages of a life where there was no boarding-house bill to be met. It is to be said that in general the fare was ample and fairly good. The great staple was baked beans, and the fireplace in the center was the home of the everlasting bean pot.

The preparation of this part of the menu was something more than cooking and partook of the nature of ceremony; with reason, since cooks were judged by the comparative excellence of their beans. A deep hole was dug on one side of the fire and filled with glow-ing embers. When the beans had been soaked for twenty-four hours they were taken out and scalded. With deliberation the cook now chose the right kind of an onion and placed it on the bottom of the pot. Then the beans were poured in until the pot was filled within six inches of the top. Slices of fat pork were laid across this, a sufficiency of molasses was poured upon the whole, and the pot sealed. The embers were now taken from the hole in the floor and the pot inserted. All space around the sides was filled and packed with hot coals and the bean hole covered up. Then fire was made over it and kept burning twenty-four hours, when the cooking was complete.

Beans and salt pork (generically, "sow-belly") were the substantialities of the menu, and fried cakes made the dessert. Upon this unadorned dietary the men thrived; there was little sickness among them.

Illicit selling of whisky, or of what passed by that name, went on throughout the logging region, but I will do the employers the justice to say that they tried straitly to stop the trade. The stuff that was sold was chiefly a form of distilled madness, and in such conditions fights, stabbings, and rows were common—at some camps. Much depended upon the foreman. If he were able to convince the crew that he had the bigger fist and was the surer shot, a semblance of peace reigned.

The solicitude of the employers about whisky did not arise from the tender heart but from the calculating mind. Whisky was bad for the total cut, which the employer yearned to have larger this year than last. It was hard to discover any other thought about the men on the part of those that hired them. Perhaps this statement is too sweeping; on reflection, I am sure it is. For what shall we say of that eminent lumber magnate, afterward not unknown in the United States Senate, who provided entertainment as well as shelter and beans for the men he employed? Every two weeks came his pay-day, whereas employers less considerate paid but once a month—if then. Every pay-day, according to tradition, this benevolent soul sent the money to the camp in charge of a sturdy and well-armed treasurer, who carried also a faro layout. This was on a Saturday night. On Monday morning the treasurer would return, still bearing the faro layout and the money.

The men themselves engineered entertainments of a less sophisticated sort—sometimes. On Sundays no work was done in the camps. Some of the proprietors were of a strict order of piety and others found that a regular resting day was sound policy in relation to annual production. On Sundays, such of the men as remained sober would get up horseplay games or haze a new-comer if they could get hold of one. But, as the character of the men seemed to decline with the years, the drinking and gambling increased, while in the near-by towns multiplied the vicious trades that preyed upon the woodsmen's earnings.

Week-days from morning to night they were busy in the woods at difficult and dangerous tasks. At night, after supper, they took their turns at the grindstone that stood in a corner, for one of the rules of their employment was that they must supply their own tools and keep them in order. I may say that this was a detail usually overlooked by the recruiter. Those that were not grinding were smoking what was probably the worst tobacco ever developed from jimson weed, burdock, and old rope. It was called Scandihoovian brand, and its sale was one of the perquisites of the employers. One could have wished at times that it was the only perquisite.

Among the visitors to the pine regions in the winter of 1884-85 was the late Bill Nye. I saw him at Minneapolis after his return and secured from him much illuminating information concerning life in the woods. He told me that the reason the tobacco was called Scandihoovian was because when it was smoked in Wisconsin folks could smell it in Scandihoovia. I asked him about the winter climate in those parts and he said that it was invigorating and full of charm for Eskimos, but undeniably at times permeated with a certain chill. He said that at night in the shack he was kept awake by a singular sound of something heavy falling upon the roof over his head. In the morning he investigated and found that it was the smoke and steam from the fireplace, which froze as soon as it left the chimney and fell on the roof in solid chunks. He said that axes could not be used in logging operations, because the sap in the tree froze to the ax-head and held it so fast it must be blasted loose. He said that if one with bare hand touched the iron door latch one's hand froze solidly to the metal and must be cut loose with knives. In the camp where he had spent most of his time six men were invalided with mangled hands because they had been careless about this. He said he sat up one night and read to them, and their sufferings beggared description. I could never find any verification for these statements, a fact that I regret because they seemed, if true, to possess a considerable scientific interest.

At the height of the business, something like 140,000 men were engaged every winter in cutting down the pine-trees of Michigan, Wisconsin, and Minnesota. At that time they embraced about every nationality and condition of life. I find reports of two English university graduates in Minnesota camps. One was a victim of rum and the other of his wife. It is said that they met one Sunday and got away by themselves and talked all day in an undertone. It must have been a strange meeting in that environment. They were not the only men of education that drifted into the maelstrom, but the greater part were ignorant French Canadians, many unable to read or write. Mixed among these would be Canadians of English stock, and it is recorded that these were oftenest the storm centers when the rows broke forth, for they would begin by expatiating on the superiorities of the Canadian form of government over the detestable conditions existing in the low, degraded United States. Thereupon some man of Yankee birth would resent these comments and a battle would follow on nationalistic lines—unless the foreman came in to stop it.

This naturally reminds me of Bob Eden, the most remarkable of all the unusual characters that the pineries attracted and having a first-class story that broke in two in the middle.

Robert Charlesworth Eden was his full name.

He was the younger son of a titled family in England, said to be a branch of the Auckland clan, for one of whose members the city of Auckland in New Zealand was named. Being a younger son, Robert Charlesworth, soon after his appearance on earth, was slated for the church and carefully educated to shine in it. The ancient family whose name he bore was proud of its place in history. It planned that Robert Charlesworth should be at least a bishop. He went to Oxford and took a degree, with honors, and then moved upon his studies in theology. I never heard how far he carried these, nor exactly what loosened the spring in his case, but of a sudden he flung away his books and his robes together, broke with the old folks, took ship, and came to America, where he drifted about for a time and finally to the pineries in the neighborhood of Oshkosh. There he probably acquired many other things, but his acquisition of most note in these chronicles was a warm friendship with the camp cook, who had a kind of poetic genius for the baking of beans.

A-Rafting on the Mississip'

A little of life in a pinery camp was enough for Eden and he came out and took a position as reporter in Oshkosh at a time when it was celebrated widely as the wickedest city in the West, a reputation outgrown, erased, and forgotten years agone. The young Englishman was clever, alert, high-pressured, and adaptable to his opportunities. He learned much in Oshkosh—with other things a command over a kind of sulphurous, vigorous, and unconventional speech that would have greatly astonished his lady mother and still more any congregation in England, if by any chance it should be heard in precincts ecclesiastical. It appears that he went the pace. Also, that he was abnormally industrious, brilliant with his pen, and vastly entertaining. He rose in the newspaper business, prospered, made money, and in 1859 was looking around for other adventures. Inland navigation occurred to him as being about what he wanted. He studied it, conquered it, passed his examination, took out a master's license, bought the steamer *Enterprise*,[5] and went to steamboating on the upper Mississippi.

For chief pilot he hired one George B. Merrick, who is to reappear in these annals, and was then approaching the mature age of eighteen, but had full papers. For cook Eden had but one choice in the world—that marvelous friend in the logging camp, the taste of whose beans and buckwheats had never departed from his memory.

The business of the *Enterprise*, if she could be said to have any, was to trade with the Indians for furs; the business of its captain was to enjoy himself. The first seems to have been indifferently performed, but the second basked in the sunlight of an inalterable

[5] Not to be confounded with others of the same name that appear elsewhere in these pages. There were first and last about sixteen steamers on western waters with the name of *Enterprise*.

THE FALLS OF ST. ANTHONY

The busy city of Minneapolis now surrounds this spot

A LOG JAM IN THE MISSISSIPPI ABOVE THE FALLS OF ST. ANTHONY

prosperity. The cargo of the *Enterprise* was ostensibly articles of barter, and in reality such a stock of beverages and provisions as no steamer had carried into these waters. Promptly on arising every morning, Captain Eden took a tumbler of Scotch whisky to clear his thoughts and start him well upon the duties of the day, and followed this with other potations of size. Whenever a good hunting-place was reached the boat would be tied up, while the entire crew went ashore under Merrick's guidance and came back loaded with game. They went up the Mississippi and then up the St. Croix, visiting every Indian encampment and dallying over barter for furs, while Eden devoted himself to an intensive study of the red man and all his ways, a subject about which he seemed to be obsessed.

Merrick knew the Indian dialects and acted as interpreter. The custom was to sit on a log, one on each side of a chief, while, hour after hour, Eden propounded his questions about Indian legends, history, customs, and ideas. He took no notes, he wrote nothing out, but he seems to have filled his head with a larger assortment of Indian lore than any other man of his times carried. Anything about Indians was in his line; also anything about rafts.

At that time rafts were being floated in great numbers down the St. Croix to the Mississippi, and some of the most famous of the old floating pilots were in the springtime of their glory, men like Joe Gardapie the half-breed, Stephen Hanks, George Brasseur, and James McPhail. It was Eden's practice to hang around Lake St. Croix until he saw a raft in difficulties, then slide up with the *Enterprise*, pull the raft through the lake without charge for the service, then sit with the pilots or a group of raftsmen, and talk about the details of their business. It seemed wonderful to him that such craft could be managed through such chan-

nels, and with the zest of a scientist he hound-slotted the
inquiry and flagged not.

He had brought along with him a library, all books
of merit, and at night, if in the mood, he would give
discourses on unusual subjects. Merrick says he was
one of the most learned men he ever encountered and
one of the most fascinating.

He stocked up the *Enterprise* with furs, returned to
Prairie du Chien, and, at the closing of the river, to
Oshkosh. The next year the Civil War broke. Eden
helped to organize a Wisconsin regiment and went
with it to the front. In a short time he was on the staff
of General Wilcox, then commanding one of the divi-
sions of the Ninth Army Corps, where he became widely
noted because of his feats of reckless daring. He had
won up to the rank of major, and his principal business was the carrying of despatches across the line of
fire. Repeatedly he did it when not a soul that watched
him believed he could get through. Yet he escaped unhurt. Oddly enough, his companion and subordinate on
these trips was this same George Merrick that had been
his pilot and interpreter on the *Enterprise*. They had
enlisted in different regiments at different places and
it was merely a freak of fate that again threw them
together.

While he was still serving on Wilcox's staff before
Petersburg and doing daily his bewildering feats in
daredeviling, Eden fell in love with an American girl.
They were married in the trenches with the shot flying
over them. The bridegroom lost no time in honeymoon-
ing. From the ceremony he went back to his wild rid-
ing, continuing to fight and to win honor. He went
through to Appomattox, saw the end, and with the dis-
banding of the army was mustered out, honored and
admired.

Then with his wife he went straight to England, resumed in some cloister his theological studies, got a sequestered nook of a parish, and lived out the rest of his days centered in the sphere of common duties, not to say humdrum, the mild-mannered and beloved shepherd of a rustic flock from which he seems never to have stirred thereafter. And so preached and married and baptized and buried and visited and ended, without having made the least use of the unequaled stores of knowledge he had swept up about the Indians, and without a sigh for the life of wild excitement on which he had turned his back. So it is said.

Chapter IV

THE LUMBERJACK

BUT to return to the logging camps. The work was hard, the management stupid, and its ways beyond knowledge. In general, the governing idea seems to have been mechanical. To arise at a specified time, whether work was to be done or not; to load in food as one would fire a boiler, and at night to herd bedward as one would turn off the steam—this seemed to be all the philosophy there was in the enterprise. At each camp was what was called a "chore-boy," usually about sixty years old, whose first duty was to wake everybody up in the morning. This he did with a cow-bell; also with a piercing voice, liberally applied. In the dead of winter the choppers, so urged forth, would reach the woods before there was light enough to work. Then they would light a fire and sit on a log until the day should dawn.

The morals of the neighboring towns declining with the morals of the woods, when the men were paid off now the most of them trooped down to the settlement and spent their wages for forty-rod whisky and in the dance halls, with which every lumbering town was oversupplied. A few hours in such a place were usually enough to make the average man a lifelong prohibitionist.

I have called the resorts dance halls, which is euphuism, and different from the name they were known by in the woods. Perhaps it is well to skip details and merely indicate the truth by saying that they were sink-holes of abomination. The women for them were supplied by a system of organized kidnapping in the cities that lured servant-girls into the country on the pretense of respectable employment at good wages. Once in the dive-keepers' clutches they were helpless prisoners and would have been better dead.

A Chicago newspaper with which I was connected, having learned at a later day that these iniquities still persisted, sent reporters to investigate and undertook a crusade against the business. I need not repeat here the accounts of women that committed suicide when they realized the situation into which they had been tricked, nor deal with other items of the traffic. I cannot, however, refrain from recording the fact that when this newspaper brought the matter to the attention of the governor of the State and asked for action, the governor protected the miscreants and denounced the reporters as liars. Of course; all persons that protest against evil as a vested interest are traditionally liars. The Women's Christian Temperance Union and other worthy bodies and individuals strove to further the efforts of the newspaper to banish the dive-keepers. They all failed.

The fights, stabbings, and shootings in the dance halls were a superfluous addition to a calling sufficiently perilous in itself. To fell a great tree in safety is a handicraft requiring swift judgment and sure knowledge. At first the felling was done with double-edged axes, but experience showed that the saw was quicker and more economical. There were two men to each tree. When they had decided upon which side they wished the tree to fall, with their axes they cut a gash on that side and then began to saw on the other, using wedges to make sure that the fall was according to schedule. One danger was that when they were about half through the tree might begin to crack longitudinally from the bottom up. If this process were not checked instantly the trunk would be spoiled and the men placed in deadly peril, for no one could guess which way the crack would run and the upper part of the tree was likely to descend perpendicularly upon them. The first intimation of the cracking would be a slight sound, hardly more than a murmur, from within the trunk. Instantly the woodsman, if he knew his business, would sing out:

"Crack! Whip the saw!"

And the saw would be swung around to one side or the other. Cutting on the side or on both sides would stop the cracking if the change were made in time.

The next danger was when the tree fell. Sometimes it did not go in the direction that had been chosen for it, sometimes it struck the branches of other trees that threw the trunk forward or thrust it aside in an unexpected direction. In either case the moment was critical to the woodsman. If the huge, unwieldy missile, weighing tons and tons, overtook him, he had no chance to escape a terrible death. The casualties in the woods were so numerous that the timber business was sometimes described as dripping with blood. This was mere extravagance.

When the tree was down, the choppers, if they had escaped alive and unhurt, sprang upon it and began to trim off the branches. All these with the upper part of the trunk were burned. It is astonishing now to reflect upon the waste that accompanied these operations. At first the loggers would take no trunk that at the smaller end measured less than eighteen inches in diameter, and even these were regarded with scorn, a fact from which the magnificence of the general growth may be gaged.

The Lumberjack

The standard log was supposed to be sixteen feet long or thereabouts, and four such logs were sometimes had from one tree. Then these were piled for the sled.

Dumping them upon the sled was another peril; hauling them with the sled to the creek was another.

At the creek the logs were piled on the bank, ready to be floated when the ice should thaw.

The piling at the bank was the most dangerous of all these motions. The first log was laid below the shelving bank of the stream and close to the ice or upon it; the others must be laid parallel to or upon this until the whole was up to the top of the bank or above it. Lifting was with a block and tackle or, in later times, with a crane. The log was swung into the air and then allowed to descend upon the pile. It was here that the danger came in. A workman of skill and experience called the "top decker" managed the operation. He stood with a cant-hook, and while the log was still in the air tried to steer it into the right position so that it would hit the pile where it was wanted. Sometimes he did this and sometimes the log swung too far and knocked him off the pile or cruelly mangled him. The accidents were so common that when the word went around the camps that another "top decker" was dead no one asked how did he die but only where was he crushed.

When the ice broke up, the logs were canted into the water and started for the raft-assembling points like Beef Slough and Stillwater, of which we are to have more hereafter. To keep the floating logs from grounding, men went along the stream with cant-hooks; or sometimes, if the water were deep enough, a man would stand upon a single log and keep his footing while he kept the log from the rocks. To any one that knows how easily a log turns in the water this will seem an embellishment of fancy, but it is historic fact.

Men actually learned to balance themselves on that most unstable foundation and so perched monkey-wise, to keep the log in motion.

An odd revelation of this difficult art occurred once at Lake Minnetonka in the early eighties. There had been a regatta on the lake and famous crews and celebrated scullers had contended. When the events were over, a local boatman offered to bet that he could row an ordinary skiff faster than one of the scullers could pull a similar craft. The challenge being accepted and tried out, the local boatman won, to the inexpressible joy of all those precincts. This emboldened a lumberjack that had seen the race to offer a bet that he could stand upright upon the seat of a single shell and with nothing but an oar propel the boat. This offer being taken, the sculler generously suggested that it might be well to secure the sliding seat as no human being could possibly keep his footing upon such a slippery contrivance. Jack scorned this notion, got upon the seat, and with a spoon-oar not only made the slim boat travel through the water but maneuvered it at his will.

At first the hauling of the logs through the woods to the stream side was done with horses. Soon it was discovered that oxen were better, and agents were sent, chiefly to the South, to buy them.

This reminds me of a strange chapter in the history of American business and at the same time of a memorable disaster.

In the early days of the development of the upper Mississippi basin, St. Louis was the metropolis and the great supply depot for everything from the head of navigation to the mouth of the Ohio. At the beginning of this era the Indians were coming up to get their rations at Fort Dearborn, now Chicago, and from Lake Michigan to the Mississippi was a stretch of prairie as flat as a board and empty as a drum. But Chicago,

Courtesy of D. Appleton & Co. From an old engraving

ST. LOUIS IN THE GOOD OLD STEAMBOAT DAYS

being the manifest key position to the new empire of the West, began to grow. Soon the railroads reached her; seventy-five years ago she started to push a railroad of her own into the prairie lands. It touched the Mississippi at Rock Island, it began to build a bridge there, and St. Louis woke up to the menace of competition.

The St. Louis merchants protested vehemently against the bridge, which was the first to cross the river, on the ground that it was an obstruction to navigation. They went to court on this and their case was thrown out. The building of the bridge proceeded—wooden. A point had been chosen where the Le Claire Rapids cease, about half a mile above the lower end of the island of Rock Island, a thing always to be distinguished from the city that bears the same name. The river was narrowest here, hence the selection, which was otherwise foolish. When the United States court on a technicality threw out the protests of the St. Louis merchants, persons interested on the same side seem to have resorted to other means, less ethical.

About twelve o'clock of a dark night the watchman on the wooden bridge heard a suspicious noise at the second span from the Iowa shore. He hastened to see what it was, and two men dropped from the bridge into a skiff below and made off into the darkness. When he reached the span the watchman found a pile of oakum and laths, with resin, tar, turpentine, saltpeter, and oil, all arranged for a fire.

But before this reversion to troglodyte warfare the bridge had been effectively fired by other means; fired and rebuilt.

One of the favorite steamboats of that day was a swift, efficient, and beautiful side-wheeler called the *Effie Afton.*

After many years and much observation, I am still

ready to maintain against all comers that the old
Mississippi River packet was among the comeliest of
the works of men's hands. Compared with her har-
monious lines and symmetrical sweep of designing, the
average Hudson steamer is a lump, and boats on the
Rhine, the Elbe, and other European waters seem without form and void. There was a certain grace about the
sheer of the Mississippi boat, a kind of jaunty and
insouciant grace, that has never been equaled elsewhere; her funnels were placed where they gave an effect of due proportion; her pilot-house rose above her
texas with a cumulative touch of the impressive and the
appropriate; her paddle-boxes were where they ought
to be; her dainty upper works were decked out with fili-
gree, like lace. Between her chimneys she swung some
bright device that added elegance and distinction, a
gilded ball, a gilded star, or other heraldry; the top
of her pilot-house might carry a pair of great deer's
horns, painted red. The stern yawl was hung aft of the
verge staff and swayed to the motion of the steamer,
a kind of rhythmic finale to a beautiful conception.
And then those paddle-boxes, if she was a side
wheeler! The painter's skill reserved its best for their
luscious adornment—a great picture in colors of St.
Anthony Falls, of Minnehaha rolling a slumbrous sheet
of foam below, of a buffalo hunt, of striking scenery
like that of Trempealeau, of Phil Sheridan spurring
to the Battle of Winchester—works of art at which the
shore people were never tired of gazing, open-mouthed.
Bravely she went, decked with flags and streamers showing clear against the white effect of her ensemble. And
then the mere motion of her—grace, dignity, power, all
expressed at once! At a distance she seemed to be swimming like a swan and with as little effort. When she
came nearer you could get the majestic march to which
her paddles revolved and the throb of her engines.

The Lumberjack

Ah w-o-o-o!—tat-tat-tat-tat-tat-tat—Ah w-o-o-o!—tat-tat-tat-tat-tat-tat, like a muffled drum beaten as the background of a piece of symphonic music.

Half the town used to gather on the levee when one of these glittering fabrics came to port; gather and stand and gaze and still gaze with delight insatiable. I would not seem to be extravagant in a matter-of-fact age nor emotional in one stern set for the impassive, but it is a fact that if the boat were new, business would be suspended in our hustling Davenport while the populace came down to stand and look and make admiring comment, mixed with comparative and exegetical criticism. Farmers, when they came to town with a load of corn to sell, would ask if there were not a steamboat they could see before they must strike the trail again.

There was such a crowd gathered on the water-front of Davenport the morning of May 6, 1856, to greet the *Effie Afton.* The evening before she had been discovered swinging up the long reach above Credit Island, but had landed first across the river, where she had tied up for the night. She was a typical packet of those times, long, graceful, immaculate, decorative, important. While yet in the middle of the stream she would whistle with pomp and circumstance, two long melodious blasts and three short ones, that set the wild echoes flying along the bluffs. Then she slowed down on both wheels—*tat—tat—tat—tat*—then stopped both and swept swiftly and silently up toward the levee. The gangplank swung out over the water, on its extreme tip the deck-hand with mooring line in hand, she came on and on—just as the uninitiated began to shake with the sudden fear that she was going to climb the bank, jingle went her engine-bells, for a moment both wheels churned backward and stopped, and the bow touched the shore as her motion was running out.

An uncle of mine was there that morning, standing

on the levee, watching, absorbed, breathless like the rest. It was a sight he had witnessed a hundred times— never mind; it was always dewy fresh in interest. He saw the passengers skipping down the gang-plank and other passengers skipping up, the freight hustled ashore and hustled aboard, the red-faced mate sweating and swearing, the lines of toiling black men, the engineer with a round stick testing his gage-cocks, "*Whist! Whist! Whist!*"—and must have thought it all wonderful, for years after he talked of it with unquenchable fervor. The pilot far aloft in his white and green cupola leaned over the wheel and looked down— cynically, I have no doubt. All pilots being superior beings, were proudly sophisticated.

Twenty minutes of this and he gave the stand-by signal to the engine-room, rang to ship up to back, started her back on both sides. She swept out, gathering headway, the helm hard to starboard. When she was far enough out, behold the pilot climbing that wheel like a squirrel, forcing it spoke by spoke against the strong protest of the water astern, up and up until he got it to the peak and over and then—he let go and it spun around with dazzling speed and the boat straightened up, went ahead on both wheels, headed for the draw, and whistled for it, one long, echoing, mellow note, D, F sharp and A, a lovely chord.

Still my uncle and many others stood upon the river bank and watched. She passed into the draw, she cleared it, she headed up against the stiff current of the Rapids. And then the sharp-eyed among the watchers were startled to notice that her starboard wheel had stopped. She swung sidewise, hit the bridge pier on one side, rebounded and hit the bridge pier on the other, hung there, careened badly until her great chimneys fell, and then before the eyes of the horrified spectators she burst into flames.

The Lumberjack

The lame starboard wheel now revolved furiously and she broke loose from the clutch of the pier, drifted under the bridge and set fire to it, and came down the middle of the river, a mass of red and yellow flame.

She was crowded with passengers. Some huddled in the bow as far as they could get from the fire, some leaped overboard and swam, some tore off doors and shutters and cast themselves afloat. In the grim and tragic history of the upper Mississippi, steamboat accidents were no novelty. The instant the fire was seen the river front on both shores knew what to do. A hundred skiffs and small boats put out. The steam ferry was making a crossing. She turned at once and began picking up the victims. The blazing wreck floated down almost to that Credit Island from which the day before the *Effie Afton* had emerged with such a dramatic stride, and there it sank. It is remarkable testimony to the swift and sure work of the rescuers that all the passengers and all the crew were saved alive.

Among the skiffs that went out to them was one owned and rowed by a boy twelve years old, a stocky, chub-faced boy that lived down by the old sawmill at the lower end of the town of Rock Island. We shall have much to do with this boy in these records and may well note his first appearance on a historic scene, because he was destined to act in a strange variety of such scenes before he should be through.

But about the oxen for the pine-woods. Tied on the *Afton's* lower deck were three hundred of them that had been bought in the southern country for use in the Wisconsin logging camps. In the wild panic that followed the breaking out of the fire, the oxen were clean forgotten, and their agonized bellowings could be heard on both shores. None had chance to escape until the fire had burned the ropes with which they had been tied. By this time a third of them had been suffocated. The rest jumped into the stream and swam toward the Iowa shore, which was nearest. Some landed in a terrible condition, having been shockingly burned about the back or side, and all were maddened with pain and fright. For the next two days the natives had an exciting time pursuing these crazed creatures through the woods and up and down the shore. In the end all were rounded up and herded into the court-house yard at Davenport, where the kind-hearted among the population strove to ease their sufferings. About one hundred of the original shipment were finally forwarded to their destination. The rest had been lost on the boat or killed on shore to put them out of their pain.

We had not heard the last of the *Effie Afton,* for her burned bones sticking up at Credit Island were fated to have a curious place in history. The company that owned her was of St. Louis origin and habitat. At the instigation of the Chamber of Commerce there, it began suit against the Chicago & Rock Island Railroad Company, owner of the bridge, for the value of the steamer, cargo, and outfit, plus exemplary damages, alleging unlawful obstruction to navigation by reason of the bridge.

The case was bitterly contested to the end, for upon it turned the struggle between Chicago and St. Louis to control the trade of the West. The railroad company employed a lawyer from the interior of Illinois already winning attention for the thoroughness with which he prepared his cases. He came to the bridge to determine for himself how much of an obstruction it was. He went above it in small boats, hovered over the spot where the *Afton* had turned sideways, set adrift wreckage and timbers to see what direction they would take in the current. He hired three experienced river pilots, the two Smith brothers and Silas Lancaster, all of Le Claire, to take him on a chartered steamboat, up through the draw, down through the draw, up through the draw, until he knew that bridge better than the man that made it.

Then he went to trial, and with the testimony of the Smiths and Lancaster and his own knowledge of the case he made an argument of extraordinary strength. I have it here before me. The point of it is that starboard wheel. Why it stopped nobody knew, but if it had not stopped, the *Effie Afton* would never have hit the bridge. Shall the railroad company pay because a wheel goes wrong on a passing steamboat? With an astonishing frankness he admitted that the bridge was something pilots must look out for and be wary about.

"From April 15, 1856, to May 6 [the day of the *Afton's* disaster], seventeen days," said he, "there were twenty accidents, and in all the time since, there have been twenty hits, including seven accidents; so that the dangers of this place are tapering off, and, as the boatmen get cool, the accidents get less. We may soon expect, if this ratio is kept up, that there will be no accidents at all."

He had in court a model of the *Afton* and strengthened his argument by pointing to it. The lawyers on the other side he caused to look like apprentice hands; in a few minutes it was apparent that about steamboats they could not tell the jackstaff from the cylinder head. One had attempted to ridicule his experiments with floating timbers and the like. "But would not a small object in a current float in the same direction as a large one?" he asked.

The case was tried in St. Louis in the face of aroused prejudice. In effect, the rustic lawyer won, for the jury was deadlocked at nine to three, and the steamboat company dropped the case. For the rest of its existence that company blacklisted the two Smiths and Lancaster on its boats and tried to blacklist them for all others.

The provincial counselor that worked so hard did much more than merely to beat his opponents in that one action. It was, in fact, a momentous first round of a long duel between two inventions of human progress. The locomotive was pitted against the steamboat, land against water transportation. By establishing the principle that railroad bridges, serving a larger public interest, were of consideration prior to navigable streams, he helped the advance of the rail transportation that was to have so great an effect upon the destinies of the new empire.

Another collateral result was of a livelier immediate interest. The decision assured the eventual triumph of Chicago, railroad center, over its ambitious rival, St. Louis, river town. Twenty years later St. Louis was second in that race, and with another decade Chicago was so far ahead that rivalry was over.

You may care to know the name of this backwoods lawyer. It was Abraham Lincoln.

Chapter V

CAPTAIN HANKS COMES IN

THE river men had reason to curse that day's work in the courts, and did so with enthusiasm and resource of eloquence. Bridges began to multiply and boats and rafts to go to pieces on them. "A bridge just has a natural grudge against everything that floats," said the pilots, and the annals of those days give them countenance. With one curious exception hereafter to be noted, the bridges were built by railroad companies in more haste to make a crossing and sell bonds than to conserve public safety. They hung their bridges upon stone piers built in the river beds and were not careful to put the piers far apart. The result was that an ordinary raft could not get through any of them in one piece; and the roll of Mississippi steamboat disasters, already too long, was swelled with many additions, some poignant and memorable.

As to this same Davenport-Rock Island bridge, which Abraham Lincoln saved, the outcome might have been good in law but it was bad in practice. Nearly sixty years later Captain Merrick, writing of it, called it "that invention of Satan and the Rock Island railroad," and declared that "no better trap for catching steamboats could be imagined." The records show that it caught more than its share, and Captain Merrick explains why.

With characteristic indifference the railroad company had built the piers obliquely to the current, and in freshet time no human being could tell how to run the lunatic maelstroms that resulted. This is what did for the *Grey Eagle*, that famous craft whose story will be told along the Mississippi shores while water continues to flow between them.

Tradition says that she was the most beautiful thing that ever went afloat: the records show that she was one of the fastest. She had a peculiar model that was worked out one winter by Captain Daniel Smith Harris, who afterward commanded her. He used to sit with his jack-knife in one hand and a piece of wood in the other, devising hull shapes. All steamers on the Mississippi, big or little, being flat-bottomed, it was supposed that the shape of the hull could make no great difference; speed lay in the engine power developed. As to this, Captain Harris had another theory. When he had worked out his model to his satisfaction, he took it to a construction company in Cincinnati, which fell upon it with joy and built from it the *Grey Eagle*, launched in 1857. She was 259 feet long, thirty-five feet beam, five feet depth of hold, had four boilers with engines of twenty-two inches by seven feet, and was for her time a powerful old girl. In proportion to her length, she was unusually narrow.

Daniel Smith Harris was a member of a notable family of pioneers that left indelible marks on the river country, even to the extent of changing on one occasion the steamboat channel.[1] They had come to northern

---

[1] They were Galena people. Galena is eight miles up the Fevre River from the Mississippi. At Harris Slough (named in their honor) they dug through to the Fevre. The river rushed through their canal, made a new road, and shortened the steamboat channel by two miles.

Illinois by way of Cairo in the fateful year 1823, the
year that saw the first steamboat on the upper Mississippi and the highest water known in many years. The
Harrises came in a keel-boat called the *Colonel Bom-
ford*, with an uncle in charge, Dr. Moses Meeker, afterward a man of note. While they were struggling
up-stream against the swift current of the flood, the historic *Virginia* came along bound upon that first trip.
Dr. Meeker tried to get her to tow the keel-boat to
Galena, but failed. The *Virginia* reached Fort Snelling
on May 19. The Harrises arrived at Galena June 10,
one month and some days out of Cairo.

Daniel Smith Harris was a boy then and helped to
push on the poles of the keel-boat. He had several
brothers. All took like ducks to the river. Daniel Smith
himself became of those pilots of whom folks ashore
spoke as Hylas might have spoken of Hercules.

One of the achievements of the *Grey Eagle* in his
hands was to beat the *Hannibal City*, up to that time
the fastest steamer on the upper river, in a grilling
race from St. Louis to Quincy. The *Hannibal City*
started from St. Louis thirty minutes in advance. The
Eagle crowded steam in pursuit and the two went almost side by side all the way, burning pitch, resin,
lard, bacon, sides, and any other fuel that was fat,
greasy, and handy. The *Hannibal City* was so plainly
going beyond her limit that the groaning of her safety-
valve could be heard on the *Eagle*, and Captain Harris,
convinced that his rival was about to blow up, ordered
his pilots to give her a wide berth. She made port with
her boilers intact, and was first to arrive, but was
beaten on elapsed time.

The *Eagle's* race with the *Itasca* was of greater historic interest. In those days there was no telegraph into
St. Paul. The first Atlantic cable had just been completed and Queen Victoria had been moved to send by

75

it a message of congratulation to President Buchanan. Both captains had copies of this message, which marked an event comparable in those times to the flight of the Atlantic in 1927. The *Itasca* put out from Prairie du Chien with the message, and the *Grey Eagle* from Dunleith, sixty-one miles farther down the stream. From Dunleith to St. Paul was 295 miles. To overcome a handicap of sixty-one miles in that distance seemed impossible, for the *Itasca* was no ferry-boat.

Daniel Smith Harris determined to chance it. He laid in a great store of soft coal and barrels of resin, which he planned to use in his furnaces with his dry oak fuel, of which he took enough to carry him through, and so cut out the stops at the wood-yards. As much as he could, he side-stepped the way freight. At six o'clock in the evening he pulled out of Dunleith. River boats then carried the mails, and he had mail to deliver at every town, but he avoided stopping by running out a gang-plank with a roustabout at the extreme end, who heaved the bag ashore as the boat went along.

The next afternoon he was in sight of the *Itasca*. From that time both boats, in the expressive steamboatman's phraseology, dug up the bottom of the river. They boomed into St. Paul almost neck and neck, but the *Itasca* touched land first. She did not deliver the message first, for Captain Harris had tied his to a lump of coal and threw it from the upper deck at an agent of his line standing on the levee. The agent caught it and spread the tidings. This was how they brought the good news from Dunleith to St. Paul—unsung: the incident sadly lacks a Browning. On the basis of the distance traversed as it then was the *Grey Eagle* traveled nearly fourteen miles an hour against a current that in some places went four miles and in some five.

The feat won her great renown wherever steamboats

ran and steamboatmen gossiped. Alas! for the vanity
of men and things!

Captain Harris was a good man and had a fine hand
at the artistry of steering a steamboat, but he had one
habit that other pilots loathed. He was captain of the
Grey Eagle, but he always insisted upon taking the
wheel himself when going through Davenport bridge
or any other particularly nasty place. Pilots wish the
captain to stick to his job and let theirs alone. One day
in 1860 he had as guest on the *Eagle* the most remarkable pilot and river man of his time, Stephen Beck
Hanks, and as they went through the bridge Hanks
said:

"Captain, do you always run this bridge this way?"

Harris said he did.

"Well, then, I'll tell you—you'll smash up on it some
day, because that isn't the way to run it."

"Not I, Steve," said Harris blithely. "I know this
boat better than you do."

About five o'clock on the afternoon of May 9, 1861,
the *Grey Eagle* came tearing down over the Le Claire
Rapids and whistled for the Davenport bridge. Captain
Harris as usual entered the pilot-house and took the
wheel. The spring freshet was on, the swift current was
running through the draw in a way of its own. It caught
the stern of the *Eagle*, slewed it around, she struck sidewise upon the head of the draw pier, and sank in seven
minutes. The ferry-boat and skiffs picked up all the
passengers and crew except seven. One of the lost was an
insane man that had been chained to the lower deck.

The upper works and texas were out of water. When
the rescuers came to the last man left on the wreck it
was Captain Harris. He was going about the upper
deck, picking up shreds and trifles and talking to himself. The disaster to the creation that was more than

life to him had unsettled his reason. He retired from the river and never returned to it. Years afterward the once gorgeous pilot-house of the *Grey Eagle* was discovered serving as a summer house on somebody's front lawn.

I tell of the *Grey Eagle* as an example of the difficulties that the bridges made for steamboating. In a catalogue of once well-known vessels and what became of them, a rather astonishing number appear to have cast their bones upon bridge piers. The water ran bewitched through these ill-constructed spans. Pilots that elsewhere could read the surface of the river like an open book and divine strange matters there, confessed that the bridges opened an entirely new school to which they must go with a chastened spirit.

So far as raft-piloting was concerned, the addition was superfluous to an occupation already beset with difficulties that seem now to disclose strange new wonders in the human psychology.

We left our pine logs to be guided or ridden singly down the smaller streams into the Chippewa or the St. Croix and so, let us say, to famous Beef Slough to be made up into rafts.

Beef Slough was a bayou or estuary, thirteen miles long, just below the point where the Chippewa River enters the Mississippi. It was wide enough to have only a sluggish current, which made it ideal for raft-making purposes. Each log was branded with its owner's mark, cut near one end with an ax, I think. Logs came helter-skelter into the slough and were assorted into booms according to the marks they bore. The men that did the assorting were specialists that worked with marvelous celerity and seldom made an error, although it took a keen eye to detect the markings as the logs swept along.

To make a raft, this was the recipe. The logs were

78

placed side by side and lengthwise of the stream. At each end of each log great holes were bored. A limb of birch was laid across, a binding withe of split burr-oak was bent over it as a staple, and pegs were driven into the holes to hold the staple fast; contrary to precept; square pegs into round holes. It was wasteful, extravagantly wasteful; there is no doubt of that. The holes spoiled the ends of the logs, and the birch and burr-oak were increasingly difficult to come by. But what cared we? The resources of the continent, bestowed upon us because of our great deserving—would they not last forever? On with the dance and the hole-boring!

Each section of logs thus bolted together extended the length of the raft and was called a string. In making up the strings, which were units of the raft, care was had to put side by side logs of different lengths, where that was possible, that there should be few even breaks at the joints. This was necessary to keep the whole thing from tearing apart as it went around the bends. But at best the texture was uncertain, and when a forward corner of a raft hit the bank the birch lashings would crumple up and the logs start forth like sheep loosed from a pen.

At each end of each string was a great sweep-oar made of a plank bolted to the butt of a young tree. A raft with ten oars at each end was a ten string raft. I have seen rafts of fifteen strings, when they covered more than three acres and looked like a vast plowed field gone afloat.

When the raft had been constructed after this fashion, the boom that had held the logs in Beef Slough or elsewhere was opened and the raft slid out upon the river.

The difficulties of managing this great mass of sluggish weight developed a class of men of extraordinary skill and often of character as unusual, men like this

A-Rafting on the Mississip'

Stephen Beck Hanks, of whom it is time that we should hear.

He was born near Hopkinsville, Kentucky, October 9, 1821, and had the straightest kind of American ancestry. Forebears of his were in Massachusetts Bay Colony about as soon as anybody else. His father's father had been a soldier in the Revolutionary army and had braved out that terrible winter at Valley Forge. His mother's father had fought under Marion in the South. After the war the family drifted to North Carolina and then to Kentucky. Stephen's father, Thomas Hanks, had a sister named Nancy. On June 19, 1806, she married one Thomas Lincoln and on February 12, 1809, she brought into the world a cousin of Stephen's destined to a momentous place in history. The Lincolns with the young Abraham moved to Illinois. When Stephen's father died of a horse's kick the Hankses left Kentucky to travel in wagons in the same direction. It was a terrific journey, through woods and over prairie trails, camping at night wherever the sunsetting caught them, and the boy, eleven years old, had to take the responsibilities of a man. It was about the only schooling he ever had, and it taught him to think swiftly and surely and to find a way out of every emergency. Other boys were pupils about the same time at the same school and many of them were to appear on the river.

The Hanks tribe, from incredible adventures, narrow escapes, and many wanderings, finally reached the banks of the Mississippi at what is now the town of Albany, Illinois, and stayed there.

This was about 1836. Three years before, the white man had vindicated the superiority of white civilization in the matter of the quarrel with Blackhawk, and this happy event having started the flood of emigrants, large numbers of them now descended upon the fertile lands about Albany until that settlement boomed. A relative of Stephen Hanks put up a kind of sawmill to supply lumber for the new houses, and Stephen went in the winter of 1837-38 to cut trees along the Mississippi for that mill. When the ice went out, he saw them made into rafts, little rafts, eight or ten logs in each, and helped to float them down to the mill. Hardwood trees they were, for little else grew there. One day a man came along from a lumbering firm in St. Louis. He was bound for the trackless pine wildernesses in the North that scarcely anybody knew anything about, and he wanted a likely young man to go with him. Stephen Hanks hired himself to this man for $200 a year.

They walked most of the way, about four hundred miles, through woods and over prairie, swimming streams and dodging Indians. Once they came upon a place where a band of Sioux had just surprised, massacred, and scalped seventy-five sleeping Chippewas, men, women, and children. At another time their half-breed guide got whisky and drank himself comatose, whereupon the white men lost themselves in a vast forest and for a day wandered miserably about in circles until they believed they were doomed to leave their bones in the wilderness, from which fate they were saved by the narrow margin of favorable chance.

This was in 1840. On the St. Croix, Hanks was put to work making rafts of the lumber from the sawmill. The method had not changed thirty years after, when I knew most about it. The boards from the mill were sixteen feet long and an inch thick. They were arranged side by side, one layer one way and the next criss-crossed on this until twenty-four courses had made an even-edged pile sixteen feet wide and thirty-two feet long. This was called a crib and was the unit of the raft. It was now framed in with pieces of 2 by 8. Holes were bored in these and stakes called "grub-pins" were thrust through the holes to keep the frame together. The grub-

81

pins projected above the cribs. To make a raft it was only necessary to fasten the cribs together with pieces of plank bored with holes to fit the grub-pins.[2]

For running the St. Croix the rafts were made of ten cribs in length and three in breadth. Each string of cribs had at each end a great oar of the kind I have described.

Below the town of Stillwater the St. Croix River broadens into St. Croix Lake, which has next to no current. To get the rafts through this was a bothersome problem. Sails were useful when the wind blew downstream, but it had a habit of blowing the other way when a raft came along. Oars were tried; also poling. Neither would work well. Rafts might be poled when the water was shallow, but in some parts of the lake it was not shallow but absurdly deep. The process finally hit upon was to take an anchor in a skiff with a line about half a mile long, go out ahead and hunt a place where bottom could be touched, drop the anchor, and then all hands pull on the line until the raft was up to the anchor. Then the yawl would be launched again and the old weary process repeated. This was kept up day and night with two crews and was no better than man-killing, but it got the raft through. Not with speed, certainly, but still the raft got through. Sometimes the anchor would stick fast in the mud and both crews would

[2] A little by-way incident in American literature pertains to this operation. In "Huckleberry Finn" *Huck* and *Jim Watson,* the Negro, capture a crib from a lumber raft that has come to grief near Hannibal, Missouri. *Jim* takes up some of the boards and makes a wigwam, and on the crib as a raft they live and float down the river. At one place, Twain makes *Huck* utter some irreverential remarks about the reigning sovereign of Great Britain and, that he may not offend the sensibilities of his many English readers, then (but not now) tender in their regard for Victoria, he makes the sovereign King William IV. This monarch of unblessed memory died on June 20, 1837. The first lumber raft with cribs that floated down the Mississippi past Hannibal, Missouri, did not appear until 1839.

be hours getting it up, and sometimes it would not let
go until a steamer came along and broke it loose.

At the farther end of the lake the current ran fairly
well into the river and the raft would go of itself.

The smaller rafts of the River St. Croix were customarily made into larger rafts to run the Mississippi;
for the ultimate market of this lumber, or most of it,
was St. Louis. In May, 1842, Hanks, being nearly
twenty-one, got a chance to go to St. Louis on one of
those rafts. It was larger than he had been accustomed
to, twenty cribs in length, six cribs in width, or
roughly 640 feet by 100. They loaded up with stores
and equipment, shipped a first-class cook, and started.
All the outfit was crude and tentative; the first lumber
raft to St. Louis had been run only three years before.
No one had yet devised a satisfactory way to moor a
raft, or, in river language, "check" it. They tied one
end of a rope to the raft and took the whole line ashore,
wrapping the other end several times around a tree.
When the line went taut it frequently pulled the tree
out by the roots. Sometimes the line broke and then the
end, flying through the air, became a perilous missile.

Not without difficulties, they won into the larger
stream. They did not dare to run at night, for in those
days no man was overconfident of his ability to take a
raft even in broad daylight through those twisted channels. Other troubles assailed them, not on the cards.
One night they tied up near what is now the city of
Red Wing. A tribe of Indians was camped close at
hand and, first and last, gave the raftsmen a-plenty to
think about. All night they swarmed over the raft,
demanded whisky and food, made threats, brandished
weapons, and (in the general belief) looked for something to steal or kill. The raftsmen were ready to sing
a jubilate when day began to break and they could
leave their dangerous visitors.

A - Rafting on the Mississip'

Hanks was of a singularly broad and philosophical outlook, but he confessed that ever afterward he had a prejudice against Indians. At that, he had fared far better than many another navigator of his times. On the Minnesota, trouble might be expected at almost any landing. Sometimes the Indians came aboard and virtually took possession, for they would not leave until they had won what they wanted—except when an engineer or captain was witty enough to circumvent them. One way was to slip the safety-valve, when the whole tribe would leap overboard in terror. But sometimes the boat must lie until the visitors were drunk.

This again suggests Captain Louis Robert.

Every week-day hundreds of strangers in the busy, cheery city of St. Paul traverse the thronged thoroughfare called Robert Street and have no notion of the origin of its name. In general it is supposed to be something truncated—Robert Smith or Robert Jenkins, with the last part cut off. In reality it does honor to one of the founders of St. Paul's greatness and a pioneer of whom any country or region might be proud.

He was a descendant of French settlers that had come to Kaskaskia when St. Louis was a trading-post in the French territory of Louisiana. About the time the first sawmill began to operate on the St. Croix he came north, and in 1844 went to live at St. Paul, then a hamlet. At first he dwelt in a log cabin with another Frenchman; then he built out of lumber from the St. Croix the first frame house erected in St. Paul. He was early in the steamboat business on the Mississippi and then on the Minnesota, where he ran for years that *Greek Slave* we have before encountered and then another still more famous boat called *Time and Tide*. He was a Territorial delegate, a commissioner under the Federal Government, and, because of his force of character and transparent honesty, swayed an extraor-

84

MAIDEN-ROCK

Valley of the Mississippi

dinary influence among the river men and settlers. He traded much among the Indians, knew their dialects and ways, lived in peace with them, and believed that they looked upon him as a father.

In the summer of 1862 he was on a trading trip to the Indian agency called Redwood, not far from New Ulm. He had transacted his business and started for home, traveling in his buggy drawn by two horses. That night the Indians, in accordance with the plans long matured by Chief Little Crow, rose and attacked the white settlers, staging the historic massacre of New Ulm. About eleven hundred whites are said to have perished that night and among them were all the people at the Redwood agency.

The Indians had no particular animosity against Captain Robert, but they wanted to get him because they regarded him as the head man and intelligence of the Whites. When they examined the dead and did not find Robert, the chief offered alluring rewards for his scalp and sent out parties to scout in all directions for him; for they knew well he had been at Redwood the day before and could not have gone far.

Robert had reached, the next morning, a place called Traverse des Sioux, about three miles from the present city of Mankato, when he was overtaken by a rumor of the Indian outbreak. As he believed that more than any other white man he had influence with the Sioux, he turned back with the notion that he could protect the people at Redwood, not dreaming that they were all dead.

A government outpost called Fort Ridgeley lay on his route, and as he approached it he discovered Indian signs that put him on his guard. He left his carriage and on foot made his way to the fort, where he learned the truth and also that the fort was surrounded by the red warriors. He saw that the situation was perilous, for the garrison was only a handful, and he offered a thousand dollars to any one that would try to get through the besieging line to St. Peters and bring help. As no one accepted his offer he made the attempt himself.

For a long time he scouted carefully around the fort only to find that there was no hole in the cordon. Next he found himself in a position of great danger, for Indians were patrolling the spot where he was crawling. To protect himself, he took off and hid his hat and wove a head-covering of swamp-grass. Then he got upon his back into a swamp where he lay with his body sunk in the mud so that only his nose was above it and protected with his woven swamp-grass. He was in that position while a band of several hundred Indians passed him so close he could have all but touched them. When they were gone he made further observations until he was convinced there was no way out, when he started to crawl back to the fort.

As he approached, his headgear and his muddy clothing looked so wild and strange that the garrison took him for an Indian and raised their rifles to shoot him, when he was saved by one man who begged the rest to hold their fire because it might possibly be a white man.

He got into the fort, took active part in its defense, and saw it relieved when the troops arrived. The Indians captured his carriage and horses and tied the silver mountings of the harness around their necks for ornaments.

But the Hanks expedition of 1842 escaped massacre if not annoyance and went its slow way down the Mississippi. The next day it reached Lake Pepin, which for trouble is to Lake St. Croix as Niagara is to Minnehaha. There was neither current nor wind and they must work with line and anchor as in the St. Croix, only

the raft now being so much larger and heavier the
dreary toil was so much the harder.

There were in fact two rafts in the flotilla, somebody
else having decided to share the hazard. For greater
ease in going through the lake the two were coupled
tandem. This gave a double man-power against the
same frontal resistance and was good judgment. Lake
Pepin, I may observe in passing, was well-known by
old river men to be the favorite summer and winter resort of the devil. It could furnish more weather to the
twenty-four hours than any other spot on the continent,
and its bad weather always had a peculiar edge of
malignity unknown elsewhere. When these rafts had
been hauled and tugged one third of the way a fierce
wind sprang up from the southward—a head wind.
They managed to make shore and for three days the
rafts lay weather-bound under the shelter of a point.
The region was wild and unknown, and part of the
crew to put in the time leaned toward exploration.
They climbed a bluff above the lake and stepped into a
huge colony of rattlesnakes just awakening from their
winter trance and all ready for business.[3] The first
thing the men knew, there seemed to be snakes on all
sides of them, behind as well as in front. By all accounts, and these quite sober, the situation was a trifle
ugly. None of the men had come armed, for this was
before the day when six-shooters were common. The
bluff was thickly wooded, and the men, picking up
clubs and their pluck, made an assault and won through
to the river.

"You'll do no more exploring," said the captain when
he had news of this adventure.

[3] Long before this, Le Sueuer, the French explorer, had reported
upon the extraordinary numbers and ferocity of the rattlesnakes
about Lake Pepin.

"There's one order we don't need," said Big Silas, looking at certain marks on his club. "I wouldn't go back there for a hatful of diamonds."

Snakes continued to be a pest. Whenever the rafts tied up before sundown the sociable creatures were fairly sure to come aboard, the inquisitive black snake and the agile rattler. At any hour in the daytime, when under way, a snake crossing the river might find his head caught between the cribs and come climbing up to see what it meant. The moth-eaten fiction about whisky as a cure for snake-bites was everywhere viewed as gospel and widely availed of—as cure and preventive. There used to be a man on the upper river known as Rattlesnake Jake, who had been bitten and rescued so many times he had become famous, and was dead before it was discovered that the marks on his leg had been made with a brad-awl.

The wind kept the Hanks outfit inert while it blew the three days assigned to it in those latitudes, and then the rafts worked out of the lake into the current again. And here they fell victims to the smilingly deceptive aspect of this jade of a river. The stream was full of islands and nobody knew where lay that elusive thing that is called the channel. They chose what certainly seemed to be the right road, broad and easy, the broadest in sight. It proved to be a trap. Beyond a curve the reach suddenly narrowed. The leading raft went aground and the second raft, bumping into it, knocked it to pieces. The rest of that day they spent in picking up fragments and working themselves out of this wicked place, only the next day to smash up again on Trempealeau Island.

It seems they had heard something of the evil repute of Coon Slough, which lies a few miles below, and when they got there they split each raft and got the halves through separately, going around the Devil's Elbow with fear and quaking, well to be understood only by persons that have seen those wizard waters boil and shoot. At Crooked Slough, another bad place, they split their rafts again, and at last, after infinite trouble and many groundings, made Prairie du Chien, the oldest settlement on the upper river, and got something to eat and a chance to rest.

Every night they must tie up and often had a maddening anxiety to find a good place and a tree that looked strong enough to stand the check line. Some days they made forty miles. Hanks records in his diary that when they were drifting past Albany, where he used to live, he took a skiff and pulled ashore to see the folks for a moment; and as he stepped out of the boat his old dog, recognizing him, almost overwhelmed him with affectionate greeting. He rowed back and caught the raft again before it had gone far. Ten days after they had passed out of Lake Pepin they tied up at Le Claire, the head of the Rapids, and took a Rapids pilot. They split each raft again and put the full crew on the first half, leaving the other, no doubt, just in front of my grandfather's place. The Rapids pilot took them safely to Rock Island in half a day and the whole crew walked back, fifteen miles, and brought over the other half. On July 12 they made St. Louis and delivered the rafts, each cut in half, to the consignee.

The next spring Hanks started from Albany back to the St. Croix, walking much of the way, and was ready to go with another raft. Meantime he had been using his wits about rafting and concluded that there was a better and safer way to check or moor. He devised and built of timbers a kind of huge cleat on the raft, with projecting arms to pass a line around. After that they took ashore only the end of the line and managed the checking on board. They took a turn around the cleat and then around the arms, and when the line went taut slackened it and eased it until headway was stopped, without smashing anything. This device was adopted at once on all rafts and saved no end of trouble—and, I think, some lives.

He says that on this trip a new misfortune beset them. There had been high water that spring and all the lowlands overflowed. This speedily bred mosquitoes in dense swarms that attacked and threatened to blind them. He devised protecting helmets of netting and so mitigated the danger, but could not end it, for the mosquitoes would still work their way under or through the netting.

He made another trip in the fall of that year and tested another innovation. The labor of getting the rafts through Lakes St. Croix and Pepin was great; and, of course, the longer one stayed in Lake Pepin the greater the chances of disaster there. So this time they took along horses, and built platforms over the cracks where the raft cribs joined. When they had sent the anchor ahead in the yawl, the horses tailed to the line and walked the whole length of the raft, pulling it along at a fair rate of speed. But this was attended with a new difficulty. The month was October, the weather intensely cold, and ice was forming in the lake. The line, wet with icy water, was extremely hard to handle. Hanks devised a simple thing, being a board with a notch cut deeply into it, by which the line could be picked up and dragged in without touching it.

On the twelfth of November they reached Sand Prairie, and moored for the night. The next morning they came out of their huts to find six inches of snow on the raft and ice forming everywhere. They made out to start, but a few miles farther it was evident that they must give up all hope of reaching St. Louis before the river should freeze. They made one more gallant attempt to fight the intense cold and snow and finally landed in a slough where they made the rafts secure for the winter. On November 16 the river froze over solidly.

They were not far from Hanks's old home town of Albany and went there to spend the winter. The crew had not been paid, none of the men had money, but the local hotel undertook to lodge and feed them on credit. Some weeks having passed without word from the employer, and the landlord growing crusty, Hanks went down to the rafts with some men and axes, chopped out of the ice as much of the employer's lumber as he thought necessary, hauled it to town, sold it, and provided the men with funds.

Before winter was over he was ordered back to the St. Croix, and the crew and pilot were left to take the raft to St. Louis when the ice should go out.

The trip back to the St. Croix Hanks made in the month of January in a sleigh drawn by mules, and traveling part of the time on the frozen river and then through the trackless woods. In the middle of Lake Pepin, sliding over the ice and snow, they came to a crack between three and four feet wide stretching clear across. This was but natural; winter or summer they always expected the worst of Lake Pepin. To go back and try to find a road through the woods was unthinkable. They unhitched the mules and made them leap the opening. Then they managed to pass the sleigh over it and went on their way. Hanks notes that when they reached their destination the mules were hairless from breasting their way through the underbrush.

Chance far more than man's prevision determined all the crises of this story, and in the hands of blindest chance was now hanging an event that was to sweep the whole business with overturn and transform every considerable settlement from Lake Pepin to Alton Slough.

Hanks was wanted in the St. Croix region to get out

91

the log drive, which was larger than usual. The winter had been notably severe, with a heavy snowfall and ice three feet thick. Spring came late; the fifteenth of May was upon them before enough ice was gone to make driving possible. They started down one of the small streams, when they were met with orders to hold their logs, because in the St. Croix River, toward which they were heading, there had come a flood and no one could tell what might happen.

It was too late. The drive had started. The flood proved to be one of the worst ever known in that region. In it the drive was caught; the logs were swept along like straws.

The mill at which these logs were to be sawed into boards that would then be rafted to St. Louis was somewhere above what is now the attractive, prosperous city of Stillwater. The mill and all the region around were flooded. Some attempt was made to catch the logs as they went shooting past. It would have been easier to catch stampeded buffalo. The whole vast drive, three million feet of logs, went by and tossed helter-skelter down the river.

Some were thrown upon the banks and stuck there, some were caught, some went into a boom that belonged to another firm.

The problem now was what to do with this magnificent timber. To try to get it back up the river to the mill was out of the question. To let it lie and rot was intolerable to the thrifty souls that owned it. In this dilemma some one suggested the sending of it down the river to St. Louis to be sawed there. Such a thing never had been done, but no good reason appeared why it should not be, if the scattered logs could be screwed together into something like a raft. Hanks was put upon this job and, working with skill and using his experience, he put together the first log raft that floated down the upper Mississippi. He herded the separate logs into strings; he fastened them together with the birch boughs and the burr-oak staples, he put the strings into a raft. Bitter experience had taught him how easily a raft, even a lumber raft, could go to smash in this difficult navigation. He aimed to make his log raft as stiff as possible, and ran long lines, A lines and others, across it from side to side and then from corner to corner and hauled them taut with windlasses.

Out of the débris of the drive six rafts were made, each six strings wide and about six hundred feet long. When Hanks was told that he was to be pilot of one of these, he seemed to have been ravished with delight.

Lake Pepin bothered his happy thoughts. Horses could not be used on a log raft, and to haul these big things through with anchor and line would be all but impossible. Hanks negotiated with a steamboat [4] and, for a price, she pulled all the rafts through the lake, being the first instance on the Mississippi of raft-towing by a steamboat.

They had started out of the St. Croix about July 2, 1844. Once clear of the lake they had no more trouble. Hanks had learned the river now. He could not be fooled by any of its tricks, and the flotilla went through to St. Louis without a break. Thirty days after they had left Stillwater he was back there.

It was the beginning of log-rafting on the Mississippi.

The new phase came upon the business with a rush. Until that time the lumber needs of the valley had been supplied chiefly by sawmills on the Wisconsin, Chip-

[4] He forgot to enter the name, an unusual oversight for him, but thought afterward it was the *Otter.* In this he seemed to have been wrong, for historically the first steamboat to haul a raft through Lake St. Croix was an aged relic called the *War Eagle,* the first of many of that name. The point is important, for the event had momentous consequences.

pewa, and St. Croix that rafted a finished product.
Now men saw a great advantage in rafting the raw
material to the spot where lumber was wanted and
fashioning it there to suit the trade. As this idea began
to take possession of them, the great industry of the
river region sprang up a giant full made. The tributary streams in the pine forests began to pour out their
log rafts and at every considerable point along the
river arose almost magically the sawmill that made lumber and fortunes with equal facility.

Chapter VI

SO LOG WAS KING

A TOWNY of mine, who was also (at times) a poet, once wrote some exceedingly bad verses in which he likened our little riverside city to a princess and its water-front to her crown. This, though far-fetched and vinous in origin, pleased local pride, always easily titillated. But no ecstasy in this mind or any other could make of the old sawmill, always the chief note in the scene, anything in the way of a jewel in that crown, for the sawmill reared itself in a mere swank of aggressive ugliness. I think there was no point of view from which it did not seem to shout aloud its multiplex offenses. It had never been painted; it was now dingy black with age. On one side it lunged into distorted rhomboids and on another wallowed into slab heaps. It gaped with huge unsightly mouths snagged with uneven teeth. Part of it was all awry and tottering; on the river side its log runway, projecting like a crude crutch, seemed to hint a worse deformity.

Yet it typified great history in the making, and throughout the town's meandering length and narrow girth was nothing to compare with it in importance. Of all this vast continental development it was at once the sign and the factor. Let be its ugliness; it had attributes that endeared it to every household. Be-

95

sides that it made homes and fostered business, in and around its weedy precincts men worked and got wages; which was well. It connected us by a chain of dollars with an expanding world; which also was well. And the quarrel of its buzz-saws and snarl of its planers, toning the nerves of the whole community to a sense of importance, dulled the remote loneliness of the frontier; which perhaps was best of all.

In those days every town along the upper Mississippi had a sawmill like this as surely as it had a schoolhouse, and three sparsely attended churches. From May to October, around these sprawling sheds, the week-day bustle never relented, the runways groaned with logs, the drying-yards multiplied their piles of fresh cut and fragrant pine. It was the happiest business ever known, for the logs slipped easily from those immemorial forests of noble white pine to the northward (believed to be inexhaustible and created for our sole benefit), and as for the lumber into which they were made—all men must have that.

It seems to be a fact that the magics of fairy-tales show tame before some of the actualities of commerce. The stupendous industry that now developed went much as *Aladdin* built the palace. Capital to support the development, men to direct it, other men to do its hard, physical adventuring, all seemed to spring from undiscoverable sources. The river town and its sawmill appeared where last year were weeds and waste. At first each mill could supply only its own neighborhood, because there was no good way to distribute the lumber it made. Then the railroads pushed over the prairie, touched the Mississippi, crossed it, dug into the vast stretches of fat black land beyond, and behold a new and dazzling world revealed; for the railroads carried with them for a thousand miles the joint product of the lumberjack, the raftsman, and the squat, unsightly sawmill.

All day long the great rafts followed one another, floating with the current of the broad, placid, and beautiful river as the business mounted (crimes or no crimes) and scattered wealth and wages all up and down the stream side. Upon it battened these new-sprung towns, while a definite if primitive romance hung upon all its activities; the romance of easy money, adventure, and peril, the finer romance of battling with nature, subduing forests, and going face to face with the wild. Chiefest of its rougher and almost Neander-thal glamours was around two battalions of its indus-trial army, those queer wild men I have described as fighting out the savage winters in the woods, and the other queer wild men that managed the rafts down the involutions of the Mississippi.

As the logs floated with about half of their bulk submerged, the raft drew maybe a foot and a half. Sometimes a few larger logs or an abnormal condition might give a draft of two feet, but one of eighteen inches was commoner. Looking at the easily flowing river, so deceptive to a landsman's eye, one would say that to find room in it for eighteen inches was no prob-lem to whiten one's hair. But this was not so much as the primer to the raft pilot's full volume of troubles. At a thousand treacherous places along the six or seven hundred miles of river that he must know with an intimate, exhaustive, faultless knowledge, there might be depth enough one day and not depth enough the next, and the pilot must know the endless secrets of all these places before he got to them.

He must know so many other things, and his knowl-edge was so vital to so many overshadowing interests, we need not wonder that before long he was a lordly creature with whom men must negotiate if they would have his services. In his pride he affected a kind of uniform, being a red shirt, a black silk cravat tied in a large square bow, and a black slouch hat. Any pilot of eminence went always gloved. Thus he received those that would avail themselves of his skill. In the eyes of the awed populace he was a noted man; he could command wages that for that day approached the fabulous, being $500 a month or more.

If he really knew his business, he might justly be proud of the mental deck-load he carried. For example, if there were three feet on Camanche bar, he must get the raft into one exact position to run safely the reef at Princeton bar, just below. But if there were four feet at Camanche, then the position for Princeton must be different or he would smash into the bank. You might think that having learned this once it would be enough for that particular spot. Not at all; because with three and a half feet you ran the reach in still another way, and every variation of depth meant another way of running. When you remember that the Mississippi is never of the same depth on two successive days, and when you multiply these troubles into every mile of the trip, you will see that time did not hang heavily upon a raft pilot's hands. All the way from Lake St. Croix to the sawmill, wherever that might be, he never knew a really drab moment. The changing shores, an illimitable procession of landmarks known only to himself, and the look of the water surface made up his chart, by the occult demands of which he ordered the head or the stern swung to starboard or larboard—port being a word unknown in my time. He had not only to steer the huge unwieldy raft, now through a storm, now through a night as dark as Egypt, but he had also to command twenty or thirty reckless, roistering, sentimentalizing savages that at the drop of a hat

would have riddled him with shot or flung him into the
stream; men that would have despised the least showing of weakness or fear as they would have resented
the least sign of up-stage authority. Everything depended upon him. At any time he might pile all his logs
along twenty miles of shore or find himself going down
the middle of the Mississippi without a crew, while of
law to sustain him there was no more than in the desert
of Gobi.

Rafts grew longer as the business found its bearings;
and then to steer them around the curvings of the channel and over the numerous and always changeful sand-
bars required a still higher order of developed skill, and
at times the swift, stern, and almost titanic labor of
the men at the great oars. In the lunacies of an inexplicable current and the quick chances of wind and
weather, skill and hard work alike would fail, and I
have seen a raft go plump into a tow head with twenty
men rowing like mad to save it and the bewitched thing
bent by their efforts almost into a great letter C.[5]

The rowing, by the way, always had a considerable
interest for persons with a strong rhythmical sense that
watched it from the shore.

Each oar worked on a peg fixed in the crosspieces
at the ends of the raft. The handles were about thirty
feet long and tapered so that a man could grasp the
small ends. Planks spiked across the logs made foot-
holds for the oarsmen. Rowing was done with excellent
unison and rhythm. The man at the end of the line

[5] In a paper furnished to the Wisconsin Historical Society, C. C.
Lincoln tells of a crew of a nine-string raft on the Wisconsin that
rowed at top speed all day to keep the raft from going into the
bank. In another paper to the same society by S. A. Sherman are
further illustrations for the curious concerning the titanic labors of
rafts' crews. In going around curves it was sometimes necessary to
loosen all the lines and let the raft bend itself into the shape of
the channel, even when it twisted into a big S and the bow could
not be seen from the stern.

gave a little signal with a kind of curling motion of his oar end. Then all raised the handles together, dipped the blades, and with the hands at the level of the eyes walked in step to the end of the plank, pushing the oars in front of them with a series of odd, surging motions, and two men on the corner oars. At the end of the stroke they gave together a final heave, lowered the handles, marched in step to the other ends of the planks, and began again.

Rough board huts sheltered the crew, placed in the center of the raft for safety's sake, the thing being so likely to hit a shore and crumble. The mess-hall was usually separate and so was the kitchen, identified by a red angle of stove pipe thrust through its side. Fare was primitive and void of ceremony, but ample, and of its kind the best the region afforded. Raftsmen knew what they wanted and got it, or heaved the cook overboard, the river being so handy.

The bridges gave crew and pilot their greatest difficulties, because of this fault of setting the piers at an angle to the current instead of in line with it. Hence there was commonly a set of water toward the mid-river piers, and the force of this drift was different at each stage of the river.

To-day you maneuvered your raft into a certain position in relation to a bridge pier and went through all right. Next week you got your raft into exactly the same position, and in spite of all hands rowing at top speed the thing went into the pier. Yet on both occasions the flow of the water, even to expert eyes, was the same. The result was that the natural emphasis of the calendar came to be reversed at towns that had bridges, and the day was marked as unusual on which a raft did not hit a pier head. Clinton bridge, for example, was planned to have piers 160 feet apart; the

LUMBER RAFT ABOUT 1866

engineers placed them at 119 feet and could hardly have done a worse job for rafting.

Even the most skilful pilots could not manage the Davenport bridge with certainty. If the wind were blowing hard across the channel, no strength and no foresight would avail. When raft after raft had been disintegrated, a pilot hit upon an invention that saved a trunkful of dollars. A few miles above the bridge was a rocky islet. He cemented into its lower edge a huge iron staple holding an iron ring more than two feet in diameter. A short distance away he provided a great iron hook, made fast in the rock.

The operation of this device will give a notion of the difficulties of raft navigation. Each raft was outfitted with a kind of strong, light, well-designed skiff, called a Quincy, from the town where it was made. Two or three Quincies were kept drawn up on the logs on each side of the raft, ready for instant use. Two had coiled upon their stern-sheets great hawsers for mooring or snubbing. When a raft was the right distance above the islet now, one of these skiffs put out. Two men rowed, one stood in the stern and paid out the line. They got to the islet, passed the end of the hawser through the ring, took a couple of turns around the great hook and stood by. When the line straightened up with the weight of the raft, it swung the raft into a certain position that enabled it to pass safely over one of the rock "chains" that beset the Rapids and so get into position to run the bridge.

But the thing demanded infallible judgment on the part of the pilot to know the instant when the raft had swung far enough, and on the part of the men ashore to manipulate the line without pulling a piece out of the raft with the jerk. Likewise, the trick was not without its perils. "Snubbing" was the technical name for it. To work it in perfection the operator must watch like a hawk. Immediately after the line straightened up taut and hard with the first pull of the raft, there came a slight easing of the pressure as the momentum of the great raft yielded an instant in the direction of the pull. The trick was to slack the line at one instant and tauten it at the next. The danger was that the line might break, and if the flying end struck one the blow might be fatal, and meantime the raft, released too soon, would drift down upon Moline Chain.

Just below the spot where the Maquoketa River flows into the Mississippi was another ugly place that raftsmen disliked—Maquoketa Slough, of evil renown. It was crooked, it was more than commonly moody and changeful, and it had an up-and-down bank with a queer swirl of water that was continually cutting into the shore and changing its contour while it shifted the channel. This was because the smaller stream ran with speed into the greater and made an eddy, and when a raft was caught in that vicious backwash and the water high, the pilot could usually see his finish. There were seven ways of running that stretch so as to keep out of the eddy, but any of them might slip from under you between one trip and another. The earth that the eddy dug out in one place it stealthily and perversely piled in another, so that on the larboard side of the channel a new bar was constantly forming. The result was that where the rafts ran in safety one season was a grassy islet the next. In June of 1866 a raft could trail all over the place and by August an entirely different channel had developed and the channel of June was a long yellow sand-bar.

Through this place rafts went at night at a time when not a light or lighthouse existed on the whole river from St. Paul to the Gulf, or thereabouts. At one

place the starboard logs forward passed within two feet
of a bluff bank. This was the case up to about the end
of the first week of July. A bar then began to form
off the lower point of the slough and the raft must be
kept four feet away, then five, then fifty, then a hundred, and by the end of the season a new crossing had
been established and the place that the rafts formerly
shaved as close as an egg they now passed nearly half
a mile away.

The question I have asked myself many times is this:
The changes in the course to be steered were grad-
ual, progressive, and chiefly under the surface. A raft
pilot went by the place in daylight the first week in
July and again the last week of the same month at
night. How did he know the second time that he could
not steer where he had steered the first time? How
did he know where he could steer?

I do not know; I never could find out. Ordinarily,
as I have explained, he would be informed about any
fixed bar or crossing by a series of marks and ripples
as he came along. A certain depth at one point meant
a corresponding depth on another. But in such an instance as this, these indications would be worthless,
because the whole conformation was dissolving and
changing hour by hour. It seems to me there is but one
solution of these mysteries. Necessity is the mother of a
curious and varied brood. The thing had to be done
and the supple human mind or spirit, or whatever it
is, driven hard by the need, found a way to do it.

The upper part of the Mississippi abounds in islands
that cut it into narrow waterways. Sometimes a raft
would fit one of these narrows about as closely as the
glove on your hand, and then to get the brute around
a sharp curve was nothing to go to sleep over. After a
time, rafts ran in the night as in the day; clear nights
if they could, dark nights if they must. Marks that are

easy in daylight are to the sharpest eyes shadowy and
confusing at night. I know a hundred places on the
upper Mississippi the threading of which by a raft on
any night, dark or clear, would seem merely preposterous. But rafts were actually steered through such
places, night after night, without disaster. Recalling
now with wonder that is almost awe what was required
of these men in lightning-flash judgment, dauntless
courage and flawless knowledge of this strange river's
ways, migrations, moods, tenses, and infinite variety, I
have honest doubt whether man's capacity for technical
efficiency was ever put to harder testing. But, as to this,
be you the judge when this poor chronicle is done.
Mark Twain made the world familiar with the difficulties of piloting a steamboat on the lower Mississippi.
They were great; the men that overcame them were
justly besung. But a steamboat pilot on the lower river
always seemed to me less of a superman than a raft
pilot on the upper.

As to these crews so liberal with knife-blade or riot,
tradition says there were unusual characters among the
keel-boat men of historic river days, rash souls (at
first) along the Erie Canal, and peculiar ruffians among
the "packet rats" of the old clipper ships. I think any
of these would have been of but pallid tint compared
with my rapscallions of the Mississippi raft.

As the business grew, their calling became more of
its own kind, and having only a casual and disdainful
connection with trades less original and more humdrum.
In the roaring days of the river traffic, when it was
the right aorta of commerce, to be anything connected
with it was to be badged with a certain distinction; but
to be a raftsman was to go in the very spotlight of
evil renown. The popular belief I have mentioned that
a raftsman led chiefly a life of crime and yearned ar-
dently to enlarge it at the expense of the orderly was

partly mere stuff, partly exaggeration, but more due
to the times and conditions in which he lived. He was
on the remote frontier line of the nation; justice there
was crudely organized, if at all; and the real law was
the new country code of the quickest hand and surest
shot. The same ferments that produced "Wild Bill"
and "Doc Halliday" on land and "Bully Hayes" in the
South Seas produced the typical raftsman of the upper
Mississippi.

But here again with some differences, as I hope to
show.

What this queer, complex, irrational thing of nerves
and tantrums that we call man will do when freed from
the restraints of law, the gaze of his neighbors, and
the habituated criticisms of a formal society is beyond
all guess.

Sometimes he goes to South Africa and, from a mild-
mannered and gentle-spoken scholar, turns into a rav-
ening wild beast with an insatiable thirst for cruelty,
like Dr. Peters. Sometimes he turns half dreamer, half
fighter, like Kit Carson. Sometimes he is all good-will,
service, and sympathy like Edward Tregear among the
Polynesians, and sometimes he is about half ruffian and
half recluse, like men I have known on the island
beaches.

In the case of the raftsman of the upper Mississippi,
there was at the beginning of the business and long
afterward all the conditions in which man is pronest
to the worst of these reversions.

But net results were not exactly what were to have
been expected.

The typical raftsman was reckless, dissolute, daring
and all that, but he was more; he was humorous with
a style of humor all his own and largely his own language in which to frame it; emotional at bottom, sophisticated on the surface; a singer, a dancer, an

improviser of wild yarns, ready with fist, dagger, or pistol; something of a poet, curiously responsive to charitable appeals, something of a Lothario, something of a pirate, something of a blackguard, and in profanity equipped with resources incomparable for richness of invention and competence of authority. And I think that in some of this his environment was reflected as much as his natural inclining in the rest. The raftsman's life was led in disorder and far from observation, but it took him into a region of singular and almost surpassing beauty where for miles he and his raft were the only signs of human effort, and the solitude was of a suggestion solemnly regenerative, all the artifices of civilization being far away. If life in such conditions lacked the grand touch of golden chances that distinguished life in a mining camp, it had something else at least as strong in human interest. For the operating and guiding of rafts down the Mississippi, having brought forth all this skill and knowledge, the guild had, after all, a certain redemption of dignity, and I have heard raftsmen comparing waterscapes with the zest of artists, if they used words artists would never have understood.

The Black River raft from which I had my introduction to this business moored in front of my grandfather's place from necessity, not choice. The town of Le Claire stood at the head of the Le Claire Rapids, almost fifteen miles long and providing navigation not only with countless difficulties but with peculiar bedevilments the river man never tired of discussing. The Rapids were not much to look at; I have heard travelers say that they were not rapids at all. These were persons that had come expecting to see boiling whirlpools, cascades, swift descents, and so on, and could discover nothing that looked different from the rest of the river.

Steamboatmen and raft pilots had another thought about it.

Elsewhere the Mississippi current ran about three miles an hour; over the Le Claire Rapids, about five. This was not enough to bother any healthy steamboat, going up or down. But something more than current made trouble in this infernal place. Elsewhere the bottom was sand and silt, shifting eternally but recording every shift on the surface of the water. On the Rapids, the bottom was rock and did not shift, but the water slipped in puzzling and unreasonable ways over these outcropping strata that were called "chains," and on each "chain" there was a different situation with each stage of water. The water ran differently, the set of the current was different, the slender path by which the pilot was picking his way among submerged rocks and reefs was different, an entirely new set of perils beset him and his craft. With the incessant changes of channel depth in this river it might be said that the Le Claire Rapids could challenge any other stretch of water in the world for perplexities. I have seen the famous descent of the Lachine Rapids in the St. Lawrence, and, if I know anything of piloting, it is dead easy compared with Le Claire as Le Claire used to be.

We noted that when Stephen Hanks had reached this unhappy spot he split his raft and took one of the Rapids pilots to help him down to Davenport. Rapids pilots were men that did nothing but study the restless humors of this part of the stream and take rafts and steamboats through it. They all lived in our town, where they were among our most respected citizens; justly, if one stops to think of what their calling meant. When a raft was split for the Rapids, the crew of the half that was left could betake itself to relaxation and refreshment of spirit, after the raftsman's peculiar

107

bent, of which you are to hear. When a raft was split at Le Claire the handy place to moor a half of it was in front of my grandfather's, because there alone a raft could lie clear of the ferry- and steamboat-landings and of the outstretched boom of the local sawmill. If there was any town that ought to know what rafts and raftsmen were, it was Le Claire, and the stretch of water front commanded by our front porch was the superior place of tuition.

Chapter VII

DAYS OF THE GREAT MIGRATION

IN this swift rise of a great industry, Hanks became a man of mark and before long a man of wealth. He was now about twenty-three years old and engaged in taking contracts to deliver log rafts to the new mills down the river. He was one of those uneasy souls that hunger and thirst after work and are never filled. In the winter he went into the woods and directed the cutting of the logs, commanded the driving and raft-making, and then got himself aboard the raft when made and piloted the thing to its destination. He was looked upon as the safest man in the business; mill owners when they knew he had a raft in charge felt that they could go to bed and sleep, because he would deliver the logs when he said he would if he had to carry them in his arms. He knew the river now so well that he could run at night. Some of his wondering crew believed he could run it with his eyes shut. For rafting lumber he received $3 a thousand feet, for logs $3.50, and twenty-five cents a thousand for the laths and shingles he carried as freight. At these rates he gathered profits.

But not without troubles and adventures. In the spring of 1847, he being then at Albany, a steamboat came along, the *Amulet*, bound for St. Paul, whose

109

pilots did not know the river above Galena and wanted Hanks to take the boat up for them. Seeing a chance to add to his fortune, he bought a load of such provisions as he knew were needed in the St. Croix region and set forth. When they reached ill-omened Lake Pepin the ice was still in the lake, but he saw a narrow lane of open water along the west bank and struck into it, clipping along at a good rate and thinking how easy it was, when the crazy wind changed and began to blow strongly from the East. This moved the ice and closed up the open lane, pinching the *Amulet*. With what Hanks described as incredible swiftness they found the boat forced upon the shore above the level of the lake, and apparently wrecked, for the ice tore open the hull for fifteen feet along the bilge. Under Hanks's directions the crew crawled down into the hold and bulkheaded this hurt. Then they jettisoned the cargo and put skids under the hull, digging down through the ice. Then they waited. Hanks believed she would still float if they could get her into the water. After a few days the ice jam relaxed, the steamer *Senator* came along and pulled them off the shore, and, when they found that she was not leaking badly, they put the cargo on board and headed up for St. Paul.

The next spring he was caught again in Lake Pepin, which seems to have been his hoodoo, but this time by a storm and not by ice. There was no handy steamboat to tow him, and he was working his raft through the lake by the long, dull process of hand-hauling. One night he was tied up under a point, and about twelve o'clock heard in his sleep the roaring of wind through the tree-tops on the bluff above him. He leaped from his bunk, called all hands, and in the darkness strove to get the raft out of the exposed place where it lay. Casting off, he had the oars worked hard at both ends until he fought his way around the head of the next point below. He had then to get into the bay beyond the point. To do this he sent men ashore with the check-line. They made fast to a tree, and the raft in that howling gale tore the tree up. They tried another with the same result. At last they found one that would stick, when the raft swung around into safety. It was a notable storm, even for that unsavory place. Just below, two other rafts of the same ownership were caught and literally ground to pieces. They even lost a large part of their supplies, and Hanks must spend the next week in helping with all his crew to fish scattered logs out of the lake and provide food for the hungry.

Such a change as we have noted among the workers in the woods showed now in rafting crews. In the beginning they had been like Hanks himself, American backwoodsmen, strong of body, straight of mind, and simple of habits. The new lot were the first contingent of the wild men that were afterward to make raftsman a word of terror to the peaceful inhabitants. The next year, 1848, Hanks had his first experience with the new type. Instead of the townsmen of his that had formerly shared his adventures, he had a crew of ruffians that got drunk whenever they dared and defied any authority but stronger force—Black River style. It was late in the autumn and he had tied up at Dubuque. His ruffians went ashore and, coming back drunk, demanded that the trip should end and they be paid. Hanks reminded them that they had shipped for St. Louis, to be paid off there. Little they cared about agreements. He told them that he was under contract to deliver the raft at St. Louis. Contracts were nothing to them either; what they wanted was their money and to be quit of the trip. He fronted a mob of them but without flinching. One ran at him with a bowie raised to plunge into his breast. Hanks, without making a movement, allowed him to approach close and then suddenly shot out his right fist and struck the raised arm a blow so powerful that the knife shot from the man's grasp and went flying over the heads of the mob into the water.

"Now," said Hanks, quietly, "we'll go to work." So they went to work.

The accounts of him agree that he had in emergencies a kind of native dignity and self-command that were rather awesome upon the average temperament. He could do more with his reserve than another with bluster. The courage that kept his blood cool and his head clear served him in more ways than one.

In 1852 he was piloting a log raft to St. Louis, when cholera broke out in his crew. It was a cholera year and the disease, or the fear of it, was unusually fatal. One member of the crew died, and at the first opportunity all the rest deserted, leaving Hanks alone on his raft. He sent to Albany for men of his own style of grit and steered to St. Louis without mishap. On the way back, cholera appeared on the steamboat and many passengers were stricken by it; but not Hanks. He went his way among the sick men to serve them unshaken, as if he knew cholera was not for him.

By this time he had gathered a fortune of respectable size for those days, but he kept on working as before, winter and summer. The winter of 1852-53 he was employed as pilot on a new and fast steamboat that made daily trips between Alton and St. Louis. Sometimes he laid over and then he would run up to Springfield to see his cousin Abraham Lincoln, who was living there, but he always arrived when Lincoln was away on a circuit.

The next summer, 1853, he started down the river with four rafts, one of lumber, the rest of logs, some of which were his own. So far he had never had a serious accident. The river was unusually high and seemed to get higher the farther he went. There was a flood in the Iowa, and when he reached the point where it entered the Mississippi the strong whirling of waters ran away with his rafts and wrecked all of them. When the flood subsided they found one of the lumber cribs sticking upright in the brush some miles from the river, and what had been a corn-field was covered thickly with the logs. Most of them never were recovered. He was under contract to deliver the rafts. After he had worked for weeks scraping in the mud to find his property, he must take what he had to St. Louis and pocket the loss. It was so heavy that he was ruined. He turned over everything he had to his creditors and when he had settled with them he found he had seventy-five dollars to his name, and his rafting kit.

The kit he stored in a warehouse at Albany. Then the warehouse took fire, the kit was destroyed, and, after so many years of hard work and honorable achievement, he owned the shoes he stood in and naught else beyond his own soul.

It was the end of his contract logging and rafting and he must begin again.

The memorials of this man are so remarkable that I hope to be pardoned if I dwell upon him; seldom in a sordid world do we come upon a character that seems in every way to stand the touch, and assuredly in the case of a raft pilot in the year of grace 1853 the touch was fairly hot. Besides, he seems to have been well worth noting as a specimen of the genus American unalloyed in an earlier day when it was closer to the blockhouse and, maybe, to the canticle. Observe, then. He had a simple, methodical but blessed habit of keeping a kind of diary or note-book, from the curt, quaint entries in which I draw material for a kind of portrait. Much more is supplied by the comments of his friends and fellow-craftsmen, who seem to have all but idolized him. In the days we are now telling of, he was described as almost six feet in height, straight, spare, blue-eyed, with a clean, wholesome look in his face and prodigious strength in his frame. Once in a store at Albany on a dare he lifted a barrel of flour by the chines to his shoulder and carried it up the hill to his home. Captain P. P. Chacey, long time a riverman, afterward retired at Fargo, North Dakota, once pulled an oar on one of Hanks's rafts. He says that between Lake St. Croix and Lake Pepin the raft ran under an overhanging tree and unshipped an oar. Four or five men were tugging at it, trying to get it back.

"Babies!" snorted Hanks. "Stand back and let a man show you." And all alone he picked up the oar and put it into its place.

He was so kind that everybody loved him, seems never to have lost his perfect command over himself, and cherished an impossible respect for what he called his duty. With other traits he was a brand from the burning, if there ever was one. In the midst of a wild, reckless, lawless environment he kept the queer streak of religious veneration that he inherited from his Puritan ancestors. He records in his diary that when he was stationed in the woods the year of his first absence from home he used to walk every Sunday morning seven miles to be at the services held in the settlement by the missionary. The lessons of youthful piety must have taken firm hold upon him, for when he was almost in middle life and had been for years inured to the ways of the new country, he set down in his diary an illuminating incident that would have been treasure-trove for the writers of the Sunday-school books of half a century ago.

It was one Sunday morning in the fall of the year, his boat had been laid up for the winter, and he had retired to his place at Albany. Before church services he walked out upon his little farm, and there, in a corner of the fence, was a covey of quail.

Old Sathanas, the ever wily, whispered to him to go get his gun; conscience replied that to kill quail on Sunday was wrong. In the struggle that ensued, Satan got the best of him, as he has so often in such contests. Hanks knew it was wicked. He knew it would be breaking the Sabbath, he knew that bitterly thereafter he would repent the misdeed; but the thought of the quail was too much for him. He got his gun and let go with both barrels and dropped eight of them. Then he went to his house to reflect with sorrow upon his iniquities and enter in his diary his self-condemnation.

He was almost wholly self-educated, but he learned to write excellent American and to make public addresses. The life that hardened some men left him, by all accounts, of undiminished kindness and sympathy. With other good traits, he had mind upon the days of his own youth. Once when he was taking a towboat up the river he noticed two boys rowing a skiff up-stream against the current and a stiff wind. He stopped, got out his speaking trumpet, and asked them where they were going. They told him, and it was more than ten miles.

"Well, get aboard," said Hanks, and he had his crew lift the skiff upon the guards. When the youths left they wished to pay him.

"Not a cent," said Hanks. "I've been a boy myself. It's all right, and come again."

He was what they called a lightning pilot, and earned the distinction. For a time in the fall and early winter he was pilot on the steamer *Governor George Briggs*, a small side-wheeler famous for speed while his delicate touch was urging her along. She used to pull out of St. Louis in the morning by the bright light and whistle for Keokuk, 204 miles away, before the sun was down, a feat that seems highly incredible but was performed many times. She was a good boat, the *Briggs;* but, according to my pilot friends, having one defect. They assured me that after every other trip she must be laid up, because she went through the water so fast the friction melted off the iron stem-piece.

He piloted log rafts, lumber rafts in the summer and steamboats in the winter, and seemed to be able to do anything except sit still in one place. From the beginning he had been marvelously advantaged with eyes that saw everything and a memory that never slipped. The first time he voyaged down the river on a raft he was noting and storing away the shape of the bluffs and the tale of the ripples. Piloting he recognized as an illimitable science, not a mere gainful vocation; and he learned to do things in it that nobody else could do. In 1850 he took an excursion party on the *Anthony Wayne* farther up the Minnesota than any other steamboat had ever gone. He had never been there himself and knew nothing about the river, but by this time he had learned to read water like large print and he kept his boat in the channel there as surely as in the Mississippi.

The new way of life into which he was now projected was packet piloting. Some report of his winter work between Alton and St. Louis had gone into the far-away. He was welcomed with joy as chief pilot on the *Dr. Franklin No. 2,* famous steamer plying between St. Louis and St. Paul.

This happened in 1854, when the river traffic was climbing to its crest. In the St. Paul and Galena trade was the fast steamer *Nominee.* She was captained by Orrin Smith and the *Dr. Franklin* by Daniel Smith

116

Harris, of whom you have heard. Between these commanders was a rivalry of long standing and some edge. It was more than sentimental; the *Nominee* was a recent comer and, being so fast and popular, was eating into business that the owners of the *Franklin* believed to be their own. You will observe that the stage was properly set for a first-class steamboat fight.

More than once there had been smart brushes between these vessels, but not enough to settle anything. Going up to St. Paul once they had been in sight of each other for a day, one taking the lead, then the other; so that they came to port with both crews eager for the finish fight next on the cards.

They left St. Paul in the evening, the *Nominee* getting away first and passing out of sight before the *Franklin* was ready to cast off. They had a hot engineer on the *Franklin;* according to the pilot-house story, he fixed a piece of scantling between the safety-valve and the deck above it and let her drive. The *Nominee* must have been likewise tearing into the work, for when the *Franklin* reached Read's Landing, eighty miles below, the other boat was still ahead. Six miles farther she stopped under a point and waited for the *Franklin,* that there might be no question as to a perfectly fair race.

Now Hanks was at the wheel. When he saw the *Nominee* lying still, he slacked up and offered her the chance to go first. Captain Smith would not take it, and as soon as the *Franklin* had passed him he took out after her with his safety-valve whistling.

After that it was nip and tuck. The two boats were about even as to build and power; the real contest was in the piloting. Hanks would not let any one else lay a hand on the wheel; he had a touch as delicate as a woman's, and knew it as well as he knew that many a race had been lost by pilots that kept the rudder drag-

117

ging. He knew something else: he knew the river better
than any other man alive and had a competent sense
of what that knowledge might mean before they should
be through.

Mile after mile the boats were almost side by side.
Both were crowded with passengers who missed their
meals rather than a moment of that fierce struggle.
Steamboat-racing is the grandest, most exciting, most
maddening sport mankind has ever known; it was easily
denounced for its dangers, but nobody could keep out
of it if a chance offered. The *Franklin* and *Nominee*
were so close to each other that the passengers could
shout back and forth, and there went up a constant torrent of taunts and gibes. Half inch by half inch the
Franklin was getting the better of the struggle, but
one could tell this only by watching jackstaffs.

At Crooked Slough, some miles below La Crosse, came
the first sharp test of piloting. It is full of islands and
short cuts. One of the cut-offs is called Paint Rock
Slough. At certain stages of water you can run it like
oil; at others you cannot run it at all, and at still others
you can bump through by grinding over a reef. It saves
about a mile and a half over the long channel. When
Hanks reached this place he knew from certain old
marks of his that the water in Paint Rock Slough was
at the bumping stage and kept to the regular channel.
The *Nominee* ran Paint Rock and had to bump and
grind her way through. When she emerged at the lower
end the *Franklin* was two miles ahead.

She had to take on wood at Guttenberg, and the
excited passengers were sure that the delay would put
their hated rival ahead. Captain Daniel Smith Harris
had another thought about that. The wood was on a
flat boat; he hitched the flat alongside, almost without
stopping.

"Now you fellows come down here and do a little hon-

118

est work," yelled the mate to the passengers. They all came and the air was full of flying cord-wood.

They made a record clean-up and cast the flat loose without a thought of what would become of it.

In those times before the electric searchlight, steamers making landings at night used great torches, which were iron baskets filled with pine chips and resin. The *Franklin* had a plentiful supply of resin when she left St. Paul—resin in barrels. They walked into it now and fed it to the furnaces with pitch, oil, and anything else they could find that would make a hot fire. Stops they must make because they were carrying the United States mail, which must go, races or no races; but they would take on no more freight than could be loaded while the mail sacks were being slung off and on. When the *Franklin* stopped, the *Nominee* shot far ahead; when the *Nominee* stopped it was the *Franklin's* turn. From Guttenberg on, the *Franklin* held the lead. When she reached Dubuque the boiler breechings were red-hot to the tops of the jackets and men on the roof and elsewhere were standing by with the fire-hose. It must have been an interesting trip for passengers of a nervous diathesis.

Dubuque ended the first lap of the race and the *Franklin* had won it by about twenty minutes. There was some wild work on the levee getting freight ashore and aboard. That was where shone resplendent the red-faced mate; if anybody had entertained a doubt of·his functions, it vanished now. His long rigmarole of biting sarcasm and blistering profanity suddenly assumed a greater importance than the President's Message.

On the levee stood a pile of barrels of flour. A roustabout would heave a barrel upon its side, start it rolling down the incline for the gang-plank, and then race madly after it, guiding it with a stick so that the momentum would carry it up the plank and aboard. It

119

seemed impossible for this process to go faster, but it did not satisfy the mate.

"Hustle those barrels! Lively now, lively! What are you going to sleep for, you black son of a petrified mummy? Think this is a nigger funeral? Go on, go on, go on! Snatch that barrel, snatch it! Don't stop there and dream about it. Are you walking on eggs? Git it aboard! Git it aboard!"

Of necessity I have left out the pith and marrow of his remarks, but they may be imagined.

The *Franklin* got away first and held the lead and slightly increased it. At half-past three that afternoon she steamed into Galena still ahead, having made the run from St. Paul in a shade under twenty-two hours, and I cannot find that the time was ever beaten.

Stephen Hanks stood at the wheel all the time and, except when they were stopping at Dubuque, never took his hands from it.

Of the good ship *Dr. Franklin No. 2*, Captain Russell Blakely was at one time the master, and that reminds me of the tragic story of Rollingstone, which on many a night in the pilot-house I have heard recounted and wondered over.

As the flood of emigrants poured west and the new empire began to take shape out of the prairie waste, the river hummed with traffic and new towns sprang up about every five miles of its course. Of some of these not a trace now remains. It is odd to reflect on this reversal of the ordinary process of development on the Western Hemisphere, and to view long stretches of silent corn-fields or empty meadow where within the memory of living men were busy streets and thriving industry. Rockingham, Iowa—did you ever hear of Rockingham, Iowa? I doubt if diligent search now would reveal so much as a brick of an old foundation wall of Rockingham, Iowa. Yet it was in its time the

future great metropolis of the upper Mississippi. It
stood on the right bank of the main stream directly
opposite the mouth of Rock River, and what made its
importance was the transfer of traffic between the Mississippi and the Rock. There were warehouses and stores
and a hotel and a fair array of dwellings in Rockingham. Once it aspired to be the county seat and perhaps
the state capital. And now it is like the city of Petra
in Edom.

It is not the only Petra along the upper river, not
by many. There is something mysterious and weird
about the way these places dried up and disappeared.
One can understand how the inhabitants, finding the
currents of trade changing, should take the trail with
their Penates, but why should their dwellings dissolve
after them? Their dwellings and their stores and their
hotels and every other sign of man's habitation? I cannot tell, but this happened; even with the old solid
warehouses of yellow limestone in which the wheat used
to be stored in the good old days of boom. I can shut
my eyes and count near a score of these between Red
Wing and Davenport; once landmarks, and now vanished like the morning dew. The Arab and his tent have
passed into everlasting proverb, but who is well prepared to have the invisible years fold up and cart away
a stone warehouse?

Read's Landing—that busy, thriving, confident little city, more than two thousand inhabitants when I
knew it. Twenty steamboats at a time have lain before
its water-front waiting for the tardy ice to move out
of Lake Pepin. Lines of stages used to start from it for
St. Paul and Mankato when the navigation was inter-
rupted. Famed for its hotels it was, in those days, its
inhabitants proclaiming that in proportion to its population it had more than any other city in the country.
They might have been right, for more than twenty

fully equipped caravansaries were in operation. The loggers used to come down with their great log drives and then tarry for days or a week in an attempt to add color to the local landscape, usually succeeding beyond one's fondest dreams. No place on the river was more famous. Read's Landing—it used to issue bonds for public improvements that were actually made. Once it deemed itself a rival of St. Paul and would have thought scorn to be compared with St. Anthony Falls. And now, I am told, it has a total population of ninety-three souls, and grass is mown in the streets that used to echo with drays and stages. The river flows past as before, out of the mystery above and into the mystery below; the old posts to which the steamboats used to tie up are still shown to the curious; and a row of old houses are the ghosts of a dead and gone traffic.

Cassville, Wisconsin—did you ever hear of Cassville? Once it was the prize boom town of the upper river and with complacency saw its future as Wisconsin's capital. The people even went so far as to build the state-house in readiness for the glad event. They certainly did. In my time we used to go ashore at Cassville to look at it as a curiosity—one end used as a hotel, a great and imposing structure of brick, not at all ill-planned nor ill-built. Reasonably, Cassville cherished this prospect; it was the liveliest city in the State and the best located. The river was the great highway. Cassville was the river entrepôt for all the region around and always would be. Handsomely it grew and throve. In anticipation of its coming glory, it was well laid out even into the pathless jungle of bottom undergrowth beyond and beyond. Cassville—it is still on the maps, or on some maps. Persons still live there, the railroad has a station and a station agent. But if the ghost of Captain Russell Blakely should come up from the old abandoned and weed-grown steamboat-landing, he would never believe that he was looking upon Cassville.

All this as a necessary prologue to Rollingstone.

It was in the boom year of 1852. The *Dr. Franklin* was then running regularly between Galena and St. Paul, loaded on her up trips to her utmost capacity with emigrants moving northwest.

One afternoon she had just pulled out of Galena, when a gentleman of port and circumstance came to the clerk's office, with an air of business drew forth his wallet, and said:

"I want a ticket to Rollingstone."

"It gathers no moss," said the clerk, who had a facetious turn. "Where would you like to go to?"

"I said Rollingstone," said the traveler with dignity.

"Say it again," said the clerk. "You ain't thinking of Prairie du Chien, are you?"

"No, sir," said the traveler, stiffly. "Not being crazy, I'm not thinking of any place except the place I want to go to, which is Rollingstone."

"There isn't any such place," said the clerk, beginning in his turn to be annoyed. "What ails you?"

"That so?" said the traveler. "Cast your eye over that," and he drew out an elaborate printed map, with beautiful illustrations around the border. It bore in uncompromising terms the statement that it was a map of the city of Rollingstone, situate on the Mississippi River, and to judge from documentary evidence a city of metropolitan moment. There were streets and buildings, schools, a post-office, warehouses, theater, and at a wharf-boat on the riverfront this same good ship *Dr. Franklin*, loading and unloading much freight and many passengers. The esthetic and the cultural were by no means neglected in Rollingstone. Streets there had beautiful curves and vistas; a large green-

123

house provided for the growing of flowers at public expense; a large lecture-hall, a public library, churches, met every need of the panting soul of man as well as of his bodily comfort. The clerk looked and gasped. He had been sailing up and down the river for seven years and never had he suspected such magnificence.

"That's where I'm going," said the traveler. "Rollingstone City, and I want my ticket."

A consultation of the boat's officers was called and the map put down among them. Not one had ever heard of the thriving city of Rollingstone; but Captain Blakely, who knew every inch of the river, surmised from the shape of the bend shown on the map that the place was on land owned by the Sioux Indians, about three miles above the spot where the great chief Wabasha had his headquarters. There was as much of a settlement as in the crater of Vesuvius. In a radius of ten miles of the spot dwelt only one white man, and if another should appear the gentle Sioux would probably make short work of him and his hair. The streets, the warehouse, the school, the wharf-boat and alas! library, church, and flower-decked greenhouse were pure imagination.

When this had been explained to the traveler, he was still unconvinced. The previous fall, he said, a small army of artisans had left New York for Rollingstone to build the houses and the school and the library and the rest of the city, and now the colonists were on their way to take possession of the place, he being the advance courier. Neither argument nor asseveration could sway him from his faith in these works, and as he insisted upon being put ashore at the site, wherever it might be, the captain left orders, before he turned in, that the boat should be stopped three miles above Wabasha's camp, which they would reach in the middle of the night.

Next morning he was much astonished to see this passenger still on board. The mate explained that when they came to the landing-place, the advance courier took one good look at it and then declared that it was not Rollingstone. He had started for Rollingstone and at Rollingstone he would be landed, not elsewhere. So he stayed on board until the boat made St. Paul, when he went ashore to learn about Rollingstone from some one that knew, for he said the officers on the *Franklin* were just numskulls and smarties.

When the *Franklin* returned to Galena, here, sure enough, were the Rollingstone colonists, about one hundred in number, men and women, all from New York City. They took passage on the *Franklin* undeterred when the honest Captain Blakely told them about the advance courier and what they might expect at Wabasha's prairie. Some had brought wagons and farm implements, all had their furniture, some of them had their canary birds and cats and goldfish.

Captain Blakely asked them if they had ever done any farming. Well, no; not exactly. It seemed that the men were mostly clerks, bookkeepers, salesmen, and the like that had wearied of a circumscribed life in the city and had broken for the open spaces. The newspapers had told them much about the wonderful new country of the West and they saw clearly it was what they were longing for—the boundless West, where life could be led close to Nature, and all that.

Newspapers were not their only source of information about these splendors. A man had appeared to lead the hegira toward the glad new day, a man that knew all about it. He had founded Rollingstone, and the school, library, greenhouse, and other delectable features were due to his foresight.

No, they had never done any farming—that is to say, actual farming on the land. But they knew all about it. All the previous winter a man had been giving lectures in New York about farming and they had attended and taken notes. It was easy. You just plow up the soil and plant the seed and it grows and then you harvest it. They had brought along the plows.

Captain Blakely must have drawn a wry face at this, but he was a kindly soul and seems to have been more worried than amused about his strange passengers. He noticed that they had nothing with them in the way of shelter—neither tents nor lumber. He asked them about that important feature of everyday living.

"Oh, there'll be houses enough," said these sanguine souls. "You see, they were all built in advance; look at the map."

Captain Blakely has recorded his speechless amazement at this response.

"Houses!" he said. "Why, there are only two white men within fifty miles of the place you are going to, and there is not a sign of a house. It's all open prairie and bottom-land. There's no lumber to be had this side of Black River Falls or the Chippewa River, a long distance away in Wisconsin. When you land, there will be no roof to put your families under; and suppose we should have one of these storms?"

It appears that one could no more dent that optimism than one could cut granite with a tallow candle. He must have been a rare persuader that filled the company with such resolute faith. All would be well because he had said it would be well.

"At least," said the kind-hearted captain, "don't attempt to land now on that bleak prairie. Come on with me to St. Paul, where you are certain of roofs to protect you and a piece of bread to eat. Then let a committee go down to Wabasha's place and report on what it finds."

He might as well have remonstrated with the wind. When the *Dr. Franklin* reached the prairie, off piled the whole outfit, wagons, baggage, canary birds, and all, with not a thing to shelter them bigger than the lee side of a hair trunk and not a sign of human habitation, except that three miles away the smoke arose lazily from the camp-fire of the great chief Wabasha.

The next boat from Galena brought another detachment of the colony; more came on succeeding steamers until there were about four hundred squatting helplessly on the river's edge. In those days there was rafting of lumber from the mills above on the Mississippi and St. Croix. The colonists got boards from these rafts and erected a few lean-tos under which they cowered. The fallacious Moses that had led them into the wilderness never appeared. I could never learn what became of him, nor what he gained from the cruel deception he practised. An experienced pioneer drifting by on a raft suggested to the wretched, shivering colonists that huts could be built of sod, and some of these dreary structures arose on the plain. A part of the troop lived in caves dug into the river bank.

Then came an epidemic of mysterious disease and carried off many. Perhaps mercifully. It seems that they had no physician among them and the nearest medical man was seventy-five miles away. The agricultural skill acquired in a New York lecture-room broke down early when put to the test. Many things were planted; few matured. Some of the settlers learned to fish and some to do a little hunting. The summer drifted by, the fall came on, and the disheartened survivors began to try to make their way back to New York. A few determined to stick out the winter. Brief experience with the cutting winds and driving snows of that latitude was enough, and when spring came the only traces of the city of Rollingstone, once magnificent on the map, were a few tottering shacks and a long row of graves.

This is the record. It is bafflingly incomplete, because it does not state that the final residue found their deceiver and choked him, but I still have hope to come upon this pleasing incident.

Chapter VIII

THROUGH FIRE, FOG, AND CYCLONE

BUT we have still much to do with Hanks and the *Dr. Franklin.*

Soon after this stout old craft had participated in the Rollingstone story and had polished off the *Nominee,* she had an encounter of another kind with the steamer *Galena* of the same line. It happened in Maquoketa Slough, which, next to Coon Slough and the Davenport bridge, had earned the imprecations of pilots. The point at the lower end of the slough was covered with a dense growth of thickets and trees, so that it was impossible to see through, above, or beyond them, and the channel there was close inshore. The *Franklin* was bound down. Just as she reached the point, the *Galena* rounded the outer edge of it, bound up. The next instant the *Galena* hit the *Franklin* on the starboard side just forward of the boilers. The crash was terrific; the *Franklin* sank at once, but quick and expert work saved every life aboard.

Man seems to learn most effectively by butting his head against his own stupidities. There had long been needed a law compelling steamboats to sound their whistles whenever they entered upon dark, narrow, or tangled places. It was the obvious thing to do, therefore nobody did it. But this disaster to the *Franklin* stirred Congress to action and the needed law got through.

Hanks continued to pilot steamers, being for a while on the *Nominee*, the boat he had beaten in the famous race, then on the *Galena*, the boat that sank the *Franklin*. It was on the *Galena* that he did a piece of piloting about which the pilot-houses resounded even down to my time.

The railroad had reached Prairie du Chien, but no farther, and the *Galena* connected with it, if she were on time. The only train out of Prairie du Chien did not run on Sunday. One Saturday the *Galena* was bowling along down the river with a large passenger list, including President Orrin Smith of the steamboat company and others of note, all anxious to get the train out of Prairie du Chien. A heavy run of freight at landings made them late in leaving and it seemed doubtful if they could make Prairie du Chien in time for the train, in which case all the passengers must lie over until Monday—either, if fate willed, at the town, or wherever they might be at midnight, for Commodore Smith would allow no boat of his to run on Sunday.

They drove her as hard as they could and hopes began to arise that they might win out, when of a sudden down came the fog.

Now the best pilots I have known surrendered to fog when nothing else on earth could daunt them. You can make out to run in rain, darkness or even light snow, but thick fog obliterates everything that it doesn't change. That mysterious book of the river's surface is all in another language when fog comes. I suppose the reason to be that in making his readings the pilot connotes the surface near at hand with the shore and the surface at a distance, and in the fog he can see nothing but the surface close at hand, and often not even that. Anyway, the rule was to anchor in a

fog; and when this one shut in, the passengers on the
Galena gave up hope and settled down to a Sunday in
Prairie du Chien or on the river, as the case might be.

The mate down below sent men forward to drop the
anchor as soon as the word should come from the
pilot-house, and stood by himself to command the job.
He took no chances in a fog. But the order did not
come. The steamer plunged on into the woolly blanket
that enveloped her. After a time it was evident that
Hanks did not intend to anchor, and then nothing was
thought of but the hazardous experiment. To make
its nature clear to landsmen, I may say that it was
much as if a man thoroughly blind-folded and unas-
sisted should attempt to walk in Fifth Avenue, New
York, from Forty-second street to Twenty-third street
at five o'clock in the afternoon, crossing the avenue
every four blocks.

Soon Hanks rang to slow down and the steamer
turned sharply to starboard. He was evidently making
an invisible crossing. The next moment he rang for
full speed ahead, and the *Galena* went on plunging
into that mass of dismal mist. Then he rang to slow
down and turned as sharply to larboard, and the wise
ones knew he was in another crossing, and next would
probably be in the woods.

Noon came, dinner was served. I warrant that the
officers and Commodore Smith, who knew well what was
involved, had little appetite for that meal. The next
moment they might go smash on a reef, or hear a snag
ripping the timbers under them, or slide upon a bar.

A crowd gathered forward on the roof and watched
with a dreadful fascination as this inspired madman
rushed them toward destruction. They saw him standing there at one side of the wheel with his eyes upon the
little patch of water visible in front of the bow as the
boat plunged and quivered ahead. Not another sign of

131

the created universe was apparent to their strained eye-
balls; only fog, a small, dimly discerned patch of
water, the steamboat tearing into it—and then fog. A
tree or snag or island would be welcome to them, and
there was nothing but thick fog. They could not even
hear a noise except the noise of the steamboat. They
saw Hanks pulling her down on one side and then easing her off on the other. When they looked at him,
serenely doing his little stunts, it seemed as if he must
know what he was about, and when they looked away
into the fog it seemed as if he was just a homicidal maniac that ought not to be at large. He never rang for
the leads; he seldom slowed down except in a crossing;
he never asked for orders or consulted with any one.
He just stood there and ripped into the fleecy pall and
went weaving from side to side, as if he were pretending to see something—the incomprehensive and reckless
lunatic.

Once they caught sight of an overhanging tree that
would have snatched the chimneys and texas off like
a cat grabbing a mouse; but it swept by harmlessly and
was gone in an instant. Once they thought they heard
the whistle of an approaching steamboat and held their
breaths. It was nothing but the echo of the *Galena*
thrown back from a bluff.

Two mortal hours the strain lasted. Off Yellow River
the fog lifted a little so they could see where they were.
Then it shut in again. Two miles above Prairie du
Chien it thinned out so they could see the landing—
and there was the train, waiting! So then, by one instinct, all the passengers, still gathered forward, fixed
their eyes on Stephen Beck Hanks.

A merchant from Chicago sprang upon a chair.

"Three cheers for the greatest pilot that ever turned
a wheel!" he cried, and the shores echoed with the
uproar.

WA-BA-SHA PRAIRIE

Site of the unfortunate Rollingstone Colony

The fame of that feat went up and down the river. Years after, when Hanks was piloting rafts out of Clinton, some one asked him how he did it. He said he hardly knew himself, but he thought it was a kind of instinct that guided him. When he had gone about so far, he knew that the next crossing ought to be near, and striking out for it held it until the darkening shadow showed he was approaching the bank, when he straightened up about where he thought should be the right place, and so came through. But it is safe to say that if the practice of steering into fogs on instinct had become general the underwriters would have poignant remarks to make about it.

April 1, 1857, he left Galena on the steamer of the same name, to go through to St. Paul if he could. When he got to Read's Landing at the foot of Lake Pepin he found that the ice was as solid as a rock, and leaving his cargo and passengers, he returned to Galena. The next trip the ice seemed in the same condition, but as he had orders to go through to St. Paul, they made a hotel of the boat at Read's Landing, April 25, and the passengers lived on it, whiling away the time as they could. Every day, Hanks would run out and take a look at that ice, and at last it seemed to him that it was about to break. The end of April had come and he felt that if there was a ghost of a chance to move he ought to get out of the hotel business and resume steamboating. The next day, May 1, he started. Twelve steamers were in sight, all ice-bound as his own had been. A wind was blowing off the eastern shore, leaving a lane through which he could creep, but when he was less than half-way the wind changed, as it had once before in the same conditions, and the ice began to fill up the narrow crack through which he was steering.

He knew well enough what that might mean, but he thought he had a way to head off the disaster. He turned the boat and headed straight out into the ice field. It was a chance, because river boats are not built for arctic ice-floes, but he went ahead and survived until he thought he was so far from shore that the ice could not beach him, when he resorted to the novel expedient of dropping anchor. It worked successfully; he lay there that night, and the next day another lane opened and he got through.

Many steamboats besides the *Galena* had been held up at Read's and were now struggling with the ice. One was caught and crushed to pieces, one was thrown high upon shore, one was jammed between two floes and her hull ground to bits under her, so that her crew and passengers must save themselves by getting upon the field of ice.

One, the *War Eagle*, got through safely, though with a slightly crippled wheel, and started ahead of the *Galena*. Unless she were passed, she would be the first boat of the season into St. Paul, which meant that she would pay no wharfage fees all that year, for such was the reward all the river towns offered to the first arrival of the merry springtide. Besides, no captain in those days, if in a reasonable state of health, could endure to be beaten. He of the *Galena* now came to Hanks and pointing out the disadvantages of trailing into port after a hated rival, suggested that the *Galena* should jam on the steam, come alongside of the *Eagle*, which was just ahead, crowd her into the shore and so get past.

Hanks promptly negatived this pleasant device and said he wasn't that kind of a pilot.

Next the captain suggested that they might come up alongside and lash the two boats together, in which case they would go into St. Paul side by side and neither would have to pay wharfage. This didn't suit the fastidious Hanks any better than the other proposal.

"I have a plan of my own," said he. "Now if you will keep any one from interfering with the *Eagle* when we go by, I can promise you that we shall be in St. Paul ahead of her."

"A boat hates shoal water," once observed Horace Bixby, philosopher and master pilot. True for you, Mr. Bixby, and it was of this fact that the astute Hanks now proposed to take advantage. Also of the other fact in physics, that when two boats are traveling side by side the action of the water between them, or some other agency, draws them powerfully together.

Some miles above Red Wing was a place called Sturgeon Bend. It had a triangular bar with the point downstream. The channel above it was divided: on the right, going up, was a course shorter and with better water (at the prevailing stage); on the left one longer and with worse water. As they drew near this point, both steamers straining hard, Hanks yelled down for more steam and threw his boat close alongside the *Eagle*. The natural cohesion drew the two together. This crowded the *Eagle* a little to larboard of the end of the bar. As soon as the *Galena* felt the water shoaling she tended to spring away from it. It was like two boats running side by side upon the thin end of a wedge. The maneuver of the *Galena* forced the *Eagle* to take the passage to the left, while the *Galena* had the better channel to the right. When they emerged from behind the island the *Galena* had a lead of three lengths and managed to keep it into St. Paul, two o'clock on the afternoon of May 2, and won the prize.

Both steamboating and log-rafting were now in full tide of prosperity. The log rafts had come to outnumber the lumber rafts ten to one, and from Minneapolis to St. Louis every town had its humming sawmill. In the winter of 1856-57 five new packets of the latest design were ordered to be built on the Ohio River for the upper Mississippi trade; the best boats that had ever been seen there, among them the *Grey Eagle* and the *Northern Belle*, both of enduring renown. The filling of the river with so many log rafts came to interfere with the easy passage of the steamboats; and as steamboats carried the United States mail, the raft was deemed by the steamboat men a lowly thing and criminal and a rank intruder. On the other hand, the lumber interests were always growing in power and arrogance and the steamboat annoyed them by getting in their way.

I have spoken of the singular change in the character of the wage earners that came over the logging and rafting industries. In these conditions, the employers being on the battle-line, civil war between raftsmen and roustabouts was inevitable.

Fighting thus became the business of the new riverman. Hanks records his protest in his diary. The affair happened at Galena. His boat was about ready to depart, when the deck crew, having nobody else to fight, divided into factions and started a fight among themselves. The next minute riot ruled; rocks, pieces of coal, and chunks of cord-wood went whizzing through the air; pistol shots began to sound, and the lower deck was a bloody battle-ground, while passengers locked themselves in their state-rooms and timid souls ashore rang the fire-alarm. The Galena police force, consisting of two men in black slouch hats, massed on the levee and read the Riot Act. Hanks remarks in his diary that the battle was stopped by the police and the officers of the boat. He does not say that he came down from the pilot-house with a club in his hand and stopped it by batting the fighters right and left, but this seems to have been the fact.

The ill-will between raftsmen and steamer men had its chief locale at Read's Landing, foot of Lake Pepin, and a great rafting place in the old days. There was always a huddle of rafts tied up there and often a string of steamboats. When a steamboat was to make a stay of any considerable period at Read's, the crew would go ashore and tank up. Raftsmen were always there upon the same errand, liberally pursued, and shortly afterward battle would rage in an atmosphere overcharged with rocks and things.

When there was no open warfare there was usually enough maneuvering back and forth between the two forces to keep life from acquiring that insipid taste. The raftsmen said the steamers intentionally broke up the rafts, and the steamboat men said the raftsmen intentionally blocked the channel, and there is no doubt that as to these particular items both sides told the truth. Natural advantage was with the rafts. All that was necessary was to anchor your raft at the right place in the steamboat channel and no boat could get through unless it had wings. Sometimes packet-boats crowded with passengers and carrying the mails would be held up two or three days in this way. Perhaps an impatient captain would try to butt his way into the obstruction. Then the raft owner would sue the steamboat company and get heavy damages. If the steamboat had thus broken loose a nest of logs, these would hamper navigation for weeks to come, and nothing is worse for steamboat health than floating logs at night, except fogs and snags. Once a great drive of logs broke loose above St. Anthony Falls and came down the river stretched out for fifteen miles, and for the rest of that summer the steamboats had to dodge the infernal things—or hit them, as the case might be.

In all these pulse-stirring phases of the conflict, Hanks, as will appear hereafter, bore his part. Once he stood in the pilot-house and turned his wheel while shot from the furious raftsmen came through the win-

dows, and some three times his coolly skilful handling
got his boat out of worse trouble. It was the gamut of
the riverman's life that he ran in these days, all the way
from fighting to fire, and back, as I must tell next.

Rivermen, if of character, come to have a peculiar
affection for the steamer on which they have served for
more than one season. On the night of June 30, 1858,
coming up the river, Hanks stood the watch from six
to midnight, when he was relieved by his partner,
Thomas G. Drenning. Hanks hopped into bed and to
sleep, but uneasily, as if he knew that something was
wrong with the boat. He had tossed and turned but a
few minutes when some one was pounding on his door
and shouting to him to run for his life, for the *Galena*
was burning.

He leaped up, got upon himself a pair of trousers,
a shoe on one foot and a boot on the other and scram-
bled down the texas gangway to the cabin.

The boat was quivering up the river under all the
steam she had, running for a landing at Red Wing.
She was already doomed and full of fire and smoke.
Hanks had swift thought upon the passengers. They
slept in state-rooms that opened from each side of the
main cabin. He grabbed a chair and beginning at the
end of the row started to batter in one door after another shouting like a maniac. Captain Laughton, who
kept his head in the face of the emergency, seized another chair and went down the other side, beating down
doors. Most of the passengers sprang from their sleep
and ran out as they were, clad in their night-clothes.
Hanks herded them to the lower deck.

River steamboats being made chiefly of tinder and
lath, the wild question tugging at Hanks's mind all
the time he was dragging out the passengers was
whether the *Galena* could make a landing before the
end. He knew there was nothing possible below Red

138

Wing—and could the boat last to Red Wing? Up in the pilot-house Drenning stood with the fire and smoke all about him, another Jim Bludso, and held her toward the landing while the engineers opened everything wide.

They touched the levee, but there was no time nor chance to run out gang-planks. Hanks and the captain threw the people ashore. Then Drenning came down from the pilot-house, singed like a cat, and with Hanks and the captain ran from the blazing boat.

There was live stock on board. Some unnoted hero had managed to cut the halters of most of the cattle and they jumped overboard, but the cries of the rest could be heard above the roar of the flames.

"Steve," said Captain Laughton, "there are passengers still on that boat!"

"Don't you believe it," said Hanks. "I looked in every state-room and there isn't one."

"I tell you there are passengers still left," cried Laughton, "and I'm going to get them."

He started to wade into the water with the intention of climbing aboard. Hanks threw his arms around him and held him by main strength, he struggling hard. The next moment the whole superstructure of the boat crashed down in a Niagara of sparks and flame. Hanks had saved Laughton's life.

The captain was right about the passengers, although he could not have saved them if he had been allowed to go. Five were lost in that raging furnace; no one ever knew how. They were not in their state-rooms, but they never got ashore.

The people of Red Wing opened their hearts to the sixty-five all but naked unfortunates that Hanks, Drenning, and Laughton had saved. Storekeepers got out of beds and opened their stores to give them clothing. Hotels and residents gave them shelter. Everybody offered them comfort and sympathy. And the next day along came a curmudgeon steamboat captain of the same line that grumbled at having to take them on his boat, and tried to gouge money from them for the rest of their uncompleted journey! The passengers must have thought that both ends of the queer human microcosm had been turned up for their instruction.

Hanks was a first-class pilot, and all right in emergencies, but one of the worst press agents that ever lived. His diary tells nothing about his great heroism on that night but only records with a kind of sigh that his wedding suit, the pride of his life, was burned with the boat. All these details about his life-saving had to be gathered from other sources.

He had odd vicissitudes of fortune. Once he suffered a reverse merely because of good nature. It was after the destruction of the *Galena*, when he was first pilot of the *Itasca*. He had a partner that was habitually late in coming on watch. This was a fault unpardonable among pilots, and Hanks should have resented it. One pitch-dark night they were coming up the river and the partner was more than half an hour late. Just as he opened the pilot-house door, Hanks hit a snag. He knew that snag well enough and was prepared to pass it in safety, but the pest had hunted up new quarters, which was the depraved and abandoned way of these satanic things, and as the night was dark he couldn't see the ripples that ordinarily betray a snag's presence, for the whole of it was under water. So a prong stuck into the boat's hold. He got her ashore all right and she was patched up and steamed again, but Hanks always viewed that accident as a dent in his record.

All experience is to the pilot so much paid-up capital. A certain part of the great prestige this man enjoyed was due to knowledge he had gained while piloting rafts and could not have gained in any other way. I come back again to the art of reading the surface of the water.

It is a puzzling fact that the page has one reading at an elevation of six feet and another from the pilot-house, twenty-five feet higher. What this meant in piloting I will show by an incident.

In tangled places, or where new bars were rapidly forming, it was the custom at night to anchor the steamer and send out a yawl with sounding poles and a supply of lanterns. The pilot in the yawl would go poking about with his sounding rod until he had found the safe channel. Then he would mark the turns by sticking up stakes, each with a lantern, signal his partner in the pilot-house, the anchor would be raised, and the boat would proceed along the lane that had been marked for it.

In 1860 a new bar was forming above Alma and all the pilots were wary of it. One night it was Hanks's watch off, his partner having the wheel. In the middle of the night Hanks woke up with an uneasy feeling that all was not well. The boat was not under way, as he knew it ought to be. He went up to the pilot-house and found they were tied to the shore a short distance above the new bar. The other pilot explained that he had been out in a yawl for two hours making soundings and trying to find a channel, and had given up the job as impossible. Hanks got into the yawl, found the channel, stuck up his lanterns, and got the boat through without trouble. The reason was that the other pilot had never handled a raft; therefore, the surface of the water read from a yawl meant nothing to him, while to Hanks it was as plain as poverty.

They used to have plenty of trouble with the unreasonable weather of the upper Mississippi. Especially in the early part of the summer, terrific squalls might come at almost any time, or even what we now call cyclones and were then known as tornadoes. The worst place for these was around Lake Pepin. In the spring of 1861 Hanks, in the *Itasca*, was backing out of Lake City about six o'clock in the morning, when almost without warning a furious storm descended. On Lake Pepin rolling seas arise with a celerity and fury that is wholly preposterous. In a few moments the *Itasca* was in a position of great peril. She was light, having almost no freight, and she rolled like a bottle. The wind caught her and swung her around broadside to the wind and waves, and all her steam-power could not turn her back, for one wheel was out of the water most of the time. Mississippi steamers are not built for seaways. The greatest perils were that the *Itasca* would be swamped or that her rolling would throw her chimneys over, when she would probably take fire. Hanks watched the chimneys swaying to and fro, while he stood on a spoke of the wheel and kept the engines full speed astern. The gale was howling up the lake and swept the boat along against all her power. An hour passed in this hand-to-hand struggle, the waves going higher all the time. The captain of the *Itasca* was a fussy man that had a lively sense of his own importance and liked to appear at landings in what he deemed the attributes of grandeur, the same being a long-tailed coat and a high silk hat. He now stood on the roof, holding to a chimney stay to keep from being blown into the lake, but still adhering to his insignia of office; and the sight of him with the tails of his coat blown out as straight as a board and his high hat pulled down over his ears would have been highly diverting to persons that did not expect every moment to be drowned. After a desperate battle, Hanks succeeded in getting the helpless craft under the shelter of a point where he could manage her again; thence to the shore and tied up until these calamities should be overpast and the passengers enough recovered from their terrors to take breakfast.

The storms used to play merry havoc with the rafts also, which reminds me of Camanche.

Camanche is a town. or the memory of a town, on the Iowa shore about half-way between Le Claire and Clinton. It was once a thriving community, shipping out much grain and produce by river boats and boasting a considerable warehouse. On Sunday, June 3, 1860, about half-past six in the evening, a large log raft was slipping peacefully through Camanche reach. The day had been exceedingly sultry, with an odd bite in the strong southwest wind. Hard work at the oars all day had kept the big brute near the channel, and the men were now resting down the easy reach, when of a sudden a great cloud as black as tar loomed over the sunset, the whole sky seemed to go crazy with whirling scud, a deafening roar of wind and thunder drew near, and the cyclone burst upon the astonished community.

Before it the works of man were but jests. Stores, warehouses, homes crumpled up like jackstraws. Two hundred and twenty-eight buildings in the town of Camanche were ground to powder. Twenty-two persons were killed outright and 119 injured. Across the river, in the town of Albany, where Hanks had his home, eight persons were killed, seventy-nine injured, and of buildings seventy-eight were demolished. The Hanks family fled to the cellar. One of the windows was open and a current of mud driven by the wind poured into the cellar and nearly choked the refugees.

As to the raft, the first thing the raftsmen knew, trees, wrecked houses, and rubbish went shooting over their heads, in the midst of which they distinctly saw a gray horse struggling in the air. Then the river seemed suddenly to go dry and they rested upon the muddy bottom. Then a vast wave, resurging from the Illinois shore, lifted them up and carried them against the wind and deposited logs and all far in the corn-fields of Iowa. West Rambo, the Rapids pilot, happened to be just below Camanche when the storm struck. He said that he saw two thirds of the bottom of the river swept as clear as a floor and then a tidal wave coming back and lifting everything before it. The vision of the horse in the air was no drunken fantasia. One was actually lifted from the Iowa shore and deposited in Illinois, more than a mile away. The track of the storm was from Fort Dodge, Iowa, to Ottawa County, Michigan, nearly 500 miles, and it wrought havoc all the way.

Weeks were required to collect the pieces of that raft and get them together again, but in the end the job was done and raft and raftsmen proceeded to St. Louis.

With other peculiarities, Hanks seems to have been fairly hard-boiled about his prejudices, one of which was in favor of telling the truth. When the Chicago & Northwestern Railroad crossed the river at Clinton, the usual outcry went up from the steamboat inter-ests that the bridge was a menace to navigation. Hanks was employed to take the old *War Eagle* through the bridge safely to show that it could be done. He managed it up and down, many times, with barges and without, and never touched anything. But when the railroad company came to him with an affidavit that he deemed the bridge no obstruction, he refused to sign. The rail-road agents showed him a handful of money for so little a thing as his signature, but he was not moved. Then the company employed him to circulate among other pilots a statement that the bridge was in their judg-ment no menace. He refused to sign the statement him-self, but he submitted it to other pilots if any of them had a different notion about it. Not one would sign, and he returned the blank paper to the railroad office.

There was low water in the season of 1865 and the boats had a hard time to get through above Lake Pepin. Sometimes they navigated the bars with only an inch or so to spare, sometimes they ground their way through the sand, sometimes they stuck fast. The crack steamer *Key City*, one of the best on the river, went ashore at Pig Eye's Bar, below St. Paul, and the *Northern Belle*, that other boyhood's dream of loveliness, stuck hard and fast at Paint Rock. Hanks took the *Itasca* up and down without an accident, though once he escaped only by a marvelous exhibition of both skill and daring.

The bow of the *Northern Belle* was hard aground at Paint Rock, but the stern had swung around with the current so that she almost filled the channel. Between her and the reef on the other side was just enough room for a steamboat to get through, and the water was so low that where she should pass the *Belle* there would be not three inches between her hull and the bottom.

The *War Eagle*, with Hanks at the wheel, came down to this place in the middle of a dark night. A pitch pine torch was burning on the *Belle*, but otherwise there was no light, so that he had to proceed upon general knowledge. He stopped his steamer and sized up the situation. If he should so much as touch the reef on the other side of the channel, his boat would swing around against the *Belle* and the channel would be completely blocked, while both boats would be wrecked. He backed up the *Eagle* until he had a sufficient runway for his perilous experiment. Then he gave her full speed ahead with all the steam she had and came tearing down upon the narrow passage. Understand, that with the wheel he had to set her exactly right, for mere inches either way would have meant ruin. Just before he reached the *Belle* he rang to stop

145

both engines. This swept down upon the shallowest
spot a surge of water and lifted the *Eagle* so that she
went through and touched nothing. It was a marvelous
piloting, in all ways as great as the exploit at Hat
Island by Horace Bixby of which Mark Twain speaks.
Only a man of extraordinary courage would have dared
it, and only a man of extraordinary skill could have
won out with it.

A resourceful man. When late in the season, he was
taking his boat north to be laid up for the winter, he
found the river choked with floating ice. This was always dangerous to steamboats, because it cut into the
hull and in a few hours would sink any boat. Hanks
ran the *Eagle* ashore above Sand Prairie and with his
men went into the woods and cut down saplings. He
had a length of chain cable on board and he wove his
saplings into the links of this chain until he had a rude
kind of buffer or fender. This he put over the bow,
winched it taut, and found he could defy the ice. He
was bound for McGregor. While still some miles below his destination he was blocked by an ice jam. He
bucked into it with his home-made breaker, managed
to open a channel, and for a day worked away, ramming
and backing. In twenty-four hours he made only three
miles, but he got safely through to McGregor, laid his
boat up, and went home by way of Chicago, "taking in
the sights," as he observes in his diary.

"I had no reason to feel that I was unnecessarily
idle," he remarks in another place, speaking about his
occupations in the winter when his boat was laid up.
One looking over his diary would be ready to indorse
the statement. When he arrived home in the fall he
often found the neighborhood in need of men to
harvest the corn. He turned to and helped out until the
corn was safely housed. Then he went into the forest
and cut stove-wood, worked in a sawmill, built houses

and barns, and took on any other light jobs of the kind until the ice began to thaw and he could go to Le Claire to get his boat from the ways.

His wage in the swift times of the Civil War and immediately afterward had been $2,000 a season. Then this was cut to $1,600, and in 1874 seems to have been reduced again to $135 a month on the ground that the railroads were cutting into the river business. Other pilots were getting $125. He refused the terms and quit packet-piloting. For years he had been in the service of one company, the Diamond Jo. He left it and retired to his home at Albany with the intention of turning fruit farmer. He imagined that he was done with the river. In point of fact, he was still to do his greatest work on it.

Meantime, the whole lumber business had been revolutionized.

Chapter IX

THE SLUSH COOK FINDS A PICTURE

WHEN Thomas Doughty landed in Le Claire three years before the Civil War, people perked up and said, "Here comes a prize." He was a good-looking young man, for one thing; besides, in his blue eyes shone honesty, and he had a way of talking that took everybody with a pleased surprise, because he was so plainly without guile. He talked well and with confidence, and was just out of college. College men were rare in Le Claire. I think he and old Dr. Gamble divided the eminence.

Back in Pennsylvania, where Doughty had been born, his family had been of some means and distinction. He had started out to save the Doughty fortunes when they began to go wrong, and had joined the great trek to the new empire of the West, having faith, much faith, but no more idea of what to do with it than thousands of others that trekked with him.

From a steamboat deck he saw Le Claire, and it looked good to him. It was then a bustling town, all for the river upon which it lived. When he sought employment it was the river that gave it. He began to heave wood into the fire-box of a steamboat.

With his native wit and intelligence he was not long for a fireman's place. He studied steam-engineer-

Courtesy of G. P. Putnam & Sons. From an old engraving

SUGAR LOAF MOUNTAIN, WINONA, MINNESOTA

ing and passed into the engine-room. Within two years he was known as one of the smartest engineers on the river—the smartest and the hottest.

That meant he would carry more steam and get away with it than any average engineer ever dared to crowd on. In those days there was faulty government inspection and little regulation, and steamboats blew up every week or thereabouts. Racing went on almost daily. There was a story that once when the boat Doughty was engineering was having a desperate struggle upstream with a rival reputed to be faster, he jammed a piece of two-by-four between the safety-valve and the deck above and nobody ever knew what pressure he got. Only, when he touched the bank at Dubuque, two lengths ahead of the other boat, the sudden increase of steam lifted the safety-valve, the two-by-four, the deck above, and upset a safe that stood in the clerk's office. By virtue of some magic, prevision, or luck, the boiler did not blow up, and Doughty became the laureled hero of the whole upper river trade.

When the Civil War broke out, with many other able river men he enlisted in the Union army and was employed as engineer on government steamboats operating on the lower Mississippi.

In this capacity his skill and intelligence made him invaluable. He became a favorite among the navy commanders under whom he served.

One day he made a singular and notable addition to the nation's military equipment.

In the World War, 1914 to 1918, you heard much about the periscope used by the deadly submarines. Thomas Doughty, Le Claire engineer, hero of the two-by-four, invented the periscope.

This is of such historical importance that we had better have the records. Rear-Admiral Thomas O. Selfridge, United States Navy, retired, is the witness. He was in command of the United States monitor *Osage*, operating on the lower river in 1863, and this is what he says about the invention:

Chief Engineer Doughty, a very capable man, presented to me a suggestion to attach a pipe to the rear outside surface of the turret of the *Osage* with reflectors made of looking-glass, whereby an observer behind the turret could see the field in front. This instrument was the first of its kind ever used on a war vessel and Mr. Doughty deserves every credit for the suggestion. It was made of a piece of three-inch steam pipe with holes cut in each of its ends at opposite sides, and pieces of looking-glass inserted as reflectors. It was secured to the outside of the turret opposite to the gun-ports. Two stationary sights were placed on top of the turret and the whole in a vertical plane of the axis of the turret guns.

Before many days the value of this device had practical testing. The *Osage*, with the inventor on board, was assigned to duty with the unlucky Red River expedition. She was a light-draft monitor, built especially for river uses. To capture Shreveport and so cut off part of the Confederacy was the object of the expedition. Banks commanded the land forces, Porter the fleet. Banks's troubles began early and continued late. His forces were checked in battles at Sabine Cross Roads (Mansfield) and Champion Hills, and he was forced to retreat. Porter had battered his way to a point thirty miles from Shreveport. When the army fell back, the fleet had to follow. This is what Admiral Selfridge says of the exciting episode that came next:

Admiral Porter directed me in the *Osage* to bring up and protect the rear. The river at this time was at a low stage, and the *Osage*, in turning a bend, ran hard aground. While endeavoring to float the vessel we were attacked by a force of three thousand dismounted cavalry under General Green.

The low stage of the river and the high banks protected the

Confederates from our fire. It was here that Doughty's periscope came in. The Confederates could not be seen till the head of their advancing columns appeared above the river bank. A fierce fire swept the deck of the monitor as the enemy, coming up in column of regiments, would fire one volley and then fall back. Standing behind the turret, I could see in the reflector of the periscope their advancing line as it appeared over the bank. Cutting the fuses of the 11-inch shrapnel to a half second, and with the elevation of the guns to clear the edge of the bank, I reserved our fire till their heads came in sight (in the periscope) and then let drive. This singular fight was kept up for an hour before the Confederates retired with a loss of some four hundred killed and wounded, including their General Green, who was killed. On the *Osage* the loss was trifling.

The college-boy engineer had saved the day and the ship.

He came back to Le Claire after the war and began to use his wits on a problem of peace that was to prove much more momentous.

Drifting with the current about three miles an hour, the raft seemed to make a long and tedious journey down to the spot where the demand for its logs became every day more insistent. Then there were those two bodies of water where was next to no current— Lake St. Croix and Lake Pepin. Unaided, a raft might be a week or two weeks getting through these places, while the big, surging, growing West was begging for lumber. To end this intolerable nuisance, Stephen B. Hanks had brought in a steamboat to push rafts through the lakes. This was comparatively easy, for the course was fairly straight and the water good. Before long the old steamboat *Minnesota* was stationed there to do nothing else. At first the towing had been literal; the steamboat had gone in front and tugged at the raft's cable. Experience showed that this was not the best way, and the steamboat was placed behind to push. At the foot of the lake the steamboat cast off and the raft resumed its slow voyage with the current's sole aid. But old raft pilots had long believed that if rafts could be pushed through Lake Pepin they could be pushed the rest of the way. Nobody ventured to try it until, as so often happens, conditions forced the experiment.

What was the first steamboat to push a raft down the Mississippi River outside of Lake Pepin?

For years controversy seethed over this point; more than one pilot-house has been overheated by it. With much evidence for each claimant, even now the historian must be wary when he approaches this part of his subject. According to the accepted version in magazines and books, the little side-wheel steamer *Union*, Captain George Winans, took the first towed raft from Read's Landing to Clinton in 1865. This is an error. Captain Winans himself wrote the story sixty years afterward, and as he was the best possible witness, I think I will let him tell it in his own way. He begins by explaining that in 1863 he was in the employ of a firm at Chippewa Falls that made great quantities of lumber and shipped it in rafts down the Chippewa into the Mississippi and so to the places where it was needed clear to St. Louis.

In August of that year the Chippewa River became so low that lumber rafts drawing but 12 inches could not navigate and three such rafts were tied up near Rumsey's Landing. With no prospect of better water, the writer was directed to take men and supplies to the stranded rafts and re-raft them making them but eight courses (10 inches) deep.

This was done, the result being four rafts built out of the three, each drawing but ten inches. In this shape they were run successfully to Read's Landing at the mouth of the

The Slush Cook Finds a Picture

Chippewa. Coupling the four rafts with two owned by Carson & Rand made a tow of 190 cribs ready to start on the 10th of September.

Supplies were placed on board, a crew engaged and an early start on the 11th was planned. We did not start simply because we did not have a crew. The men had discovered that there were no extra hands in the town and when I went to the Landing to investigate I was informed that it would take $4 a day to secure their valuable company on the trip. As the regular wage had been but 75 cents a day up to that time we did not negotiate.

In the winter of 1862-1863 John W. Harding and Seth Scott had built a small geared side-wheel boat at Durand, Wisconsin, proposing to operate her on the Chippewa River. The boat was named *Union* and owing to a mistake in design drew 18 inches of water. As there were but 14 inches in the channel of the Chippewa by July 1 the *Union* could not navigate.

Her owners took her to Read's Landing and did such odd jobs as they could find on the Mississippi. She was idle on the day my speculative crew struck. As the subject of running rafts with a boat had been discussed for two or three years whenever a bunch of pilots got together, it occurred to me that the present would be a good time to try it. Finding I could get five men to go I boarded the *Union* and soon made a bargain with Seth Scott for the services of himself and boat for $7 a day.

We got to the raft with the boat with five men a little past noon and by evening had a temporary arrangement made by which we could handle the boat behind the raft.

Owing to the low water there was no probability of another raft starting for a month and the gentlemen on strike got so uneasy that they sent word that evening they would go for $1 a day. Not feeling quite sure of the boat proposition, I agreed and before the next day's close I was very glad I had done so.

Early on the morning of the 12th of September, 1863, the first raft to be towed by a boat below Lake Pepin left the

153

shore opposite Read's Landing in tow of the steamer *Union* of 28.59 tons burthen—George Winans, pilot; Seth Scott, engineer; Louis Weber, cook.

Everything started out finely. I had a double crew on the bow and the boat did much more than I had expected, but I soon discovered that our apparatus for handling the boat was not sufficient and it broke down before we were out of sight of Wabasha. Shipping up the stern oars and sending part of the crew back, we floated until we made repairs. At Tepeotee, however, it was wrecked again and before the crew could get back, the stern swung down and the boat went aground. Her wheels were too large and struck the bottom and before the engine could be stopped the pinion stripped more than half of the wooden teeth out of her core wheel. We had no extra teeth aboard and Winona was the nearest point at which we could get them. This meant a delay of at least three days, the season getting late, and two strings of lumber to be delivered at Hannibal, Missouri.

We got the boat off the sand, lashed her alongside and went back to the old, inglorious method of floating. The *Union* was left at Winona and Seth Scott remained and made repairs and then ran back to Read's Landing, while the raft continued in the same old way.

Items in my expense account show that the experiment cost the Lumber Company $86. It also confirmed my long entertained belief in the ultimate success of the raft-towing steamboat.

He floated his raft, leaving parts of it at various destinations. When he was below Keokuk and above Warsaw, one crib got loose and landed on a sand-bar. There was a small side-wheel packet running between Warsaw and Keokuk, and Winans hired her to tow the lost crib into Warsaw, its destination, and the rest of the raft to Hannibal, Missouri, the last port on its itinerary. The packet did this successfully in one day and was the second steamboat to push a raft on the Mississippi proper.

The Slush Cook Finds a Picture

The next year, 1864, the rivers were still low. The *Union* passed under the captaincy of Cyrus Bradley. In September he took a contract to tow a raft with this boat from Read's Landing to Clinton, and, profiting by Winans's experience, rigged up winches to maneuver the steamer back and forth. With these he made the trip successfully and delivered the raft at Clinton two days earlier than it could have reached there by floating.

"That," says Captain Winans, "was the first raft that went through to its destination towed by a steamboat."

The next year, 1865, July 20, he saw the little side-wheel steamer *Tiger*, Captain Jack Chapman, not much bigger than a skiff, going along with a raft past Read's Landing. She was not towing it; it was towing her. She was lashed across the stern of the raft and used instead of stern oars. Two days later they tried the experiment of placing her straight behind and pushing with her, and went so to the end, being the second real journey of steamboat and raft from headwaters to sawmill. The same year Captain Bradley took a raft down with the little steamer *Active*. In 1866 he brought out the side-wheeler *Minnie Will*, and after that the towing or pushing of rafts with steamboats ceased to be a novelty, though it did not begin to be a success.

All these steamboats were side-wheelers. They could somewhat increase the speed of a raft on a straight stretch of water, but they could not manage it around the curves and over the crossings. The great oars were still used forward and aft, and in every place of difficulty it was the raft that handled the steamboat. Under these conditions, it was by sheer luck that the outfit got through without smashing up, and the great majority of lumbermen and raft-handlers preferred the safeties of floating.

At Le Claire, the raftsman's capital, the inventor

155

of the periscope watched all these experiments and believed he saw the flaw in them. The idea grew upon him and he worked out plans for a boat that he thought would be a success at raft-pushing. He was a good talker, a singularly good talker, because he always believed what he said and so could make others believe it. Early in the winter of 1865-66 he had succeeded in interesting other persons in his project and a temporary boat-yard was constructed just above our unsightly old sawmill at Le Claire. To finance his pet project had been his greatest difficulty. He had saved a little money; back in Pennsylvania some remnants of the Doughty family fortune survived. He put everything he had into his boat and his relatives were glad to venture with him. So far as he could see, the investment was as good as wheat; it could not possibly fail. The lumber business was growing to overshadowing size, the rafts almost banged upon one another's heels, and a boat that could push them in half of the time required to float them would be like a gold mine for dividends.

So he built his boat that winter. It was seventy-five feet long, sixteen feet wide, three and a half feet deep, which meant that she was small, even for that day; but, in Doughty's opinion, large enough. She had but one boiler and two engines, with eight-inch cylinders and twenty-four-inch stroke.

She was built, launched with acclaim, proudly christened *Le Claire*, and in the spring days of 1866 started for the St. Croix River to push down her first raft.

It was her first and last. Upon the vast, awkward thing she was trying to urge along, the revolutions of her small wheel seemed to have no meaning, and as soon as she got into a ticklish place the whole outfit went into the bank and to pieces.

With it went Tom Doughty's hopes and the last

of the family fortune. He had all but mortgaged his furniture to build that boat and strained all his credit. His pet plan collapsed upon his head, and the inventor of the periscope found himself penniless and in debt.

Wise men that from the first had deemed the experiment impossible now applauded their own great foresight and showed why rafts could not be handled that way. The moment you tried to push them they tended to swing crosswise of the current and then the current slung them into the bank. That was evident. Floating was the only way.

But all the next year and the next, restless and indomitable fools continued to experiment with the idea George Winans had demonstrated. They tried it with side-wheel boats, thinking that, as you could go ahead with one wheel and back on the other, when you got into a tight place you could swing the raft. This proved to be just another fable. They kept the great sweeps at each end of the raft and the great crews to work them, but these mostly opened up new lines of misadventure. In the summer of 1868 I saw the little side-wheel steamer *Annie Girdon* towing a raft with the sweeps and the oarsmen at them, down the reach above Princeton, Iowa. There was a rather tangled crossing. To try to swing the raft into position the pilot rang for full speed astern. The after-oars were manned to help. The sudden rush of current as the steamer was reversed flung the oars violently against the oarsmen and knocked three of them overboard. One was struck in the face and received a broken jaw. Another was said to have been knocked unconscious and lost, but I think this was unfounded.

At any rate, it was demonstrated that, with a steamer towing, the oars were a source of danger and must go, but there was nothing to take their place. The solution of this problem came in the usual manner of step by step. The captain of the *Girdon,* I think it was, hit upon upon the idea of placing capstans, called crabs, on the after-corners of the raft with lines running to the stern of the pushing steamboat. At a signal of the whistle, the crew would wind in on one crab and slack away on the other, thus changing the angle of the boat in reference to the raft and assisting in the steering. It was crude, it was clumsy, it was not wholly safe, but it demonstrated that the way to steer a raft was to make the steamboat a rudder as well as a propelling force.

Still, the thing did not work well. Wisdom in observant landspeople was more than ever convinced that Tom Doughty had been dreaming dreams, and the floating raft alone was possible on such a river. When a steamer arrived at a destination with a raft it was hard to say whether the steamer had brought the raft or the raft had brought the steamer. In difficult places like Maquoketa Slough the raft would frequently smash on a bank despite all the furious beating of the steamer's wheels. Too many disasters of this kind made owners and bankers wary of the whole project.

Of a sudden all this was changed and the great new era in rafting arrived, one might say, overnight.

This brings into the story its most conspicuous and redoubtable figure, a man with a career like the romances of Oliver Optic. Once before we have crossed his path when as a boy he put out in his skiff to help the people on the *Effie Afton.* Now he comes in to stay and so pat we had better stop to look at him with some attention.

His name was Samuel R. Van Sant and he was born May 11, 1844, in a neat new cottage at the lower end of the town of Rock Island, where his father was employed as an expert shipwright in a boat-yard. It seems extraordinary that the two men that loom most in this narrative should have the same old American

158

background. Like Hanks, Van Sant could trace his ancestry to the beginning of things in America. A member of his family was one of the four purchasers of Manhattan Island in the early days of the Dutch possession, one forebear served through the Revolution, another through the War of 1812.

The house in which Samuel Van Sant was born overlooked the river, then beginning to swarm with traffic. His first consciousness was something about the river; he grew up with that singular and passionate attachment to the river I am to speak of later; he had it in his bones, both acute and chronic. The first dollar he earned he spent for a skiff on the river. His thoughts and plans turned instinctively to the river. His first adventure was on the river, and, incidentally, if he had not been possessed of this spell in its utmost power it would have been enough to turn him from the river forever.

He was about nine years old and beginning to help around the house and the boat-yard. One afternoon his father sent him to the sawmill for an ax. It was raining and he took an umbrella. The large steamer *Denmark* was passing, upward bound. Her swells loosened a skiff and sent it floating down the stream. Common law had it that whoever found and rescued a floating skiff could claim salvage or take possession of his find. Sam had a skiff of his own near-by. He leaned the umbrella against a tree, leaped into his own boat, and put out after the derelict, caught it, took it in tow. Then he started for home. The wind was blowing hard and swept him backward. After a time he saw he must cast off his prize if he was to win against wind and current. His next discovery was that even when he had freed his boat and was rowing his best he was being carried farther away.

Darkness was coming on. He made out in the dusk

159

an island with something that looked like a house. He got to shore there, pushed through the underbrush, and discovered that the house was unoccupied.

By this time night had come and he could not tell which way was home. The house was a wood-chopper's shanty. He went in and found a bedstead and a mattress but no bedding. He fastened the door as well as he could, put close by him an ax that he had found, and lay down. The night was cold. When he could no longer stand the cold he would put the mattress over him and lie on the bare boards beneath, and when he could no longer stand the bare boards he would put the mattress under him and lie in the cold. All night he listened with terror to the howling of wolves and the hooting of owls. He thought there could be no more sun, the daylight was so slow in coming. When it began to make the hut clear he acted a scene that would have delighted Horatio Alger, Jr., or the gifted author of the Rollo books. He looked over the things that had been left in the shanty and found an old Bible. So he read a chapter and said a prayer and always averred afterward that he felt much better. When the sun had come the wind had gone. He could see which way his home lay. With a clam-shell (fresh water and large) he bailed out his skiff, got in, found he could make headway now against the current, and rowed home, where he arrived just as his father was about to have the river dragged for his body. When they had discovered the umbrella standing against the tree they gave up all hope. Their neighbors had come to condone with his mother and offer sympathy.

He went to school, was like the other boys of the neighborhood, half mad about the river and anything connected with it, and put in his spare time at the boatyard picking up scraps of river lore with all the trades

that took part in the making of a steamboat. It seemed
to him that a steamboat was the grandest thing in the
world, and to build or steer one the only legitimate
object of human life.

When he was thirteen the captain of the packet
James Lyon, a friend of his father's, invited this promising cadet to make a trip to St. Paul as the guest of
the boat. Samuel nearly exploded with joy and pride.
Before the *Lyon* had whistled for the bridge, he had
been all over the old craft and knew the officers. Next
day the second mate was taken ill and the watchman was
made second mate. What does Young Hopeful do but
apply for and get the vacant watchmanship? Included
in his duties he found the cleaning, filling, and hoisting
of the red and green chimney lights. By comparison all
other motions and labors on that steamboat he deemed
unimportant to navigation.

Some time after his return from the voyage, the Burlington ferry-boat, the *Jo Gales*, which had been repaired at his father's yard, wanted to go home but had
no fireman. Sam volunteered to fire her, took along a
boy chum to help, and made Burlington all right. The
money they got for this work they expended joyously
for a ride on the *Grey Eagle* back to Rock Island. It
was a distinction to have so much as touched the moor-
ing-line of that glorious and famous vision.

The next season he secured his first regular employment on his beloved river, being engaged as fourth or
"slush" cook on the ancient packet *Lamartine*. His
duties were to peel the potatoes, scale the fish, chop
the wood, and wash the dishes. All that summer he
worked at these tasks.

One thing about the *Lamartine* interested him as
much as the changing scenes on the river. On the side
of the vessel, near one of the paddle-boxes, was a large

161

picture painted in striking colors and showing a man in the act of throwing overboard from a steamer a portmanteau or valise.

In a peculiar way this picture connected him for the second time in his life with the Hawkshaw of the West, a gentleman whose doings were so illustrative of the times and the country into which the slush cook was born that he must have further exposition. We have had the difficulties through which the emigrants struggled out to the new empire that the steamboat and the raft made possible for them. Better than anything else I know of, the narrative of this Hawkshaw person reveals what the new country was when they had reached it.

Chapter X

GOOD BUSINESS ON THE *LAMARTINE*

THE Valley of the Mississippi from its earliest settlement has been more infested with reckless and blood-stained men than any other part of the country, being more congenial to their habit and offering the greatest inducements to follow their nefarious and dangerous trade."

So concluded a competent authority of the times, writing in 1849.[1] The judgment seems to have been ably sustained, having even the indorsement of the chief magistrate of the State most affected. "Horse stealing, murder, counterfeiting and robbery were common throughout Illinois, according to Governor Ford. Citizens were in the habit of banding together for protection because they could not get it from intimidated or dishonest juries." The governor was quoted as saying that his fellow-citizens of Illinois, "with some honorable exceptions, were, in popular language, hard cases." [2] Assuredly, he was in a position to know.

Farther to the South, Murrell's band of outlaws with others had left large red spots on frontier history, but nothing worse than the things done in and around the governor's domain. In the region between the Missis-

[1] "The Banditti of the Prairies," p. 9. It was published in 1850.
[2] M. R. Werner, "Brigham Young," p. 175.

sippi and Illinois rivers from 1840 to 1846 was a reign
of terror caused by a league of criminals that robbed
and killed, and exerted upon what public authority was
then existent a strange and apparently incurable paral-
ysis. So many bold robberies and murders had taken
place in this region, and the organization of the brigands was so powerfully intrenched, that in the autumn
and winter of 1844 all Governor Ford had said about
the banding of citizens for protection came to be exceeded. Orderly men armed themselves as if for war,
barred themselves into their houses, and sat all night,
their guns across their laps, awaiting attack. Some
particularly atrocious crimes against isolated settlers
were followed by the robbery of the Frink, Walker &
Company stage near Rockford, by an astonishing attempt, nearly succeeding, upon the Federal land office
at Dixon, and then by the murders of Miller and Liecey
in Lee County, Iowa, not far from Keokuk.

Miller and his wife and Liecey and his wife were
new arrivals that had come with the great tide of emi-
gration from the East. They had money in hand and
bought land outright, a fact that made them marked
for the bandits. The two families occupied one house
together. In the middle of the night the outlaws descended. After the men had been tortured to make them
tell where their money was hidden, both were shot.
Miller died at once. Liecey lingered for several days.
This crime, coming so soon after many others, aroused
the country-side with new terrors.

There was then living at Montrose on the Mississippi
some miles above Keokuk a young man named Edward
Bonney, whose antecedents and way of life are left un-
revealed to us; luckily, perhaps, for there were those
that said he had been no better than he should have
been and those that said he had been worse. For reasons that he never confided to the public, he interested

himself in the pursuit of the murderers of Miller and
Liecey, and soon showed a detective skill that caused
him to be looked upon (by some persons) as a marvel
of cunning. He learned that in searching the premises
around the Miller house, men had found a cap, trimmed
with fur and having no vizor. Bonney remembered, or
said he remembered, that three weeks before in Nauvoo, Illinois, then the Mormon capital, he had seen a
youth wearing such a cap. He went to Nauvoo and
sleuthed among the inhabitants there with such skill
or luck that he was able to identify the youth he had in
mind as one Hodges, living with two brothers on the
outskirts of the town. Next Bonney found a man that
had seen two of the Hodges with a third man rowing
toward the Iowa shore the evening before the crime.
Then he found another that on the morning after the
crime had seen one of the Hodges coming from the river
bare-headed.

On this evidence, Bonney went to the chief of police,
or head watchman, and demanded the arrest of the
three Hodges.

Nauvoo was populated mostly with Mormons. The
Hodges were, or pretended to be, Mormon elders. All
Mormons were then nervous and excited because of the
persecutions they had suffered. It was certain that if
the arrest were attempted in the daylight a rescue would
follow. With a posse, Bonney and the police chief went
to the house at night, surrounded it with guns, and
made the capture.

The three prisoners were to be arraigned the next
day before the justice of the peace, who was a Mormon.
Bonney was satisfied that, in view of the strong feeling
aroused by the arrests, the prisoners would be either
discharged or released on nominal bail, when they would
escape to the gang and be safe. Therefore, he played his
cards with skill. He asked for a postponement of the

hearing for two days, which was reluctantly granted. Then he went quickly over the river to Lee County, Iowa, where the grand jury was in session, and where he secured indictments of the accused men.

This automatically sealed up the case for the time being, because the men must now be held pending the arrival of the requisition of the governor of Iowa.

He next sought out the prisoners' lawyer, and talked with him, apparently with nimble and persuasive tongue, for he succeeded in showing this counselor that as the prisoners were certain to be extradited as soon as the governor of Iowa was heard from, it was to their interest as innocent men to waive extradition and go to Iowa to meet their accusers. As soon as he got them to Iowa he had them taken before Liecey, who was still alive. Liecey identified two of them as the murderers, and died the next day.

The two he recognized were the younger Hodges, William and Stephen. No evidence being found against the oldest, Amos, he was discharged. William and Stephen went to trial. A strong effort was made to arouse the Mormons to save them. Another brother, Erwin Hodges, living miles away in the country, came to Nauvoo and demanded action in behalf of the accused, threatening otherwise to reveal the secrets of the church and its rulers. He was murdered almost in daylight in a public street of Nauvoo. No inquiry was made into his death. It was said that Brigham Young forbade any investigation and assured the Mormons that it was none of their business.

Stephen and William Hodges were tried, convicted, and hanged. The murders had been committed by three men. Who was the third? Tom Brown. What became of Tom Brown? According to the accepted version of the story, he had escaped. Afterward people became

166

exceedingly curious about this Tom Brown, and some of them made odd remarks about him.

This was in the spring of 1845. In July the western country was startled by a crime much more sensational than the Lee County murders.

Colonel George Davenport, for whom the city of Davenport, Iowa, was named, was a stout old pioneer, a veteran of the War of 1812, a successful Indian trader, and the proprietor of many keel-boats. He lived at first in a log house on Rock Island, but, prospering greatly (and, it appears, deservedly), he built on the island the most pretentious dwelling in the western country, known far and wide as Colonel Davenport's villa. In 1823 he qualified for an enduring place in such annals as these by appearing as the first notable pilot of a notable steamboat. The immortal *Virginia* arrived, bound for Fort Snelling. The prospect of the Rapids was too much for her hardy captain and he sought help. Colonel Davenport took the strange craft up to where the town of Le Claire was afterward built. It must have been a voyage of incidents, for it consumed three days.

By 1845 a considerable village had grown up at what was then called Stephenson and is now the city of Rock Island. On July 4, 1845, its inhabitants held a celebration of Independence Day and all of Colonel Davenport's family except himself went off to have part in the joy. He was sixty-two years old, but, because of his outdoor life, he was in the prime of health. While his family was gone, a band of men landed upon the island, shot and beat Colonel Davenport, and plundered his dwelling. He died of his hurts that night, but not before he had been able to furnish some description of his assailants.

Because of the prominence of the victim, this crime

167

aroused the whole prairie country. Colonel Davenport was beloved by all the whites, and among the Indians had a commanding influence because he had practised upon them the eccentric device of treating them justly. It was now felt that murder as a trade had been carried far enough in those parts, and a resolute effort was put forth, stimulated with large rewards, to find these assassins.

Bonney was loosed upon their trail. He tells us that the Hodges were really enrolled in the gang that had terrorized the Middle West and that from the first he believed the slayers of Davenport to be members of the same organization, which he determined to run to earth. As his life was already in danger because of his activities in the other affair, he felt he must have a refuge for his wife and children and moved them from Montrose to Rock Island, where they found shelter for a time under the hospitable roof of John Wesley Van Sant.

Sleuth Bonney on the trail provided himself with several thousand dollars in the genuine but unsigned notes of the Miners' Bank of Dubuque. It was the time of "wildcat" money, when the counterfeiter enjoyed an almost unexampled prosperity. With the bills as a passport to the underworld, Bonney journeyed forth, traveling much upon steamboats, which he knew were favorite haunts of criminals, and particularly upon our old friend the *War Eagle*, popular boat of the day.

Either Mr. Bonney was a fictionist of rare gifts or the criminals of his time were minded like children. Take a specimen from his account of his sleuthing. He is on the *War Eagle* bound down from Dubuque.

Soon after leaving port, a young man addressed me by my name. I did not at first remember him.

"My name is Young," he said. "I was sick last winter in Loomis's tavern at Nauvoo and saw you occasionally in the

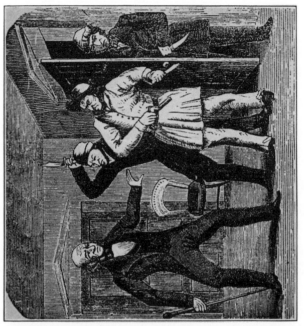

BIRCH THROWING THE PORTMANTEAU OVER-BOARD

Original illustration from "The Banditti of the Prairies" by Edward Bonney

MURDERERS ATTACKING COLONEL DAVENPORT

Original illustration from "The Banditti of the Prairies" by Edward Bonney

bar-room." I finally remembered hearing of him as one of the gang at the time of my search for Tom Brown.

"Seeing we are old acquaintances, Mr. Young," I said, "suppose we go into the saloon and take a social glass."

"Agreed," said he.

"What kind of speculation are you in now-a-days," I asked as we touched glasses.

"Nothing in particular. I have been at work a little at a few miles from Galena. A little while ago I was up as far as Prairie du Chien on a little operation."

"I think I am not mistaken," said I, "in taking you for one of the *right stripe?*"

"Well, I don't know. What do you call the right stripe?"

"Pshaw! you know what I mean."

So Bonney produces his alleged counterfeits and Young says he will be able to handle much of the false bills when Bonney gets them signed. Young has brought in the names of four of his confederates, a man known as Judge Fox, one Birch, and two brothers named Long—John Long and Aaron. Bonney asks if these men will probably want a supply of his counterfeits, and Young says they will. Then Bonney proceeds to ask:

"Will they *raise* much money this summer?"

"They have made some pretty good raises recently."

"I suppose they raise some good horses?"

"Yes, and they look up some first rate sights."

"Some of the boys made a good raise lately by Colonel Davenport. They were smart enough not to be caught. I have no idea myself who they were."

"Oh! I know all about that."

"Who were they?"

"Judge Fox, Birch, John Long and Aaron Long are the men who robbed Colonel Davenport."

"I was told that Davenport in his description spoke of only three men."

A-Rafting on the Mississip'

"Very true! Three were all he saw. But Aaron stood watch outside while Fox, John and Birch were at work in the house."

This guileless youth, according to Bonney, then proceeded to tell the probable road the murderers had taken and where they were likely to be found, for they had hidden themselves in remote parts of Indiana and Ohio.

Bonney started off upon the clues thus furnished and traveled for weeks in what was then the backwoods country. By pretending sometimes to be a counterfeiter and sometimes a horse-thief, he wormed himself into the organization. He says that it included a sheriff, a clerk of a county court, a special agent of the United States Treasury Department, other public officers, and many men in many places that were ostensibly honest and respectable merchants.

One other thing he pretended to be. He passed himself off as Tom Brown, the mysteriously escaped murderer from Lee County.

After wild adventures and many narrow escapes, he succeeded in running down Fox, the leader of the gang, and arresting him. As he wished to be on the trail of the others, he turned his prisoner over to a man that had lately been United States marshal of Iowa, and departed in the pursuit. Near Sandusky he got Birch and John Long and carried them to Detroit, thence by rail to St. Joseph, and so by boat across Lake Michigan to Chicago. How about requisitions? you instinctively ask. Already thought of and provided for by the careful Bonney. He carried with him requisitions signed by the governor of Illinois, with blanks left to be filled in with not only the names of any persons Bonney might choose to arrest but the names of seven Western States! That was all. It must be admitted that this was an unusual person.

There was then no railroad west of Chicago. The

journey to Rock Island must be made by stage. Birch and Long had taken their arrest quietly, assuring their captor that they would be rescued and he would be killed as they passed through Illinois, the gang's chief domain. Bonney was accompanied by an officer. They had their prisoners handcuffed between them. All night they sat with pistols pressed against the stomachs of their captives, telling them that at the first attempt at a rescue both would be killed.

About midnight two armed men on horseback rode up and looked into the coach, apparently waiting for a signal. None was given. The riders repeatedly rode close to the stage and looked in. Birch and Long did not dare to stir and the next day the stage rolled into Rock Island.

On information obtained by Bonney, Aaron Long was arrested near Galena, a wretch named John Baxter in Wisconsin. Then at a thieves' hang-out near Nauvoo they took Granville Young, the youth that had revealed so much to Bonney.

About that time news came that Fox had made his escape and was again at large. Bonney said the former United States marshal had played false.

Justice, when it moved at all in those days, went on swift wings. The murder was on July 4, 1845; the trial of Birch, the Longs, and Granville Young began on October 6, and on October 19 the Longs and Young were hanged. There was not the least evidence connecting Young with the murder. They hanged him on general principles. He had admitted that he had been a horse-thief. That was enough—in those times. Bonney records no qualm at the fate of his fellow-passenger of the *War Eagle* to whose glib tongue he owed so much.

Birch made a confession and was allowed to have life imprisonment instead of hanging. He had not been in

the penitentiary two years when he escaped and was
never afterward heard of. Baxter's iniquity consisted
in worming his way into Colonel Davenport's confidence
and then revealing to the gang how much money the
Colonel had and where he kept it. He was tried twice
and convicted each time and finally saved by a special
act of the Illinois legislature. Some others of the gang
received penitentiary terms. Fox was never again captured, and there is no record of proceedings against
the sheriff, clerk of court, or honest tradesmen.

Still one other figure in the story was left unac-
counted for. It was Tom Brown, the mysterious third
man in the Lee County murders. How about him? Well,
there were persons that said Tom Brown was nobody
but Edward Bonney, and they had Bonney indicted on
the charge; also on an accusation of counterfeiting.

On the second charge he was brought to trial and
triumphantly acquitted. The indictment for murder
was never tried. The governor of Illinois and certain
well-known citizens of Rock Island gave Bonney a
clean bill of moral health. He himself declared that the
charges against him were manufactured by members
of the gang, seeking revenge. He may have been right
about this, but there are some things the impartial inquirer now encounters that he wishes Bonney had
cleared up. For instance, how did he, if a blameless
citizen of correct walk, come to know so well the language, ways, haunts, and devices of criminals? Also,
who was Tom Brown and why was he never run down?

The picture on the *Lamartine* that had so much peculiar interest for the fourth cook was a picture of
Birch, one of the banditti. He was shown in the act of
throwing overboard a portmanteau or valise.

According to the universal belief of a later day that
still survives and occasionally works its way into print,
it was a veritable representation of an actual occur-

rence on the *Lamartine*. Bonney, by this legend, had arrested Birch and was bringing him to Rock Island. Birch arose in the middle of the night, laid hold of his valise, containing incriminating evidence against undetected members of the gang, threw it into the river, then cast himself after it, and was never seen again by officers of the law.

This is the story. It would be interesting to know how these perversions originate and are circulated and magnified. Birch threw a valise into the water, but it was Bonney's, not his own; and not on the *Lamartine* but on the Lake Michigan steamer crossing from St. Joseph. Bonney and Birch traveled on the *Lamartine*, but under different conditions from those in the story; different and more interesting.

Bonney says he had learned in his travels (and Birch in his confessions, or one of them, confirmed the discovery) that Fox had buried a great treasure at a lonely place in the bluffs of the Des Moines River. Bonney wanted to recover this hoard and took Birch and an officer to the spot. The cache was exactly as Birch had described it, but the only treasure they found was an American half dollar and two Spanish quarters. Somebody had been before them and removed the plunder. Bonney surmised it was an agent of Fox. Bonney and Birch went back to Rock Island on the *Lamartine*, but Birch's escape took place two years later and was from the penitentiary.

Yet the story and the picture were good advertising for the old *Lamartine*, which is said to have been in need of such adventitious aid; also of a scrubbing-brush well applied. Travelers were willing to change their plans or wait over only to be able to say they had ridden on such a famous boat and seen the famous picture. Clever press-agenting did not begin in the twentieth century.

173

Bonney wrote a book about his adventures, a once famous book called "The Banditti of the Prairies." It is a good book, too, for a detective story, not more than one third of it being highly improbable and another third fishy.

The house in which Colonel Davenport was murdered has been preserved by the Government as a historic relic. It stands not far from the greatest of the arsenals of the United States.

The picture on the old *Lamartine* had a peculiar interest for the fourth cook because he had seen the hanging of the murderers. Not knowingly, but as an infant in arms. The whole population had turned out for another reason than to see a gruesome spectacle. It was widely rumored and everywhere believed that on the day of the hanging the gang was to make a descent upon the town and destroy it. There were troops at the hanging-place, and troops meant safety. Not a house was left tenanted that day.

Chapter XI

AFTER TOM DOUGHTY WENT SMASH

SLUSH cooking on the picture-adorned *Lamartine* was not much of an occupation to one that aspired to command. It did not last long for Young Hopeful. Other engagements of a more dignified character came next and, just as the prospect opened for learning the river, the Civil War broke.

The day after President Lincoln's call for 75,000 men was published, Samuel R. Van Sant, aged sixteen, stood in the line at the enlistment-place. He was rejected for youth. In a few days he tried again and was told that if he could bring a written consent from his father he would be accepted. Father, being besought, sternly refused. Son sat down to a siege that lasted some months and was stoutly resisted. At last, the father learned that a friend of his was forming the Ninth Illinois Cavalry, so he said that if Samuel would go with this friend he would surrender about that matter of a consent. Samuel seized the chance, served in the Ninth Illinois Cavalry throughout the war, was in many hot engagements, fought hard and well, and sent most of his pay home.

When the war was over, he resumed his schooling, went to a business institute, then to Knox College, at Galesburg, where he completed his freshman year.

When he came home he found that his father had secured a quarter interest in the boat-yard at Le Claire, head of the Rapids.

"Why don't you own it all?" observed Samuel, whose mind turned toward the main chance.

John Wesley went aghast. "All? Why, I haven't a cent of money. It was all I could do to get this one fourth I hold."

Like many another good man he had been bankrupted by the great panic of 1857 and the memory still beset him.

"I'll get you the money," said Young Hopeful. He had just come of age. John Wesley laughed.

Hopeful went away and talked the matter over with certain friends of his. He always had this happy faculty of making people believe in him. This time it was worth gold to him. He got the money, bought out the other partners, and founded on faith, hope, and credit the firm of J. W. Van Sant & Son, that lasted more than forty years and all that time made the river towns buzz with talk.

At first, and for a long time after, it was all but overwhelmed with debt. The yard had been bought on nothing but promises; every month or two there was a note to be met, and young Captain Samuel must jiggle incessantly on the financial slack-wire while he strained every nerve to get the business that alone could keep the new firm from going, with spectacular accompaniments, plump upon the rocks.

The hideous old sawmill lay just above the Van Sant yard. It was here that Tom Doughty was building his rafting boat. Captain Sam watched it with anxious interest. Also he watched the disastrous experiments of that boat and others in the towing of rafts. Turning the matter over in his quick-firing mind, he came to the

176

From an old engraving in Harper's Weekly

THE RIOT ON THE DUBUQUE

conclusion that he knew what was the matter with these ventures.

To push a raft through the water and hold it up against the stream, more power was required than anybody had applied to the job. He planned a boat that would have such power. Next he saw that a side-wheel boat would never do the trick. When you tried to back with a side-wheeler, the wash from her wheels poured against the raft, so that it was like a man trying to lift himself by his boot-straps. Besides, in steering a raft with a steamer it was often necessary to twist your steamer at almost right angles with the raft, and then the wheels would walk into the raft, or the wash break it up. What was needed was a stern-wheeler—with plenty of power. He planned that kind of a boat. He saw that the secret of managing the raft safely around those sharp curves and over the bad crossings lay in shifting quickly the angle of the boat in relation to the raft, and he looked for something to take the place of the slow and clumsy crabs.

John Wesley Van Sant had learned to have much faith in his active, resolute, pushing son, but this proposal in the teeth of a notorious failure next door made him wary. Besides, there appeared no possible way to finance it. All this the younger man took blithesomely. In the end he had his way, and the steamer he had planned was begun.

It was a desperate hazard. There was no money to pay the ship carpenters; management must fire them with so much faith in the enterprise that they would wait for their pay until after the boat should begin to earn money—if ever. There happened to be close at hand a supply of excellent timber. Good white oak grew upon the river bluffs. Across the river, near Port Byron, stood a grove of these beautiful trees, and the winter before the Van Sants had cut and transported a choice of them.

Captain Sam's plans called for one hundred feet of length, twenty-one feet beam, four feet of hold; engines of twelve-inch bore and four-foot stroke; to be built in Cincinnati by the same house that built the engines for the lower river packet *Natchez*, famous for speed and her forever besung race with the *Robert E. Lee.*

The first object was power, and to secure plenty of steam they decided on a boiler unusually long, tubular, with lap-welded flues of a length of twenty-four feet and a corresponding diameter. They found that boiler flues were not made that length. Nothing daunted, they braised on four feet at the end of each flue and made a contraption that many said was impossible and one that worked perfectly.

In Cincinnati, Captain Sam had made a contract for the machinery on terms that he thought favorable. One fourth of the price was to be paid on the spot, one fourth when the machinery was ready to be shipped, and the rest ninety days later. When the hull was well under way, Captain Sam journeyed to Cincinnati to look over the machinery.

He saw at once that something had gone wrong, and learned that, despite the contract, the builders had positively refused to deliver the machinery until it should be paid for in full.

The trouble was, they had been making some quiet inquiries about the Van Sants and the town of Le Claire and the results had not been exhilarating. No one could successfully conceal the fact that the Van Sants were building an experimental boat, and on a shoe-string at that, being well-known to be without means. As for the town in which they lived and moved, the disgusted investigator returned the damning fact that there were in it more saloons than business houses and nearly as many as there were dwellings. In summer it was visited by riotous raftsmen and in winter housed a horde of the unemployed.

The enterprise staggered toward the reef. Captain Sam had agonizing visions of going home and confessing defeat and failure, and how he could meet the shipwrights that had done their work on credit he could not imagine.

In the course of his wanderings around the engine-shop he made the acquaintance of the foreman, one Bowman, who seems to have had human qualities. Captain Sam revealed to him the clove-hitch in which he found himself.

Mr. Bowman, with an inquiring eye, looked the captain over. Then he led him to the office of the concern and said:

"This young man has kept his part of the contract and we should keep ours. I will guarantee that he will make his payments all right."

On these terms the machinery was delivered and shipped.

Meantime, the winter was nearly done, spring was coming on, and the ice in the river began to honeycomb. There was no railroad to Le Claire, but one ran from Rock Island along the opposite Illinois shore. The boiler sent by rail reached Port Byron, and lay there. Meantime, the building of the boat had proceeded to a point where the boiler was needed.

All winter, teams had been crossing on the ice. They had now ceased to venture, the ice being deemed too thin and the spring break-up too near. But persons still ventured across afoot.

If he were to wait for the ice to go out and navigation to be resumed, he might have to wait three or four weeks, and the season would then be so far advanced that even if the boat were a success she could earn noth-

179

ing to meet his pressing obligations. It was horrible to think of the ice giving way and throwing the precious boiler to the bottom of the river, and it was maddening to think of meeting his creditors with nothing in the till. He chewed his mustache for half a morning and decided to take the risk.

To spread the weight he built a sled of timbers six by eight inches and thirty feet long, spiked together. On this (with his heart in his mouth) he saw the heavy boiler deposited. To avoid adding to the weight of the boiler the weight of a horse, he devised a harness with traces fifty feet in length. He himself took the reins, and started.

The course was nearly a mile. There was not a foot of it that was not overshadowed with imminent peril. The ice cracked more or less and was plainly rotten. There was a spot in the middle that looked as if it might give way at any time. Van Sant's heart stood still when he came to it. The big sled went upon it, crept over it— was clear of it, and went triumphantly to the shore. The driver's spirits soared like a balloon when he saw the horse he was driving begin to ascend the bank and knew that even if the thing collapsed now it was in a place where the boiler could be fished out.

It didn't collapse. The boiler reached the boat-yard in safety, was put in position, and when the ice went out the engines were fetched. Being now made ready for the government inspector, the new boat was named the *J. W. Van Sant,* and so was triumphantly launched and lay off the boat-ways with flags flying and steam up.

On any raft she might try to tow there would be no thumb-handed devices of crabs. Captain Sam had adopted for his boat a steam capstan placed on the forecastle. Lines from this ran aft through pulleys and thence to the corners of the raft. By turning the cap-

stan the angle of the boat was changed and the raft
was steered. It was the forerunner of the double-barreled
"steam nigger" afterward in general use, which was a
donkey-engine placed just forward of the engines and
manipulated in answer to bell signals from the pilot-
house.

But it was yet to be shown whether in actually controlling rafts the new boat was in any degree better
than her predecessors, and, if she failed of that test,
Van Sant & Son would pass from the affairs of men, for
in would come the sheriff with his writ.

May 6, 1869, the *J. W. Van Sant* started up the
river after her first raft. She carried with her a passenger destined to play a notable part in the coming
revolution—and after it. Frederick Weyerhaeuser was
his name. Forty years later men were to celebrate him
as potentially the richest man in the world, being owner
of a priceless domain of indispensable timber.

The manner in which he was projected into the business that made him a prince among the wealthy is
calculated to foster faith in the theory of luck as the
controlling factor in human success: therefore it ought
not to be retailed to the young. Among ourselves, I do
not mind saying that Frederick Weyerhaeuser stumbled
upon riches as a man might bark his shins on a log
going down the lane of a dark night.

Oddly enough, it began in a way with this same
Captain Van Sant when the captain was about thirteen
years old. Steamboats used to come to the boat-yard at
Rock Island to be hauled out upon the ways and undergo repairs. Early in 1857 the famous and beautiful
packet *Prairie State* was lying there ready, after extensive restoration, to start voyaging. She was in charge
of her mate, one Ben Howard, afterward a noted commander on upper and lower rivers. Mate Howard had

taken a fancy to young Sam, who was always eager to do something connected with steamboating. Howard berthed on the boat but dined at a hotel up-town.

One Sunday about noon he said to his young pal:

"Sam, I make you captain. Take charge of this boat and keep her in order. I'm going up to the hotel to get my dinner."

He had been gone about twenty minutes, when Captain Sam, marching to and fro on the boiler deck and alone, saw the steamer *Kentucky No. 2* heading up for the yard. In a few minutes it was plain that she intended to land alongside the *Prairie State*.

Captain Sam climbed to the roof and ran up and down shouting warnings.

"Don't land here, you can't land here! Keep her off, land down below, you can't land here!"

Officers and crew on the *Kentucky* regarded this apparition with great amusement and made fast to the *Prairie State*.

The next moment something went wrong on the *Kentucky*. I do not know whether the bump against the *Prairie State* opened her fire-boxes or whether the cook spilled grease, but she burst into flames.

The wind was blowing hard on shore. Before the *Kentucky* could be cast off, before, I think, the crew had any idea of what was happening, the *Prairie State* caught fire and both boats were one sheet of flames.

Close by lay an old sawmill with piles of dry lumber. As nothing could be done to save the boats, all efforts were concentrated upon saving the mill. It came out intact but badly damaged. Two German working-men bought for a song what was left of it. In the next three years running at top capacity it could not produce the lumber that was demanded of it, and the two thrifty Germans began to heap up riches. They were Frederick Weyerhaeuser and Frederick Denckman.

Mr. Weyerhaeuser was now at his own suggestion a guest on the *J. W. Van Sant* to see how the new rafting experiment would pan out.

The raft had wintered in Cat Tail Slough below Clinton and belonged to Weyerhaeuser & Denckman. The *Van Sant* got astern of it, Captain Sam on the roof, outwardly calm and inwardly quaking, for the existence of J. W. Van Sant & Son hung all upon the venture, and if it went wrong he should have for the rest of his earthly existence the haunting thought that he had ruined his father as well as himself.

They made fast at the stern and started down, and the *J. W. Van Sant* handled just like a skiff, said the pilot. Without a hitch she steered the raft around the curves and over the crossings. It was evident that the secret lay in her great wheel and great power. When she started to back she could swing even the lumpish heavy mass of a log raft.

But the triumph was not complete until Rock Island was reached. The mill at which the raft was to be delivered was the old mill at the lower end of the town, the same old mill that had started the Weyerhaeuser fortunes, the mill so narrowly saved when the *Prairie State* burned. In it Captain Sam had worked as a boy for fifty cents a day, and now, by a freak of fate, it had become a crux in his life, the goal upon which so much depended for him. To get a raft into the boom at this mill was no easy task, and the custom was to hire the steam ferry to assist. When the Davenport bridge had been successfully threaded, Weyerhaeuser was for signaling the ferry-boat as usual.

"We don't need any ferry-boat," said Captain Sam. "We can do this trick ourselves."

So he set the *Van Sant* back as hard as he dared and swung the raft toward the Illinois shore and so into the mill boom.

Mr. Weyerhaeuser was delighted and said the problem had been solved; all rafts would now be towed instead of floated. He wanted a steamboat built at once after the *Van Sant* pattern and Sam smilingly awaited the order to build her. It did not come. Mr. Weyerhaeuser was a good business man. He found some place where his boat could be more cheaply built and went there for it, using, however, the Van Sant design.

The revolution was on. In the turn of a hand the business, so great before, began to go beyond all forethought. A few years later seventy stern-wheel raft boats after the *Van Sant* model were pushing rafts on the Mississippi. The 500 feet of length for a raft came to be despised. Rafts twice that length were successfully handled by stern-wheel rafters, built like the *J. W. Van Sant;* and the firm that had started the revolution struggled and bumped along for years, enlivened with a close and adequate prospect of the bankruptcy court.

Much ink and more suspiration have been expended upon the question which was the first steamboat to tow a raft. About one thing is no question. The *J. W. Van Sant* was the first boat designed and built for the raft-towing business and successful at it.

The glad new day of swifter rafting and greater profits was not ushered in without disasters and a many of them. A long time must elapse before pilots could get perfectly the tricks of the new device. They were men that had piloted the floating rafts and piloted them well; but the handling of a pushed raft was another story. Oars were now discarded. Everything lay in the maneuvering of the steamboat. On a difficult crossing the donkey-engine would pull the stern of the steamboat around until it lay at a certain angle with the raft. Then maybe the engines were to back and haul the stern of the raft into a position where the reef could

be avoided or the crossing made. Or maybe the donkey-
engine was to be revolved the other way and the stern
of the steamer brought into another position when the
wheel was to go ahead and the raft shoved into the
channel. The heart of the difficulty was to learn when
to make the maneuver and how far to go with it, and
many a raft was smashed in that tuition. Pilots found
they must begin all over again. Before, there had been
steamboat pilots and raft pilots. Now these dissimilar
functions must be united and the joining was not easy.

One of the attendant troubles was something only a
riverman would think of. Floating-raft pilots were all
down-stream men. But river surfaces viewed up-stream
and river surfaces viewed down-stream are two different
texts.

That strange order of human beings, the Rapids pilot, now became indispensable. Nobody else could handle boat and raft over that stretch of bewitched water.
Once an excellent floating pilot, having been raised to
the pilot-house, was trying to land a raft on the Iowa
shore at Le Claire. It fetched up against Illinois two
miles away and must be tied there until a Rapids pilot
could come and get it out of its mess. On a stern-wheel
boat are four rudders; on a side-wheel boat but one.
To learn how to handle those rudders on a raft boat
was almost an educational course by itself.

The *J. W. Van Sant* had in its first days enough of
all varieties of mishap. When it attempted to pick up
a raft, the pilot did not back the steamboat quickly
enough and she tore into the logs a third of the way
before she was stopped. When he tried to back out of
the wreckage, he backed so hard that the boat broke
her lines and got away. Bound up-stream after her second raft, while going through Coon Slough, the tor-
tuous place I have mentioned before, the inexperienced
pilot, just at daybreak, allowed the steamer to be caught

185

in one of the troublesome side currents and banged into the bluff side of a reef. She struck so hard that the furnace doors flew open and burning coals were thrown out. Thus the boat took fire at the instant that she sprang a leak from the dent in her bow. There was lively work on the *J. W. Van Sant* for the next twenty minutes, and the bankruptcy court loomed again, but they got the fire out and tarpaulined the leak at the same time and limped up to La Crosse, where the *Van Sant* went on the ways.

When she floated again she found employment towing down several rafts that had been laid up in winter quarters; also in towing barges. She was a powerful boat, but to keep up her steam on coal alone was difficult. Captain Sam picked up a lot of kindling-wood from the sawmills and used that to help the steam-making.

One day they were towing a barge over the Rapids, having plenty of steam and going at a railroad clip, safety-valve open and roaring. Just as they passed the Davenport bridge the engineer discovered that his feed-water pump was not working and the boat was about to blow up. The government island of Rock Island was on the larboard side, but no boat was allowed to land there. Despite this rule, the pilot ran the *Van Sant* ashore and all hands leaped off in terror to escape the coming explosion. An armed guard ran toward them ordering them off the island and threatening them with his gun. Sam Van Sant, in a few gurgling words as he tore along, made him to understand that the boilers were about to blow up. He dropped his gun and ran with the rest, history recording the fact that he was the first to reach the top of the bank. The engineer had thoughtfully drawn the fires before he skipped ashore. Officers and crew stood at a safe distance waiting for the fireworks. When it was evident that there were to be none, they gingerly returned to the boat and discovered what was the matter. They had been traveling at such speed that the barge alongside turned up a great bow wave and uncovered the intake of the pump, so that it drew only air instead of water.

But for all the mishaps, that one season demonstrated the success of the *J. W. Van Sant* and of the new way of rafting. With that discovery slowly vanished the whole picturesque race of raftsmen as we used to know them. The crew of the *Van Sant* did all the work needed on the raft. *McAndrew's* viscount loon thought steam had killed romance at sea. The steam windless certainly abolished the old-time song-singing, whisky-drinking, and prank-playing raftsmen. But not before I had a satisfying look at them.

Chapter XII

RAFTSMAN JIM AT HIS WORST

SURELY the wise and the thoughtful that write so confidently about man and his ways of fortune-making have often overlooked one element of his success that comes near to top all the others. I mean the happy conjunction of the right time, the right conditions, and the right material, with the right man, and these must be beyond mortal control. In a calm review of the gigantic lumber industry of the West, the main part of its phenomenal development seems at each crux to have been minor to any human agency. Just at the time that, following Stephen Beck Hanks's experiment in 1844, log rafts began to chase one another down the crooked Mississippi, came the discovery of gold in California and the huge Western surge of peoples that filled the empty solitudes and by a new magic built cities. The logs could not come down fast enough to meet that demand, and a great employment opened for hardy spirits and none other. Rafting in the old floating days was nothing for weaklings. The sheer labor was often so great that, watching the great oars quivering under the strokes of men in a place of peril, I wondered that the flesh-and-blood machine could sustain such efforts. Recur again to the remoteness and lawlessness of the new country, and we can see some of the reasons for an unusual segregation in the human family. Some, but not all.

In one respect, at least, common report did these men wrong. It was a tradition that, besides being by birth and nature depraved, they lived in a state of perpetual souse, thereby needlessly augmenting original sin. This was not true, for the simple reason that drunken men could no more navigate a raft down the intorted Mississippi than they could walk the slack-wire. But rafts, as they floated along, would frequently tie up at a town for supplies, or because the raft must be split for a dangerous reach, or for other reasons; and it was then that the rum demon came from his lair to supply arguments to prohibitionists.

The raftsman's beverage was whisky—neat, and often home-made. It was a powerful decoction. Raftsmen themselves said it would take the hair from a buffalo robe. One of the stories they used to tell with the mien of men reciting the burial ritual was to the effect that once a crew landed at Bellevue and, getting more than usually drunk, the town locked itself in its cellars. Rummaging about an empty back yard, a raftsman came upon what he deemed treasure in the shape of a still from which the liquor was still dripping. He went back to the raft, fetched an empty bottle, and filled it with fluid that he described with joy as the finest corn whisky he had ever tasted. It proved to be lye. The frugal pastor's wife had an up-ended barrel in the back yard which she had filled with wood ashes preparatory to soap-making.

"Hey! Don't let that stuff drop like that on your boots!" I heard one raftsman say to another that was passing him a bottle. "I spilt some on my new shore shoes last week and it ate the uppers off clean down to the soles."

"Was them shoes tanned with oqueejum?" asked

the other in a quietly interested way, as if he were seeking scientific knowledge.

"No, sir. That there leather was tanned with the best hemlock bark, and the shoes cost me $3 in Red Wing."

"Now, say, my friend"—gently remonstrative—"don't you know better than to buy leather tanned with hemlock? What you want is leather tanned with oqueejum and then whisky can't eat it. You see, whisky and hemlock, they get together on social terms, same's you and me, and then the whisky does its deadly work and swallers the leather. But whisky and oqueejum's enemies and when they meet whisky gets licked every time. That's why I keep my stomach lined with it. Oqueejum's made from the bamjam tree which grows in India to a height of more than a thousand feet. Its wood is so hard they have to cut it with a cold chisel. It stands to reason that it's stronger than hemlock. Try some on your stomach and then your liquor won't get to your head like this."

The essence in their badinage was always this straight face and the grave earnest look; infinitely they scorned the man that could laugh at his own humor. The most extravagant conceits must be delivered without the batting of an eye, or in their judgment all point was lost to the world.

When a raft crew's visitation was over in one of these towns, and timid souls crept abroad again, I observed a certain note of admiration as they viewed the traces of their late unwelcome guests. There was the beer-saloon sign nailed across the Presbyterian church door, the parson's buggy roosting in a tree, and old Mrs. Disney's cow painted green with paint feloniously extracted from McKane's paint shop, and to-morrow they would be talking of these things with chuckles and mirthful head-shakings. But the next raft that tied up on our water-front was none the less awesome.

Raftsman Jim at His Worst

When raftsmen had delivered a raft at its destination, say Muscatine, Burlington, or St. Louis, they must be returned to the pineries on up-bound steamboats, taking what was called deck passage, equal to steerage on the ocean. In the meantime, they had employed their leisure in celebrating with many libations a prosperous voyage, so that usually when they selected the steamer upon which they would ascend the river the cabin passengers had reason to remember the trip. Fights were of almost hourly occurrence; among themselves, if one could not be provoked with the steamboat's crew. Sometimes they arranged shooting matches on the lower deck, at which nervous passengers, remembering that the upper structure of a river steamer was not much better than cardboard, took to their prayers.

The roustabouts or deck-hands on these boats were usually black men, and often (before the Civil War) they were slaves. It was not hard for a gang of fierce-looking outlaws, ugly drunk and armed to the teeth, to subjugate these, but the mate offered a different problem. An old-time swearing, hell-roaring, red-faced Mississippi mate, with his tongue hung in the middle and both ends attuned to profanity, having constitutionally no fear of God or man, was not always suppressed even by the wild men of the rafts.

This brings me back to the *Galena*, the famous packet and floating palace that Stephen B. Hanks piloted in the grand old times. She was built in 1853 at Cincinnati and has manifold claims to glory. For example, the next year, when the Rock Island Railroad was completed to the Mississippi River, it chartered five of the best steamboats afloat and invited an astonishing list of the nation's notables to be its guests on a trip to St. Paul and return, and the *Galena* was one of the five. But what I started out to tell about her was her celebrated battle with the raftsmen.

A-Rafting on the Mississip'

They were an ugly lot, and not Black River men at that, but from the St. Croix, reputed to be more orderly. They came aboard at Burlington for Read's Landing, foot of Lake Pepin, and had not been five minutes on the lower deck before it was plain that the officers were due for trouble that trip. Nothing was right for the raftsmen. They objected to the places where they were to sleep, they objected to the food, and they objected to the second steward, who tried to pacify them. As they underscored every complaint with drawn pistols, life seemed to be vivid in that part of the world.

The first night passed without disturbance, but the next morning it was evident that the pleasing beverage known as forty-rod had been circulating freely, and about ten o'clock the raftsmen started to rush the boat and take possession of it.

The *Galena* happened to have a mate that was a son of Anak for size and of Belial for fighting. He had with him about six men from the crew that were of his own views concerning life and proper behavior, and with these he made a sudden charge upon the rioters. The mate's army was the smaller, but it had an advantage in being sober and another in knowing exactly what it wanted to do. Each man was armed with a club in one hand and a pistol in the other. Providence this time was on the side of the surest hitter. After a furious struggle the raftsmen found themselves disarmed and beaten, some with broken heads and some insensible.

They were now told that if they kept still the rest of the voyage they would be carried to Read's Landing; otherwise they would be bundled ashore as and where they were.

Peace reigned on the *Galena* the rest of that trip, but as the raftsmen went ashore at Read's they swore revenge. The place was full of their confrères in the drinking and fighting line, and from that day the

Galena was marked for the ill-will of all the rafting world.

The next time she came along upward bound, part of her crew went ashore, ostensibly to be treated for thirst but really, no doubt, looking for trouble. They did not search long. A contingent of raftsmen was on the same errand and in a few minutes a fight started between the representatives of the two industries. The steamboat men were worsted and driven back to their vessel. The captain of the *Galena* stepped ashore to protect them and the raftsmen knocked him down and started to beat him to a jelly, when he was rescued by an armed sortie from the boat.

Hanks was in the pilot-house, for the *Galena* was overdue to start. He was one whose courage had been attested many times in many ways, but it seemed to him well to be heading away from that locality about that time. He rang to back, and the packet was sliding into the deep water, when the raftsmen with shotguns opened fire. Some of the shot came through the pilot-house window. Hanks stuck to his post. The *Galena's* express messenger with a revolver returned the fire and dropped a raftsman; but by this time the steamer was out of shot-gun range and peaceably proceeded.

It was well enough known to all on board that when she made Read's on her return down the river the raftsmen would start the second round of the fight.

As to that, the captain took no chances. In some way he managed to get a carronade and a supply of ammunition; also twenty-five army muskets and a becoming quantity of bullets. The carronade he mounted on the upper deck; the muskets he stacked forward on the deck below where they could not escape observation.

When the *Galena* rounded-to for Read's Landing on her way south, the captain himself with his gunner stood by the carronade; all the crew that could be spared from other duties was drawn up beside the muskets. The raftsmen's army was gathered at the Landing, about two hundred strong, and ready to attack with pistols and rocks as soon as the *Galena* should make fast. When they saw the carronade and the muskets they conceived a different purpose. The packet put her freight and passengers ashore, took other freight and passengers aboard, and backed out into the stream. As she started, a chorus of hoots, groans, and curses arose from the raftsmen's ranks and a volley of stones broke cabin windows, but that was the extent of the action.

The adventure must have been reported up and down the river, for a few trips afterward, while the *Galena* was lying at Hastings, fifty-two miles above Read's, another battle broke loose with raftsmen. The excuse was trivial, but any pretext would have served. At Hastings the *Galena* had shipped a new chambermaid. I never could get the rights of the story, but the row centered over this woman. She had been employed at one of the local hotels, where she had been a great favorite, and people said she had been enticed away, or something of that kind. Raftsmen caught a part of the *Galena's* crew, beat one of them so badly that he was left for dead, and then started to rush the steamer. Along the river bank was rich store of handy missiles, and in a moment the air was full of flying rocks and crackling with the breaking of glass. Hanks once more got his boat out of range.

They went their way to St. Paul. On their return they stopped at a landing some miles above Hastings and here came aboard the member of the crew that they had left for dead at the hands of the mob. He had feigned death until the mob departed. Then he had crawled under a lumber pile, waited until dark, and so got out of town.

While he was under the lumber pile this man heard
the mob planning to seize the *Galena* on its return and
burn her. Having such a warning, the captain again
secured the carronade and put it on view with the
stacks of rifles and the gangs of huskies. At Hastings
the mob had gathered as foretold, but once more the
sight of the artillery seemed marvelously to cool hot
courage, and the *Galena* got away with no worse bombardment than curses.

I hate to record the fact, but it appears that the vic-
tors were not generous in their triumph. Some weeks
later the *Galena* happened to meet the same raft crew
conveying a raft down the long reach above what is now
the city of Clinton. The raftsmen made the identification first and signaled it with a volley of epithets. By
way of riposte, the *Galena* cut close to the stern of the
raft and smashed two oars there. It was not heroic, but
perhaps it was human nature.

Some of the roistering, boozing, fighting, and Cain-
raising denizens of the raft were known by fame from
one end of the business to the other, and may be said to
have merited the distinction. This reminds me of Dave
Mills, whose mere name in the days of my boyhood was
a sign of terror and who, in the estimation of the law-
abiding, surpassed for pure deviltry anything that ever
came out of Black River.

The town of Prescott, Wisconsin, was a harbor for
rafts and a pet resort of raftsmen. It was known in
those days as one of the toughest places in all the river
region, a fact you would never suspect if you were to
visit it to-day. The population amounted to about
eight hundred, all of whom, including the preachers,
lived by virtue of the river business, and not otherwise.
There was a steam sawmill at Prescott owned by the
firm of Pewitt & Loehner. The head of this firm, Mr.
Coleman Pewitt, was one of the wealthiest citizens in

those parts. He was also city marshal and police force.

It was the practice of Mr. Mills, when he had forti-
fied himself with about five drinks of tanglefoot whisky,
to draw his revolver in whatsoever thirst palace he
might then be and begin to shoot it at the mirror back
of the bar, or at any other attractive target; and, if
the proprietor or bartender objected to these outbreaks
of a playful nature, Mills held it a point of conscience
to beat up the objector. He was six feet two inches in
height and a bull for strength.

In the course of his pursuit of an amusing life he
came by raft one day to Prescott, where, having twenty-
four hours or so of unoccupied time, he shot up all the
saloons in town and disabled most of the bartenders.
Then he encountered Mr. Coleman Pewitt, marshal and
police force. George Merritt once told in a public address the story of what happened next, which I sum-
marize as a picture of the life I am trying to recall.

It seems that Marshal Pewitt, patrolling the town in
moments of vacation from his sawmill, observed the
frolicsome Mills on pleasure bent, and, being in the
habit of carrying in his coat-tail pocket a pair of hand-
cuffs of trustworthy make, slipped these upon the visitor unaware and had him a prisoner, forthwith marching him to the town calaboose on the top of the bluff.

The problem that then confronted the citizenry was
what on earth to do with the captive. It was admitted
that if he were released he would probably beat up all
that had previously escaped his attentions, and it was
also well enough known that to keep him locked up and
feed him would empty the town treasury.

In this dilemma Mr. Pewitt proposed an appeal to
Homeric standards. Let Mills be released and he would
undertake to fight him to a finish. If Mills won he was
to be made city marshal and take up his abode in Prescott, Pewitt at once resigning in his favor. If Pewitt

won, Mills was to be put upon the first steamboat that touched at Prescott with the understanding that if he ever returned he was to be shot on sight.

Rest and some hours of quiet having by this time somewhat cleared the mind of Mr. Mills, this proposal was expounded to him and accepted with joy. As nobody had ever been able to stand against him in a fight, he considered this contest as already won.

City Marshal Pewitt was much smaller in stature than Mills, being no more than five feet ten; but he had led an active outdoor life, mostly at handling logs, and his muscles were as hard as rocks. Besides, he had never impaired his strength by excessive devotion to the wine bags, and he had a little scheme of his own.

Before the arbitrament could be carried out, it was thought well to submit it to the judgment of leading citizens, because, if Mr. Mills were to become city marshal, they would have a natural interest in the fact, and if he were to be shot they might be useful witnesses before the coroner or other busybody.

Accordingly, the case was laid before the best men in Prescott with a request for their deliberate verdict. Of these good men and true, John Martin, as keeper of the best saloon and biggest gambling dive, had naturally, in view of his commercial interests, the right of priority. Mr. Martin, being consulted, said the plan was good and should be carried out. It was next submitted to and approved in turn by Norman Dunbar, who kept the leading grocery; Hart Broughton, leading hotel man; Charles Young, leading physician; Lime Smith, leading drayman; and L. H. Merrick, leading steamboat agent. The first snag was struck when the project was broached to the Rev. Mr. Richardson, pastor of the Methodist Episcopal church, who was so lacking in public spirit and the true sporting instinct as to object strongly. He said that what was proposed was ungentlemanly, unethical, and contrary to all the usages in the admirable State of Connecticut, from which he had lately emerged.

Mr. Richardson, being in the minority and, of course, far outweighed by the opinion of Mr. Martin, the plan proceeded; a ring was formed and Mr. Mills released from bondage. Before a select circle of the best people of Prescott he faced his opponent.

Each now assumed the attitude observable in all the prints of pugilists, the crouching position, right arm raised, left by the side ready to strike. The referee shouted "Go!" and the men began sparring and feinting, when of a sudden Mr. Pewitt lowered his head and drove it with great violence into Mr. Mills's midriff.

The Terror of the Bar-rooms fell at that mighty stroke and lay upon the earth gasping "for great lack of ease," as John Ridd hath it, referring to another occasion like this. He had scant time to recover, for the agile city marshal was upon him, hammering him with his fists and then inserting a thumb under one eye, which he seemed likely to dislodge. On this the Terror of the Bar-rooms yelled for mercy and the fight was over.

The best people of Prescott, who had witnessed it with interest, now reminded Mr. Mills of its terms; reminded him in simple but expressive words of one syllable that he could not fail to grasp. He admitted that they were right and the assembly adjourned to Mr. Martin's emporium, where they drank together sociably. When the next steamboat arrived Mills went aboard. He scrupulously observed his part of the contract. Often after that he was on boats or rafts that passed Prescott, or landed there, but he never came ashore. He would stand on the guard and chat amiably with City Marshal Pewitt or others, but he never came ashore.

Raftsman Jim at His Worst

Otherwise, neither his manners nor his morals underwent reformation. A few years later, being angered about something, he and his partner, one Joe Gates, attempted to shoot up the town of Read's Landing, and the citizens rallying with shot-guns a pitched battle ensued in which Mills was wounded.

When he recovered he went one day to a saloon in North La Crosse, where he began his entertaining revolver practice on the mirror. The bartender did not orally object, but reached under the counter for his own pistol, with which he shot Mills dead.

Then the barkeeper offered to pay the funeral expenses, which the town authorities said was right handsome of him and rendered further proceedings unnecessary.

With the coming of the steamboat as a raft-pusher the old style raftsman began to fade from the landscape he had made so picturesquely animated. The crew of the raft boat being now the crew of the raft also, was composed of a wholly different human element. The raft boats out of Le Claire were manned by young townsmen of ours that everybody knew and whose backgrounds were all for order and the straight walk; young Americans, sober, intelligent, and often ambitious. More than one career of distinction began on those boats. As for character, I recall that when there went over the West a strong movement to organize the underlying temperance sentiment, the entire crew of one of our boats wore blue ribbons—from pilots to strikers.

The economies of the new order were manifold. Rafts were no longer plaited with birch boughs, staples, and costly hole-boring. A frame surrounded the outside and within it the logs were held together with hawsers and then with steel cables, drawn tight with steam winches. A great saving was effected in man-power.

A - R a f t i n g o n t h e M i s s i s s i p'

Whereas in the floating days from twenty-five to thirty men were required to handle a raft, the steamboats managed with eight or ten.

Consequently, a horde of former raftsmen, now out of work, was let loose upon many a river town and speedily climaxed the terror of their name. Mr. A. D. Summers, who was a boy with me in Le Claire, has written a graphic and amusing account of the time when an army of the idle raftsmen and other tramps took possession of the old stone quarry (where we used to play scrub), and for many days lived upon the contributions of the householders. A gang of them called one evening at his father's house. Mr. Summers, under instructions, indicated the wood pile in the back yard as furnishing an admirable chance for exercise preluding the evening meal.

"Hell!" said the leader, "do you suppose we are looking for work?" and led off his cohorts in a state of outrage. When rain came, it was their custom to sleep in barns. One night fifty of them were in the loft of the barn of Mayor Schwarm. About daybreak some one had occasion to enter the place. The raftsmen got the notion that the visitor was the advance guard of a posse and broke for the stairs. At the foot a calf was tethered. The first fugitive tripped over the rope, the second fell over the first, and most of the contingent piled up on the floor in a tangle of struggling legs and arms before the eyes of the astonished visitor, who was only a boy and fled in terror.

Just before the coming of the steam raft-pusher closed the long day of the floating raftsman, he put upon river history a hideous red smear that still underscores the worst ever urged against him.

In July, 1869, the packet *Dubuque* of the old Northern Line, one of the best boats that ever ran on the Mississippi, took on board at St. Louis four raft crews

200

numbering about one hundred and twenty. They had deck passage with certain harvest hands, number unknown, that were bound for the wheat harvest along the upper river. Harvest hands were also more or less of the jungle. Of cabin passengers, traveling up-stairs, the lists were full, for this was a popular boat.

She reached Davenport on the evening of July 23 and tied up for the night. There seems to have been low water and the captain was unwilling to run the Rapids at night.

Many passengers went ashore; among them the raftsmen and harvest hands, who tanked up on the usual beverages.

At daybreak the *Dubuque* pulled out. Half an hour later a big raftsman, in the belligerent lees of intoxication and followed by a crowd of his compeers in the same state, climbed the companionway to the upper deck and demanded breakfast in the saloon.

The steward was a colored man; the waiters and deck-hands were of the same unfortunate race.

The steward explained that only passengers having first-class tickets were served on the upper deck and that breakfast for the others would be served on the deck below.

The raftsmen jeered at this information and tried to push their way into the saloon. The steward opposed them. In the scuffle he got the big drunken raftsman close to the companionway and sent him reeling downstairs.

His companions swore vengeance. Raftsmen were not to be insulted by Negroes.

They trooped to the captain and told him that unless the impudent "nigger" steward was punished they would set fire to the boat.

River men had one handy and common way of settling disputes. The captain, who realized the danger he was in, tried to quiet the rioters by reminding them of their favorite tribunal. Let the raftsman and the steward meet on the forecastle and fight it out with their fists.

The raftsman refused to fight a black man. Part of the deck-load was baled hay. The rioters now approached it with lighted matches to set it afire. All were armed; every raftsman went armed in those days. While part of the mob threatened the captain the rest sought out the deck-hands to kill them, for by this time had come the strange and terrible frenzy that we have since seen in many a race riot, and madness reigned.

The terrified deck-hands had scattered into hiding-places. Raftsmen relentlessly trailed them. An incessant fusillade of pistol shots produced wild panic on the upper deck. The boat was now fighting the swift current of the Rapids. Even the coolest of the passengers could see nothing but death ahead of them; either the boat would be fired or she would be wrecked on a reef.

A colored man had hidden in the forward hold. The raftsmen hunted him out. He eluded them and ran aft, followed by a cursing crowd. At the end of the afterguard he suddenly turned, whipped out a knife, stabbed to the heart one of his pursuers, and leaped into the water. Two men that had been fishing in a skiff started to row to him. The raftsmen fired at his head as he swam along. I cannot tell now whether they hit him, but, just before the skiff could reach him, he sank from sight and the mob cheered.

The barber hid in a closet. A rioter dragged him forth and stabbed him with a bowie-knife. He ran aft and begged a woman passenger to save his life. She hid him in her stateroom and bound up his wound. The rioters trailed him by his blood to her door and demanded their prey. She stood like a statue and poured upon them a torrent of such scorn that they sneaked away.

A deck-hand hid on the after-guard. Strange as it may seem, the boat continued all this time to make her regular landings. At the town of Hampton, Illinois, this fugitive attempted to escape. He was discovered and beaten into the water, where he was pelted with missiles until he sank and drowned.

The captain had managed at Hampton to get a passenger ashore with telegrams for help to be sent to the sheriff of Rock Island and other authorities. When the *Dubuque* was again upon her way, three more deck-hands were stabbed or shot and the bodies thrown into the river. Now the rioters sought the captain and demanded that the boat be run ashore, every black man on board be disembarked, and the voyage resumed with themselves as deck-hands. But they made a condition that the captain and officers should make no resistance, the boat should be run as they directed, no arrests must be made, and no information given. If the captain refused, the boat would be fired.

He consented to these terms and ran the boat to shore, where all the black men were landed. After this the rioters were quiet and the boat proceeded.

At Camanche, a few miles above Le Claire, the truculent ruffian that had started the trouble slipped ashore and disappeared.

Clinton was the next stop. The rioters by this time became impatient and demanded that the boat should speed up for St. Paul without stopping. There was a railroad bridge at Clinton and its draw was closed. The captain of the *Dubuque*, to gain time, told the rioters that the draw could not be opened. While they were arguing about this, a special train passed over the bridge, and the next the rioters knew a company of

regular soldiers from the Rock Island arsenal marched
down the levee. In answer to the captain's appeal they
had been sent by train up the Illinois shore. At the
sight of the uniforms and rifles the rioters broke and
ran for a vacant warehouse. Soldiers and the gathering citizens surrounded it. The commandant sum-
moned the men to surrender. They made some show
of resistance but finally gave in and were marched
in irons back to the *Dubuque*. With all her passengers
she started back to Rock Island. The passengers were
desired as witnesses.

The trial was short. Eleven of the rioters were convicted on the spot and taken to the penitentiary. Some
days in the county jail was the sentence for the rest.

But the man that launched that day of horror, the
ringleader that slunk ashore at Camanche, was never
caught. All the country was scoured for him, vigilantes
rode in every direction, the telegraph was used, and
all to no result. Once the scouts got a trace of him.
Far in the interior he had stopped at a lonely farm-
house and asked for a drink of milk. Then he disappeared. On the river he had been well-known for years
as "Pock-Marked Lynch." In behalf of my river and its
renown, I set down with emphasis that he was not really
a riverman. He was a parasite. His business was to
carry a faro layout up and down and relieve raft
crews of their wages. He had a partner named Frazier,
who managed to escape at Clinton. Years afterward
interest was revived in this story by a report that Frazier had returned to the river and had been seen and
recognized. If so, his visit was brief. As to Lynch, his
description was widely published, but so far as any
record shows he was lost to the sight of men.

Chapter XIII

OTHER PHASES OF RAFTSMAN JIM

IF in the face of the fairly eloquent testimony of the foregoing examples I continue to maintain that my rascals of the raft had sometimes a redeeming substratum of sentiment and poetry under their rowdyism, I may be judged merely eccentric. Yet I have reasons. I knew the floating raftsmen. Not many men now alive had first-hand knowledge of them. Besides, there were raftsmen and raftsmen. As to which, perpend.

To impressionable minds, of all the singular, mysterious spells that pertained to the Mississippi River the strongest came about the windless and cloudless sunset of a summer day. I do not believe there are such sunsets elsewhere in northern latitudes, not even on the Bay of Naples. Their only peers within my knowledge have been in the South Seas. The mirror of the river held the sky's burning and gorgeous colors, the unutterable bronzes and imperious reds, along with the Courbet green of the bluffs or of the willows on the tow heads; and there was an almost unearthly quiet abroad, a kind of competent and pervading self-sense of exaltation in so much beauty. The air was like glass; I could see a man in his shirt-sleeves leaning out of a window of Johnny Woods's house, across the river on the Illinois side, and hear the bell of the **Port Byron** Congregational church. In the midst of this idyllic and luminous quietude a great raft would come without a sound down the long Le Claire reach, drifting through the bronze, crimson, and dark-green without disturbing them by a single ripple; and then, of a sudden, there would float over the water the sounds of a fiddle, or maybe an accordion, playing "Buffalo Gals," and we could easily make out the crew sitting in a semicircle rapt upon the solitary musician.

From Princteon down to Le Claire, about five miles, the river ran almost straight, and if the rafts came slowly they came easily; but a mile below my grandfather's house the stream turned sharply to the west, and when a raft approached that point we could hear the queer, hoarse voice of the pilot booming weirdly through the stillness. "Forward oars, there!" and then came the creaking of the great oars upon the thole-pins, and the red and green bow lanterns upon the head of the raft would slowly go from sight around the point.

I brought my narrative in the first chapter to the place where I was sitting on a rock below my grandfather's house, listening to the singing and whooping of the wild men of Black River that went on all day.

It was not always hymnody of a kind to edify the youthful mind, but I am bound to say that, when there were children about, the raftsmen, if they happened to be sufficiently sober, would put some restraint upon both their language and their lyric offerings. They had a singular and absorbing passion for music—crude music, but still something approaching melody. Most rafts carried fiddlers as conscientiously as they carried cooks.

A few of the old songs and their tunes still run in my memory. Those that provided a chorus or an opportunity to dance a few steps between the stanzas were the favorites. "One-Eyed Riley" went like this:

> He was prime fav'rite out our way,
>> The women folks all loved him dearly;
> He taught the parsons how to pray,
>> An' he got their tin, or pretty nearly.
>>> He's the man they speak of highly!
>>> W-a-h-hoop!
>>> Riddle, liddle, linktum!
>> [*Pause—then all together, fortissimo*]
>>> One-Eyed Riley!

ONE–EYED RILEY

He was prime fav - 'rite out our way, The

wo - men folks all loved him dear - ly; He

taught the par - sons how to pray, An' he got their tin, or

pret - ty near - ly. He's the man they speak of high - ly!

Rid - dle lid - dle link - tum! One - Eyed Ri - ley!

A-Rafting on the Mississip'

THE BIG MAQUOKETA

We waz boom - in' down the old 'Mis - sip, One
splu-geous sum - mer day, When the old man yells, "Now
let her rip! I see the Ma - quo - ke - tay." But
we jest sez, "We're up to snuff an' don't keer what you
think; That cros - sin' ain't got dep' e - nough." Cap'
Jones jest took a drink! Dry up, yer darned old
li - ar, 'Cause his in - nards was a - fy - ar!

Other Phases of Raftsman Jim

The music now goes on without stopping, the air is repeated, and they dance out the measure until they come to the chorus:

> W-a-h-hoop!!
> Riddle, liddle, linktum!—[*pause*]
> One-Eyed Riley!

When "tum" is reached, all the boot-soles must slap the floor together. Then the dancers remain rigid until the refrain, which they deliver with roaring enthusiasm, "One-Eyed Riley!"

"The Big Maquoketa," flowerage of an undiscovered river laureate, was sung to an alteration of an air once a favorite in the politest circles.

> We waz boomin' down the old Miss'ip',
> One splugeous summer day,
> When the old man yells, "Now let her rip!
> I see the Maquoketay!"
> But we jest sez, "We're up to snuff
> An' don't keer what you think;
> That crossin' ain't got dep' enough"—[*pause*]

> Cap' Jones jest took a drink!
> [*Spoken:*]
> What? Water? Yes, water.
> [*Sung:*]
> Dry up, yer darn old liar![1]
> [*Spoken:*]
> Not water? Yes, water.
> [*Sung:*]
> 'Cause his innards was a-fy-ar!

"Raftsman Jim" was a narrative of somewhat dubious adventures of a youth that embodied the ideals

[1] Liberal translation here.

of gallantry and daring supposed to typify the calling. The air was pilfered. I can recall a few stanzas. One went thus:

> So her pop sez "Nay,"
> And he lopes away,
> And bobs right back the very next day;
> And he shuts one eye,
> And looks very sly,
> She gives to her pop the sweet bye-bye.

[Chorus]

> There ain't no cub as neat as him—
> Dandy, handy Raftsman Jim!

As in the other instance, the air was repeated after a stanza, when everybody danced, ending with four slapping steps sounding in unison and the roaring of the refrain:

> Dandy, handy Raftsman Jim!

RAFTSMAN JIM

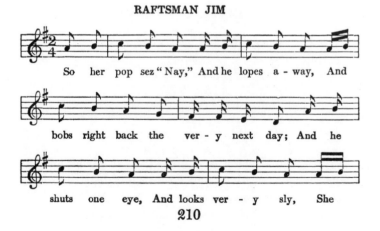

So her pop sez "Nay," And he lopes a - way, And

bobs right back the ver - y next day; And he

shuts one eye, And looks ver - y sly, She

Other Phases of Raftsman Jim

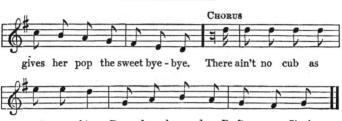

gives her pop the sweet bye-bye. There ain't no cub as

neat as him, Dan-dy, han-dy Rafts-man Jim!

But at all times the standard favorite was "Buffalo
Gals." I have been told that this song originated on the
old Erie Canal and landed early on the Mississippi in
the keel-boat days, before the advent of steam. If so, it
is the eldest of these lyrics, and certainly it had the
widest vogue. From Pembina to New Orleans men sang
it and danced to it; taken by its lively refrain and the
pleasant alternations in its recurrent phrasing.

If the words had been twice as boshy—a thing that
would not be in nature—that refrain would still have
carried them. I offer the text with a sense of humilia-
tion; and yet I have found this song on old Broadway
programs as having been sung to audiences that ought
to have known better, and there is evidence that East
and West it was the darling of its times.

> As I was lumb'ring down de street,
>   Down de street,
>   Down de street,
> A handsome gal I chanced to meet—
> Oh! She was fair to view.

> *[Chorus]*

> Buffalo gals, can't you come out to-night?
>   Can't you come out to-night,
>   Can't you come out to-night;
> Buffalo gals, can't you come out to-night,
> And dance by the light ob de moon?

A - Rafting on the Mississip'

I ask'd her would she have some talk,
  Have some talk,
  Have some talk,
As she stood close to me. [*Chorus*]

I ask'd her would she have some dance,
  Have some dance,
  Have some dance.
I thought that I might get a chance
To shake a foot with her. [*Chorus*]

I'd like to make that gal my wife,
  Gal my wife,
  Gal my wife.
I'd be happy all my life
If I had her by me. [*Chorus*]

As the lumber business and log-rafting expanded under the favorable sun of the rising empire, and as the railroads effected a concentrating of the industry at their crossing points, Clinton, Burlington, Winona, Dubuque, Davenport, Rock Island grew rapidly. Profits were comfortable and fairly certain; the whole river region began to resound with industry and rejoice in easy money. Then came, of course, the harpies and parasites—in swarms. Rivermen's dance halls, drinking saloons (and worse) lined the water-fronts of the cities.

From the small towns, publicity and the danger of vigilance committees excluded the worst phases of this commerce, but a kind of floating resort that anchored in sloughs or behind islands could long defy both commentary and law. Commonly, such migrants hung to their harborage until some intolerable outrage had awakened dilatory authority or the neighbors arrived with dogs and guns. Then they cast off and floated to another obscure and safe haven.

BUFFALO GALS

As I was lumb-'ring down de street, down de street, down de street, A hand - some gal I chanced to meet, Oh! She was fair to view. Buf - fa - lo gals, can't you come out to - night? Can't you come out to - night, can't you come out to - night? Buf - fa - lo gals, can't you come out to-night? And dance by de light ob de moon?

A-Rafting on the Mississip'

Despite its intimate connection with the river, the town of Le Claire was orderly and law-abiding. None of these wandering resorts ever made fast to its shores, but about two miles above and out of its jurisdiction was an island, and the slough back of this island made a good refuge for such skulkers. Sometimes a man of this order would come to town to buy supplies. I have since seen crude fringes of life in about all the climes of earth and have never known anything equal to these abandoned ruffians. In my distinct recollection of them there is a touch beyond human likeness. I have known better men to be hanged for less reason, and I think, after one fair look, any observer would believe them capable of any atrocity.

In all remote, new, and unorganized regions men are prone to revert for a time toward savage standards; but, for an adequate reason, not even the roughest mining camps produced criminals as reckless as these. The mining camps had the restraining fear of Judge Lynch and a surrounding community with some addiction to a moral standard; river rascals being exempt from observation were also exempt from restraint. Only once I heard of retribution descending upon them. A big log raft was tied up in Bad Axe Slough. A floating dance hall was a short distance above. Three raftsmen that visited it were slugged and robbed, one being mortally hurt. The raft went its way; but when its crew returned north they alighted at McGregor, forty miles below, and searched the back waters until they found the gang that had done the robbing. Exactly what happened that night was not well known; but the boat was burned as it lay and no one in that region heard again of its inmates.

Altogether, these crafts were hotbeds of crime. Poker Flat at its worst never knew anything so absolutely lawless. The brigands that conducted them

214

drugged raftsmen, robbed with impunity, and often murdered at their pleasure. Within the space of a week three bodies came ashore with stab or pistol wounds done in some of these traveling hells. The boundary line between the river States ran along the center of the steamboat channel. To escape ordinary arrest, they had but to steer to one side or the other, and if extradition were sought they could be miles away and beyond identification before the lumbering justice of those times could come up with them.

Once, also, there came to my notice a singular and incongruous commentary on another side of this wretched business. I was standing one day on the river-front at Davenport, watching the smart steamboat *Josephine* manage six barges through the bridge draw, when from up the stream hove in sight one of these floating dives bearing in river parlance a generic name not to be repeated in print. It seemed to be composed of two long flatboats fastened together and covered, except at its ends, with low, one-storied deck structures. Forward and aft enough room had been left to work two sweeps. It drove with the current under a bridge span and so down.

As it came opposite the now empty steamboat-landing, there was a stir among the loungers to see a young woman of strange appearance come running along the bank with her eyes fixed on the drifting flatboats. A thing more out of place among the freight piles and burlaps of a water-front can hardly be imagined. She was dressed in an evening gown of heavy silk, deep green in color, without sleeves, elaborately trimmed with gold braid, and having a train that she must carry in one hand. I have often wondered where that dress came from; its like had not been seen in our town or time. She could not have been more than twenty years old, she was far from ill-looking, and she seemed not of the kind one would expect to see in the conditions that quickly developed. She had no hat, and her luxuriant hair, of a notable depth of red, was well arranged upon her head. She was panting with fatigue evidently, as much as with an intense excitement. The light slippers on her feet had once been white, but were now stained with mud and torn as if with the rocks. Her dress too looked as if she had been running through bushes.

"Row me out to that boat!" she gasped. "I'll give you this," and she waved a five-dollar bill.

Old Joe Arp, the boatman, had been sitting on the bow of his skiff pulled up on shore. He roused at the sight of the bill and took her aboard. They were within perhaps a hundred feet of the dance hall, when a rear door opened and there stepped out the ugliest scoundrel I had ever seen. He had a rifle, which he laid suggestively in the crook of his elbow, and he said to Arp in a low voice:

"You git away from here—and do it quick."

The woman sprang up in the boat and nearly upset it.

"Oh, Bill," she cried, "dear Bill, take me back, take me back, Bill!"

The rifle came up to the ruffian's shoulder. "You git for shore, or I'll blow you full of holes," he said. "Git!"

Arp said afterward there was something in the man's voice so coldly cruel he would have sheered off if there had been no weapon. He lost no time in making for shore. The woman held out her hands beseechingly. The rifle continued to cover them until they were far away. Then the man went into the house and shut the door. On the bank the woman fell to crying upon a pile of burlaps. A half circle of river-front men stood and looked on in silence. I noticed that nobody jeered. Presently, she arose and wiped her face and passed in her conspicuous gown up the river street. She was not seen in that town again. I never knew what became of her. Rivermen said she had run along the bank all the way from above Le Claire, following the dance-hall and pleading and crying. That was a distance of fifteen miles.

But I had in mind to tell about that immortal lyric of the river, "Buffalo Gals."

Some attempts were made to improve upon this poor fustian, one of which for a peculiar reason came to celebrity.

A few miles below McGregor on the Iowa side an irascible old gentleman named Dee kept a wood-yard for steamboats; also an ever-ready rifle and a collection of dogs. He had a daughter, known all up and down the river as the Corn-Fed Girl, who was at once the dream and the despair of every batty poet from Pig Eye's Bar to Alton Slough. These, undergoing for her sake the pains of composition, caused the odd corners of many a local newspaper to echo with lame numbers. To win a sight of Mary Dee while the boat stopped for supplies at the wood-yard was a feat of distinction, usually achieved, if at all, at some risk from guns and dogs. Mr. Dee, I may say, was a retired riverman; it is likely that he knew what he was about when he kept his daughter secluded like a nun.

When a boat headed for the Dee yard, officers and passengers made bets on whether without being shot or bitten they would or would not succeed in getting a glimpse of the fair recluse, and the expedients resorted to made the basis of many a well-spun lie in the watches of the night. Sometimes ingenuity or persistence succeeded. A commercial traveler from St. Louis was supposed to have played the lowest trick on innocent womanhood. He had a suspicion that while Mary was locked up in the house she might be watching the visitors unobserved. He placed himself with his back to a window apparently engaged in most earnest conversation with Pop about the coming election and the state of the nation (Pop being an unconverted Copperhead), while he unfurled a copy of "Godey's Ladies' Book," and of course Mary came right out.

For myself, I may say that for a long time I heard these reports and sniffed at them. Rivermen were notorious for fervent imaginations about such world wonders; in their view anything that wore skirts was divine. Besides, there was, and for years had been, competition among Le Claire, La Crosse, and Dubuque on this subject, each asserting itself to have the prettiest girls and each advancing the claim on what seemed to the judicious mind but trifling warrant. But once when I was making trips on the old steamer *St. Croix* in a capacity something like that of a supercargo, we came one Monday morning unusually close around the point below the Dee place. The river was high, and Uncle Joe, the first pilot of the *St. Croix*, was hunting slack water. So we boomed unperceived upon the wood-yard, and there was Mary hanging out the washing with her sleeves above her elbows.

Well, there was no doubt that for once reputation was justified, a thing I have seldom observed since. She was a great beauty, and no mistake. She had the Irish deep-black hair, Irish blue eyes, a face of almost classical contour, a white skin set off with a delicate pink glow—all this away out here in the wilderness. I could understand, also, how she won her peculiar name. It was in right of her statuesque figure and her air of exceeding wholesomeness. After this, I suppose it will be needless to remark that I fell with the rest.

But about the addendum to "Buffalo Gals," I have spoken of my towny that had the amazing and fevered vision of our water-front as a diadem. He now pro-

duced some execrable verses about the invisible siren
of Dee's Wood-Yard, and as he adapted them to the
tune of "Buffalo Gals" (more or less), it became a
habit of raftsmen to roar them out as a serenade when
the raft hove in sight of the Dee place. A single sample
will be enough:

> Oh, the Corn-Fed Girls, they are the best
>> In all the West
>> They are the best,
> And of all the tribe that I have seen,
> May Dee, she is the queen.
>> [*Chorus*]
> Corn-Fed Girl, see the moon shine bright,
>> Ain't you coming out to-night?
>> Ain't you coming out to-night?
> Oh, Corn-Fed Girl, ain't you walking out to-night
> With your hand laid in mine?

The rest of the story of the Corn-Fed Girl went
at first as might have been expected. Yes—you are
right; she eloped. It happened, however, contrary to
form, that the man for whom she left the parental
roof was not wholly unworthy, a circumstance to ex-
cite remark anywhere. When Mr. Dee's emotions had
passed the dog and gun stage, he admitted that the
joke was on him and turned in his blessing.

Chapter XIV

CAPTAIN PLUCK TAKES CHARGE

TWISTING back and forth like a snake along the broad shallow bed of the upper Mississippi is a trough, deeper than the rest of the bottom and, of course, hidden from sight. This trough is the steamboat channel. It may be less than a hundred feet wide in a place where the total width of the river is half a mile or a mile, and it may turn and wind about like a drunken man while the visible total of river goes placidly and deceitfully straight. A raft afloat without a steamboat had, because of its lighter draft, a considerable latitude of motion. When it was pushed by a steamboat the boat, except sometimes in high water, could not stray far from that unseen trough below it.

This was one difficulty about raft-pushing and enough to keep any pilot from going to sleep at his task. Another was that in some places the trough turned perilously near one shore or the other, so that while the steamer was all right the raft might be hitting the bank. Or, where there was a tow head or a strong current, the raft might pull the steamer out of the trough, yet itself be safe. To these and many other complexities was added those maddening problems I have mentioned that were made by changing depth.

How steamboat pilots kept their vessels in the trough

220

I have indicated in the foregoing examples. It was partly by a complicated system of shore marks known only to themselves; partly by reading the surface of the water, which they alone could translate; and partly by some queer uncharted mind motion that we have called a sixth sense, a sense that enabled them to know in the darkest night exactly where they were and where their fantastic road led next; to know, not within feet but within inches. But a steamboat pilot had to think of a craft maybe two hundred feet long and thirty feet wide. The pilot of a raft pushed by a steamboat had to think of this and also of the huge sluggish field of logs ahead of him and to calculate how both were to be managed in safety through a black pall without a dependable light.

I have stood at night in the pilot-house of a raft boat and peered out ahead and around me, and so far as I could see at all, we were steaming into an indeterminate waste of dun-colored mist. Away down ahead, apparently a mile off, glimmered the little lights, one green, one red, that marked the forward corners of the raft; farther away was the spark of one of the Government's crossing lights that were the everlasting jest of the pilot-house but served no other purpose. On one side of us I could make out a long, shadowy outline that seemed on scrutiny blacker than the rest of the prospect. This, I was assured, was the line of the river bluffs. On the other side, farther away and dimmer, was another such line. The river was a gray sea, before and behind us—faint, nebulous, mysterious. Sometimes in this weird twilight I could make out a darker body, or thought I could. This, I was told, was an island. It might have been a weasel, a camel, or a whale for all I could see.

In front of me, at one side, stood Uncle Joe, the pilot, loafing over the steering-wheel and placidly smoking a corncob pipe, the perfect figure of assured competence. We had been talking about sleep and dreams.

"No," said he, "it's funny how some men sleep on a hair-trigger and some you couldn't wake up with a cannon. One time I was in the old *Tigris* [1] when we were towing empty grain barges to Red Wing. In those days Red Wing was the biggest original wheat market in the world; you wouldn't think it now, maybe, but it was. We had four barges, two ahead and one on each side and making slow work bucking the current. I was taking her up Fulton Slough. There was three feet on Sycamore Chain, so I knew I was all right, and just as I got to the head of the slough, here comes—"

Clang! Clang!

Down in the engine-room I heard the bell for the donkey-engine strike twice. Without a pause or a ripple in his smooth flow of talk, Uncle Joe had pulled upon the bell-rope. Instantly the quiver and quaver of the machine began as the *St. Croix* was drawn around into a sharp angle with the raft.

"—the old *Prescott* with a couple of sand flats. Of course, she hadn't any business to be there bound down at the head of that slough—"

Clang! and the donkey-engine stopped.

"—so I gives her the warning toot good and strong—"

Jingle! Jingle! goes the bell in the engine-room. He had pulled another rope, and the great wheel astern stops and then begins to back.

"—and the next thing I see, she wasn't under control—"

---

[1] There is some error about these names I have been unable to rectify. I cannot find record of a steamboat *Tigris* on the upper river. Possibly the pilot said *Tiber*, but the *Tiber* was owned in Winona. As to the *Prescott*, I think he referred to an earlier *Prescott* than the towboat built in 1870 and bearing this name. There was a steamer *Tigress*, but she was sunk in the Civil War.

Jingle! the wheel goes ahead again.

"Yes, sir. There she was waltzing down the head of the slough at her own sweet will, and me just below with all those barges and the channel there ain't seventy feet wide. That was one time when Uncle thought he was slated for trouble."

Clang! and we haul around the other way.

"What did you do?" I say.

Clang! The donkey-engine stops.

"Nothing. You know you can't turn around in those sloughs, nor back your way out of them. So, of course, I just stops and then backed dead slow until the forward barge hit one of the flats. Then I went ahead strong and pushed the whole outfit up on the shore into the woods and clipped out into the river. But while we were pushing 'em, one of our deck-hands hopped aboard, and there in a chair in the clerk's office sat the clerk, fast asleep. The *Prescott* had been hired to tow sand for a contractor, the contractor hadn't showed up, the night before all hands had gone up to town to have a time, and the clerk was left on watch. Well, there came on one of those big, roaring he-storms that night and broke the *Prescott* and the flats loose and blowed them out into the river, and the clerk, he sat there and slept through all that row, thunder, lightning and all, and never woke up.

"Soused," I say.

"No, sir—"

Clang!

"—he wasn't soused. That man never took a drink—"

Clang!

"—in his life. But he could outsleep the dead. He could give *Rip Van Winkle* cards and spades. But what I started to tell you was what come of that sleeping. The *Prescott* had been sold to some fellow back on the prairies, shoemaker or blacksmith or something [immense disdain] and so he sued us for running his blame' old boat ashore—"

Clang! Clang!

"—Well, in those days you could tie up a steamboat on a sheriff's paper. You can't do that any—"

Clang!

"—more, and the next six weeks we had a lively old time dodging the sheriff's boys. One day one came aboard with his writ, or whatever they call the thing, and started to read it, he having attached the bowline or something, and my partner, who was in the pilothouse, started to back hard and broke the bowline and carried the sheriff off to Cassville, which was out the State and set him ashore—gently, of course. But every time we showed up around those parts there'd be a sheriff's man looking for us with a paper in his hand. Got to be kind of annoying, as you can see for yourself. A steamboat can't always be carrying sheriffs off. So, one day our lawyer, a smart chap in Keokuk, says —that's Glenhaven down there to labboard—well, he says: 'Attach nothing! Why don't you fellows bring suit against this owner (meaning the shoemaker, or whatever he was) for salvaging his blame' old boat and things?' So we done it and that called off the sheriff, because the next thing this carpenter knew the officers was chasing him. So then the most of us was in favor of calling it even and quitting. But the people in St. Louis where our boat was owned said not in a thousand years and they started in to make the blacksmith pay and I never could find out how that came out."

Clang!

And so on, hour after hour, one crossing after another, twisting from side to side as the boat threaded the circuitous windings of the trough down under the water, weaving a pattern and shaving disaster first on

one side by say three feet and then on the other by
two, and the raft, 600 feet long and 250 feet wide,
swung and maneuvered into. marks that were to me
wholly imaginary. I dwell on these things because of
the profit to the spirit, for thus do we win a new respect for man and his capacities. Recalling achievements I have seen by raft-steamer pilots, I do not know
where one could well draw the limitation. "Glory to
man in the highest, for he is the master of things," and
any of them seem possible to him when faced with their
necessity.

"There's no backing out of those places," said Uncle
Joe. He was speaking verity. In some of the sloughs or
reaches the raft would take up the navigable channel
and leave but a slip of water on each side. Then a steamboat bound up would meet a raft in one of these narrow-
squeak aisles and the wonder was, not that there were
occasional disasters on the upper Mississippi, but that
any boat got through alive.

Once I had this brought home to me so I could understand it. I was out on the middle of the raft one
day when we were coming down below Copper Creek,
where the river is all tangled up with more islands than
there are gunmen in Chicago and the channel twisted
around like a politician's smile. Of a sudden I was aware
that the *Clinton*, the crack packet of the day, was coming up the slough and was already caught in an apparently helpless position. The channel was narrow, the
raft filled the whole of it except a thin strip on one
side, and even this was disappearing as our logs swung
down toward a long, bluff island. I stood a fascinated
and breathless observer of what seemed inevitable disaster, for there was not a chance on earth for the packet
to turn and run out of that trap. Already the open
water seemed less in width than the beam of the steamer
coming on. One of the most beautiful steamboats on

the river and crowded with passengers was about to be wrecked before my eyes.

I heard her jingle bell ring peal after peal; distinctly I heard her pilot discharging down the speaking tube profanity hot enough to melt the metal. With every pound of steam she had she went tearing through the narrowing passage and cleared it just in time. Her larboard wheel missed the last logs by not more than a foot and her stern planks by inches. Half a second more would have done for her. Her pilot said afterward that about the middle of that slender lane he had not a foot of water under her bow and once he felt her touch and thought all was over, but she ground her way through without sticking.

Meantime, J. W. Van Sant & Son had been doing some piloting of their own along other lines. They started with what seemed to them a colossal debt, for those three shares in the firm had to be paid for from profits, and the building of the new steamer on credit had been termed by Wisdom a merely mad bid for the bankruptcy court. The thousands of dollars that it had added to the debt load kept father and son awake at night. Ship carpenters and other workers had still to be paid. At one time Van Sant & Son owed everybody in Le Claire, and as for their notes at the bank, they were kept in the air as a juggler whisks his oranges. They owed not only big bills for big things but every tradesman in the town; they owed Butcher Rothmann for the meat that came to their table, and Jimmy Davenport for the sugar and tea. They owed Dave Carr the barber for cutting their hair, and Mr. Schwarm, the mayor, for three pairs of shoes. Captain Sam never walked out of his house in the daytime without being reminded of his desperate state. He couldn't have thrown a club in any direction without hitting a creditor.

Captain Pluck Takes Charge

In the midst of this turbulence, with his head just above the water, he did two things that left breathless all that knew the inside facts about the firm. He bought on credit from the Northern Line the stern-wheel packet *James Means* to make a rafter of her, and he proceeded to lay down the lines of another steamer to be built at the Van Sant yards.

In all this he was not crazy, as some of his head-shaking friends declared, but acting on a profound faith. He had seen enough of the performances of the *J. W. Van Sant* to show that there was to be a great future for such boats. Already she was making money. Two boats would make more money and three be better still. Besides, the boat-yard in winter was crowded to its capacity with steamboats that came to be repaired, and he foresaw a great business along these lines; if only bankruptcy could be avoided.

The new steamboat was launched at the yard the beginning of the season of 1872 and carried many improvements over her predecessor. She was called the *D. A. McDonald*, a name destined to a peculiar place in river annals.

Soon after the *McDonald* was ready to steam away on her first voyage, the Van Sants heard that at Evansville on the Ohio River a stern-wheel boat called the *Hartford* was to be sold by the United States marshal, and from all they could hear she seemed about right for towing a raft. Why not have four boats instead of three? Captain Sam took the chief engineer of the *McDonald* and went down to Evansville to buy that boat, hiring a good man as the engineer's temporary substitute.

The *McDonald*, having demonstrated the wisdom of her designer, was much in demand and had now been chartered to a towing company at La Crosse. She had whisked one raft down the river and was scrambling back after another. On the fifty-eighth day of her young life she was just below the town of McGregor, Iowa, when the engineer in charge came to the captain and said:

"Captain, this boat ought to run to shore and tie up. The water in the boilers is foaming and we ought not to go any farther with it."

"Tie up? No, not we!" roared the captain. "This boat's got to make La Crosse before the saloons close to-night. We drive right ahead."

He was drunk.

"It isn't safe," said the engineer. "We're likely to blow up any minute. We'd better stop and tie."

"You listen to me," said the captain. "We run right on. Hear?"

The engineer was timid, and all for obeying orders. He should have drawn the fires and let the boilers cool without further reference to the roof, for in this the law would have amply sustained him. He went away shaking his head. Eleven minutes later the larboard boiler let go with a roar, followed the next instant by the starboard. It seemed as if everything above the main deck on that steamer melted away like wax. Sixteen persons were killed outright. Among them were the drunken captain and the second engineer. The survivors clung to the wreckage and were picked up by the tow-boat *Jennie Brown*, which happened to be close by.

Captain Sam coming from Evansville was bowling along below St. Louis when at a landing he bought a sheaf of newspapers to cheer his lonely hours with the news, and there on the first page with black headlines was the story of the disaster.

The spot where the *McDonald* sank was a short distance below the McGregor bridge.

This structure, a pontoon owned by a singular character named John Lawler, consisted of boat hulls anchored with gear chains and supporting a framework on which were railroad tracks. At the steamboat channel a span was left open by dropping down a hull on an anchor chain. When a train was to be passed over the bridge, a steam-engine worked a winch that pulled the open span against the current into place. The Chicago, Milwaukee & St. Paul Railroad used this device as the crossing of its Northern Iowa line and paid John Lawler a neat sum for every car that traversed the river—in the summer time. In the winter, the pontoon boats were removed and the railroad company laid tracks upon the ice and so crossed.

Lawler, a Scotch-Irishman of stern aspect, was thrifty, active, capable, and much respected. He had done steamboating on his own account, and had been owner of the packet *Northern Light,* said by some judges to have been the most beautiful steamer that ever sailed the upper river, and poetically mourned when she hit a rock and sank. He was now the owner of the *Jennie Brown* and some other small craft.

Van Sant and father went at once to McGregor to look at the wreck of the *McDonald.* Against all expert opinion, father was of the belief that it could be raised and saved. His plan was much derided by those that knew about such things and saw plainly that it would never work. He procured two barges and anchored them one on each side of the sunken hulk. Then he got six heavy chains and passed them one by one under the *McDonald.* This was difficult without divers, but he maneuvered each chain in a bight until he got it under the *McDonald's* nose and then worked it back and forth until he had it where he wanted it. Next he laid great timbers lengthwise on the barges and made the chains fast over them. Then he put jackscrews under the timbers and began to lift, three inches on one side, then three inches on the other.

A - Rafting on the Mississip'

After a time, Son saw that this process would lift the hull clear in another day, and that it would be necessary to have a towboat at hand to keep the outfit from being washed away and lost. Therefore, post-haste to Lawler to see if he could hire the *Jennie Brown.*

"Take her for as long as you need her," said the bridge owner, and plunged into a calculation of how many cars at so much a car the railroad was likely to pay for that month.

The *Jennie Brown* stood by, and at last the jack-screws, three inches at a time, brought the wreck up so it could be seen.

It was worth seeing, onlookers said, though nothing but bare hull and engines. Everything had disappeared above the main deck. The force of the explosions had even wrenched the hull timbers, which was why she sank so soon. This was not wonderful. The explosions were so tremendous that pieces of boiler were picked up nearly a mile away and some never did seem to come down.

The *Jennie Brown* now took in tow this limp and shattered thing, still supported by the two barges, and started with it down the river for Le Claire. The first day they made as far as Dubuque and tied up there for the night. By noon of the following day they made Le Claire all right, and before night Captain Sam had the satisfaction of seeing the battered hulk out upon the ways and surrounded by a neck-craning and curious crowd.

The next day the shipwrights were at work upon it to make this rag of a steamboat once more into something that could float and earn money.

But the next day began also a season of grinding anxiety for the owners of the wreck. J. W. Van Sant & Son were up to their chins in debt and from day to day staving off bankruptcy. They had more than merely worked hard; they had toiled like cart-horses, they had followed all the time-worn injunctions to honesty, industry, and sobriety, and the rest; their boat-yard had been far from unsuccessful. But they were stoop-shouldered under the load with which they had started. And now there was this bill for the *Jennie Brown*—standing by and towing and all; perhaps she would charge salvage, and at that thought Captain Sam shivered and visualized ruin. With a heavy heart he took himself to McGregor and stood before the redoubtable John Lawler.

"Well?" said the king of the pontoon, hardly looking up. "What now?"

"I have come to ask about the bill for the *Jennie Brown*," says Sam, mouthing gingerly.

"Ain't any bill for the *Jennie Brown*," said the king. "When men show the pluck you've shown, the rest of us ought to help them along."

Besides the *McDonald*, a new boat was on the Van Sant ways, another new rafter, for father and son now had visions of a great Van Sant fleet—if they survived. Like the others, she was built on a shoe-string, and even at that the builders had not enough money or credit to swing her, and brought into the enterprise two other citizens of Le Claire. As she progressed, they came to the point where boilers were needed.

New boilers were needed also for the *McDonald*, the old ones having been scattered over a mile or so of rich bottom-land, and the question for the penniless builders was how to get four new boilers at once, without money.

The boiler-maker, a St. Louis man, had the contracts, but not a hand would he stir on them until he had his cash, or its equivalent. He knew something about the financial status of the Van Sant tribe.

Captain Sam started for St. Louis to argue with him.

Just as he was leaving, his brother Nicholas rushed after him, shouting:

"Don't go! Come back! The *Hartford* is sunk!"

It was so. She had been sunk by the ice in the slough up the river where she had wintered.

The year was 1873—the great panic year. Never was the business outlook gloomier.

Captain Sam went up to the place where the *Hartford* lay, saw that she could be raised and started the work on her. Having been a packet, she had more cabin than a rafter needed. He brought up from Le Claire a gang of men and a number of hay-wagon racks that he had placed on sleds. Now he cut off half of the cabin from the *Hartford*, loaded it upon his sleds, slid it to Le Claire, and placed it upon the *McDonald*, which had no cabin at all.

He then went to St. Louis to take up the argument with the boiler-maker. This astute person was still adamant about cash, but offered a suggestion. The boat-yard did repair work for steamers of the Northern Packet Line, a concern with much money. Happy thought! Get the Northern Line to make an advance.

This modest request Captain Sam took to a meeting of the packet company's directors. It met with a stern refusal. The by-laws forbade anything of that kind.

As he was going away with defeat to-day and ruin next week, Captain James Ward, president of the company, whispered to him:

"Wait for me in the anteroom."

So he waited. And after a time Captain Ward came out and said that while the by-laws forbade any advances to anybody, there was nothing in them to prevent the company's acceptance of drafts to be payable in the future.

On this hint, Captain Sam made out his drafts, the

THOMAS DOUGHTY

Inventor of the periscope; pioneer in stern–wheel raft boat making

WOODING-UP AT NIGHT. A MISSISSIPPI PACKET AT A WOOD-YARD

boiler-maker took them for pay, and the boilers were delivered.

The new boat needed a name. In view of the finances of her builders, Captain Sam had called her ironically *The Poverty* and by that name she had been entered on the firm's books. She was now approaching completion, being entered at the supervising inspector's office at Galena as a boat with name to be supplied. This did not suit the inspector, and he began to press for a name. The builders racked their brains in vain to find one. *Poverty* was no name for an American boat that expected to do business. She was of unusual merit, too, they believed, this one, and ought to have an unusual name. One day when Captain Sam was out of town, there came from the inspector a telegram demanding a name and no more delay. In her husband's absence, Mrs. Van Sant opened the despatch, took paper and pencil, and answered it:

"The name of the boat is the *Le Claire Belle.*"

It was, and under that name for seventeen years or such a matter she steamed up and down the Mississippi, delivering rafts and making money. More than one season she returned in profits all that she cost to build. The average life of a Mississippi River steamer was five years. The *Le Claire Belle* lived more than three times that span.

Meantime, there was the *McDonald*, rebuilt, reboilered, and better than ever, one of the sprucest boats that ever turned a wheel, and looking for rafts and things to tow. If the *Le Claire Belle's* luck held and the *McDonald* shared it, the firm might hope to get to its feet, provided only that its creditors would give it a chance to live. And just at that time one of them was heard from. He came in with mortgage papers made out to support his claim by impounding one of the boats; papers all made out and ready to sign here on the dotted line.

"I'm not going to sign," said Captain Sam when he had read the documents.

"Why not?"

"Because there will be no preferred creditors here. If we go to smash, everybody will be treated alike."

Once the *McDonald* towed a lumber raft to Alton and cleared $3200 on the single trip. By the time she had returned to Beef Slough for another, the glad tidings had spread that there was money in the till, and one of the creditors speeded to Beef Slough to lay his hand upon it. Captain Sam was there before him. The creditor used freely the tropic word and cheery smile of congratulation. Then he mentioned his little account and said he expected it would be paid now.

"It will not be," said the captain.

The smile faded as the creditor demanded to know why not.

"Because your claim is for money advanced. The first men to share in this money will be the shipwrights and carpenters at Le Claire. They lent us their work; you lent us only your money."

At the Davenport National Bank was a grim old cashier named Woodward, commonly known as the Watch Dog, it was so hard to get past him with anything. The Van Sants were carried at this bank in large amounts and this a panic year, when everybody was nervous. Captain Sam went to see Watch Dog Woodward.

"I can't pay that note now," he said. "I am going to pay it some day," and he explained the exact situation in the raft-boat business. Mr. Woodward listened without comment, all the time appraising the captain with searching scrutiny. When the recital was done, he allowed the note to be renewed, not once but many times.

Captain Pluck Takes Charge

Misfortune seemed still enamored of the Van Sant parts. An excellent firm hired the rescued *Hartford* on comfortable terms, and then failed and could pay nothing on the charter. The house in which Captain Sam lived burned with everything he owned. His one child, a daughter, died of diphtheria. The general condition of business was so bad that building lessened even in the new empire, and there was a falling off in the demand for lumber. Still he fought on.

Three years of nip and tuck struggle followed with varying fortunes. In May, 1876, the *McDonald* took a contract to tow ice barges from up-river points to St. Louis. The weather was delightful. Captain Sam was always a great hand for good company. He took Mrs. Van Sant with him on this trip; also a party of friends from Muscatine. As the *McDonald* was heading down for the draw of the bridge at Keokuk, the captain was standing on the upper deck forward. He did not like the way the boat was being handled for that draw. It seemed to him that the pilot was not making enough allowance for the swirl of the high water. A captain was not permitted to tell the pilot how to run anything. Captain Sam hopped below and called his mate.

"Get all the passengers out upon the barge," he said. "I think we're going to hit the bridge."

They had time to get most of their guests to a place of safety, when the captain's foreboding came true. The strong rush of the water past the draw pier caught the boat and swung it sidewise. The impact drove the guard of a barge under the guard of the steamer, where it broke through the hull. About midships she crashed into the stone pier. Once clear of that, the pilot headed her full speed for the Iowa shore. There was not time enough. The water poured in through the crushed side and she sank below the bridge.

Her upper works were still intact, and if she could be raised she might ride the river again.

The United States Government was then doing extensive work on the Keokuk Rapids and employed large flatboats to carry stone and machinery. That night one of these flatboats, loaded with heavy stone, broke loose in the high water, swept down the river, struck the wreck of the *McDonald*, and shaved off everything down to the boilers.

J. W. Van Sant & Son were still heavily in debt. And there lay their chief money-earner, inert in the mud.

This time she seemed done for. The oldest rivermen took a look at what could be seen of her and said the case was hopeless. So strongly ran the current at that spot that before any salvagers could get to work there would be nothing left to salvage. Commodore Davidson, the head of the packet line and one of the best steamboatmen on the river, was all of this opinion. Captain Sam telegraphed to St. Louis and brought up a professional wrecker, an expert of renown, who spent forty-eight hours in earnest deliberation and for a fee of $1000 announced the same judgment.

"If you can get the boilers and engines out of her, it's as much as you can do," announced this thoughtful person, and shook a solemn head.

It is worth something to be descended from a Revolutionary hero. By this time the Van Sant fighting blood was up. Captain Sam sent the expert home with his $1000 (borrowed) and a headful of scornful speech. Then he brought down from Le Claire two barges and a choice of men from the boat-yard and resorted to the tactics he had used before.

The show was just before Keokuk's front door, without admission charge, and was greatly enjoyed by all. "Van Sant's Folly," it was relishingly called by the discerning, and the only question was whether the fool was to be washed off with his ridiculous works, supposing him to succeed in freeing the hulk from the silt in which it was embedded. There was astonishment when after two weeks of incessant toil with chain and jackscrew the hull of the wreck began to appear between the two barges.

Astonishment gave place to another emotion when it was seen that the wreck thus supported was moving shoreward. Directly in front of it was the city's levee or landing-place, and the city council clearly perceived that it was the intention of this wizard person to beach the wreck there and so leave it upon Keokuk's doorstep. Resentful aldermen introduced an ordinance forbidding the wreck to be brought within a hundred feet of the shore. By great good luck, an old riverman that knew the Van Sants was a member of the council. Giving his personal guarantee that the wreck would not be left on the levee but be taken away as soon as possible, he succeeded in preventing the slamming of the door in the hardy wrecker's face.

Presently the hulk came duly to the bank, unsightly with mud and weeds and with everything swept away above the lower deck. The handy men from Le Claire patched up the hole in the side and pumped her out so that she would float. Then they rigged up a queer jury steering-wheel and a whistle, made steam and found that she would turn over all right. The next thing Keokuk knew, about four o'clock of a bright summer day a strange-looking craft without pilot-house or upper works was whistling for the bridge draw.

In this guise under her own steam she passed up the river to Le Claire and was not much better when she began again to tow rafts.

For this exploit the river town newspapers unanimously voted to change the name of the man that pulled her out of the river slime and made her go again. He was no more Captain Van Sant, but Captain Pluck.

"Passed down, steamer *D. A. McDonald,* Captain Pluck, with raft, Beef Slough to Alton.

"Passed up, steamer *D. A. McDonald,* Captain Pluck, St. Louis for Stillwater."

But two voyages to the bottom of the river seemed to Captain Pluck enough for any steamboat. When he came that winter to rebuild the *McDonald* he got an act passed through Congress changing her name to the *Silver Wave,* under which poetic suggestion she plowed the Mississippi for many years, brought down many rafts, made much profits, and with coin justified the grim tenacity of her master.

His profound faith in the possibilities of the business, a faith in which he sometimes stood almost alone, was vindicated in other ways. In 1842, when Stephen Hanks went into the pine wilderness, there were in the whole great St. Croix region but two sawmills, one at St. Croix Falls, the other at Marine. On the Mississippi below the St. Croix there was hardly one mill that really deserved the name. Thirty years later Hanks counted 135 sawmills between St. Paul and St. Louis that he had seen erected and buzzing their way into fortune. Besides these, scores had been built above St. Paul and on the tributary streams. Out of the great boom at Beef Slough, mouth of the Chippewa, issued now in a season from 400,000,000 to 600,000,000 feet of logs. In one season, that of 1873, 680 rafts passed the Davenport bridge and were estimated to have contained 275,000,000 feet. As sample days, on June 5 of that year eighteen rafts passed the bridge; June 6, eighteen; June 7, seventeen; June 11, sixteen. Fifty-four acres of logs in a day. Six great lumber manufacturing points above Davenport daily consuming their quotas of logs were gages of the new empire.

Chapter XV

THE PILOT AND HIS WAYS

ONE trait all rivermen of my time had in common, if so be that they were not mere ruffians or roisterers. It was a great, absorbing, dominating, vital, and, to the outsiders, unexplainable passion for the river. To say that it was a fondness for the river or a liking for the river—that would mean nothing. What they felt was more like a lover rejoicing in his first love, only this was immune from satiety and did not change. I know I shall be thought extravagant, but not by those that knew the life I am writing about. The peculiar fascination that this stream exerted upon all its devotees approximated the uncanny. "Alas! they're mad," said my towny, the poet, who had read the classics and could quote or paraphrase with equal circumstance. It was hardly a figure of speech.

Other men had interests aside from their daily work. My pilots had none. Other men, or most other men, have a tendency to quarrel with their jobs. The Mississippi River men were on terms of intimate comradeship with theirs. I have never known a lawyer past forty that was in love with his profession nor a doctor that adored doctoring nor a carpenter that wanted to get up in the middle of the night and plane boards. But to a pilot his craft was all in all. It was not these hours of labor for this handful of pay that he might have bread; it was a romance that never grew tiresome, a joy that never lost its savor. He had for the river all the tender attachment susceptible men have for the recollected scenes of their childhood, for the old haunts, the old swimming-hole, the old-time playmates. I have known pilots to whom the river, year in and year out, seemed more than wife, home, or child. Suppose a riverman to climb to a way of life much more remunerative —become a lumber magnate, as some did, or a prosperous merchant, like many others. He was never done wishing himself back and sighing whenever the time came when he knew the ice would be going out.

Even if he took the wings of the morning and buried himself in earth's uttermost parts, the spell was ineradicable. For him no life had taste or tang but the life of the river. I do believe that many a raft-steamer's deckhand had more profit of living than all the millionaires. The lore of the river, and the endless talk about the ways of running the river, and the subtlety and danger of the river, and recollections of the look of the river, and times when the south wind was blowing lightly at night and the moon made silver-tinted crepon of the river, and crisp days in fall when the red haws on the islands hung over the river, and Indian summer when the haze was tender with the river, and the thought of the ever-haunting song of the river, and the swift changes of the mood of the river (that jilt, that unfathomable coquette!), and the everlasting flowing of the river, out of the mystery above, into the mystery below—not the clash of thrones nor the music of the spheres had by comparison a passing interest. Let any man with any touch of the poetic or emotional in his being make so much as three trips on the river and he was done for. From that time the spell had him fast. If thereafter he should be wandering in Polar soli-

From an old engraving

THE MISSISSIPPI

Sunrise below St. Anthony's Falls

tudes or the Libyan sands, he would have visions of that marvelous stream; perhaps in the early morning or evening, with its unruffled surface superbly colored, or maybe in July the smell of it would come to him when the wild clover was ripe on the tow heads or along the shore. It would haunt him, the river; he would see it in his dreams sliding its smooth and silent current past the islands, out of the mystery above the point into the mystery below the bend.

Some of the glamourie I could account for by referring it to the river's stretched-out panorama of shore and sky-line, always changing, always good. It was the bluffs framing this vista that made the Mississippi different from all others. When the glaciers melted they poured forth vast torrents of water that must have flowed for centuries with almost unimaginable power and had beds miles wide along which the present rivers are by comparison but trickles. The banks of the glacial floods are the bluffs of to-day and guard every inland stream, big or little. Usually they are of clay and not much to look at. Along the upper Mississippi, all the way from Bellevue to Point-no-Point and beyond, the glacial river tore its way through strata of blue-gray limestone, leaving long lines of precipitous cliff. Between these walls winds the present river, sometimes near to one, sometimes to the other. Now the steeps are half overgrown with vines and brush; now they stand out bold and bare. Except in a few spots the formation is nothing like a gorge, for the walls are two or three miles apart; and it is not regular, for sometimes the ramparts disappear where a tributary comes in; but everywhere the beauty and the variety of it are remarkable. In some places the cliffs are like cathedrals, sometimes like castles; sometimes they show in different lights a dazzling play of color. Compared with this gorgeous picturing, not the Rhine, the Elbe,

the Danube, nor any other river in Europe has a word
to say to the Mississippi. Take but Queen Bluff, towering 683 feet—the best on the Rhine seems timid to
that solemn pile of geologic architecture. And in beauty
Trempealeau surpasses the little Lorelei as much as
Maiden Rock surpasses it in a reality of romantic interest; for the story of Weenonah is no myth. And what
shall we say of Frontenac and Diamond Bluff, Chimney
Rock and that weird and unforgetable splendor, the
Sugar Loaf?

Then the towns were better than other towns—or
seemed so to me. Dubuque, the metropolitan, the well-
ordered, the sedate; McGregor in its picturesque cove,
Lansing under its towering hill, Clinton the adorable.
Mauger the sawmills—and bother them! They marred
but did not spoil many a good bit of back-drop scenery.

To pass to and fro before so variegated a showing
and much of it of a charm so potent was soul-stirring;
as well as I know anything, I know the power of it
was reflected in many a riverman's psychology. He
might not know how, he might not be willing to talk
about it, but he felt it; any man not a block or a clod,
or mad or drunk, would feel it.

In his occupation, also, the pilot had the queer exaltation that pertains for us mortals to the meeting
with difficulties and the triumphing over them. To be
confronted with a piece of snarled-up river: to study
it out and attempt it and conquer it and bring all
through in safety with one brain and one pair of hands
—there was something to make the blood bite and the
pulses sing! And yet, certainly, as to pilots there was
something more.

Ah, landsman, landsman—you can make nothing of
this; it will be all alien and comical to you. But, landsman, you never steered a steamboat—you don't know,
you haven't a guess! Even if your life has been crowded

with triumph and brightened with good fortune, it is but a barren waste, never having known this. You don't know the deep-reaching and soul-satisfying joy of the steering-wheel, of the intimate and electric contact it gives you with one of the most beautiful and wonderful of man's creations. To stand there and feel the throb of her tingling through your finger tips; stand there and commune with her silently as if with something living, breathing, palpitating, responsive to you and your thought—why, the life of Jenghiz Khan was pallid by comparison! Every moment she has a different mood, and you understand it and in your soul talk with her about it. When she is restless you soothe her with a spoke or two. When you get up toward the head of the bar, she fights away from it for deep water and you coax her along and along and get her to go where you want her to go. She wrestles with you, and it is your will against hers, and you subdue her and bring her back to her marks and are good friends with her again.

No, there's nothing known to man like piloting on the Mississippi River. I have been on most of the famous rivers of the world and none of them is worth an old shoe compared with the Mississippi. There's that mixed-up crossing above Gordon's Ferry, and the upper bar is working down so that the crossing is becoming closer and closer. You get your jackstaff on the mark, and she hates that bluff reef that you must hug, and tries to spring away from it; and you fight her down to submission and never let the jackstaff move from the trunk of the old dead white oak until you are across. Then you straighten up and go picking your way like a lady crossing a muddy street, zigzag, now here, now there, slow bell, full speed ahead, weaving a course like a ballet-dancer, and she answers every time, just as your will tells her—oh, no, there is nothing like piloting a steamboat on the Mississippi! The poets are always pretending that ships and floating things have souls. Why, half the pilots do not need to be told this; they know it well and can prove it.

I was not much better than a half-baked amateur at it, but the memory of its raptures has never left my finger ends. To this day I had rather take a good steamboat through Coon Slough than hold any other job I ever heard of. By comparison to be king of England must be like washing dishes.

They never lost their feeling about it, the grand old boys of the steering-wheel. Long past the age of eighty, Joseph Hawthorne, famous old scout of Le Claire, resisted all inducements to retire and took annually a berth on a government steamer just to have the wheel once more in his hands. Captain Walter A. Blair, who commanded many famous vessels, owned one of great beauty and renown, and was accounted the smartest captain and one of the ablest pilots of the age, admired and applauded—behold him at seventy-four or more taking a job as pilot on a new towboat only for the same pleasure. I know old rivermen that have reached high positions in the State and the Union, places of historical interest, places of enduring importance, glory, fame, and income—they would drop all for a few hours in a pilot-house again. I have the documents to show. Why, here is Major John E. Rowland, for years an active and upright riverman, went to London, made a career, achieved success, and in his seventieth year wrote, "The only ambition I have is to get back to the Mississippi." Right, right! Every thrall among us knew exactly how he felt.

Commonly of a winter, three hundred or four hundred rivermen would be laid up at Le Claire and among them a choice gathering of pilots—Rapids pilots and all others. About the center of the lank riverside town

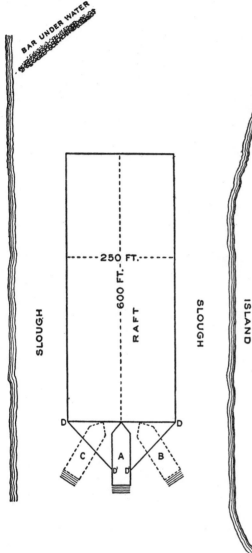

MAIN SHORE

BAR UNDER WATER

SLOUGH

250 FT.

600 FT.

RAFT

SLOUGH

ISLAND

D   D

C   A   B

D' D

THE RAFT AND THE RAFT BOAT

A. The boat pushing the raft on a straight course; B, C, at an angle to steer the raft around a bend; D, D, D', D', the lines from the after corners of the raft to the donkey engine or "nigger." In the situation shown here, it would seem to make no difference whether the boat were hauled into position B and went ahead or into position C and backed, but in piloting the choice might be of vital importance, depending upon conditions of depth, current, channel and the position of the raft in reference to the next bar below or the next crossing, and it was his knowledge of these varying conditions at hundreds of points that made the pilot's work and wisdom so remarkable.

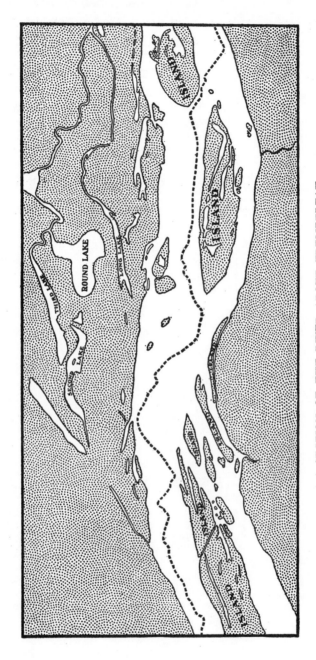

A SECTION OF THE RIVER ABOVE TREMPELEAU

was a billiard saloon—I cannot now recall the name of
the proprietor—that was the favorite resort of these experts. In this place met day after day their council in
plenary session to debate the one topic inexhaustible
—the river, the river, the river, and how to run it.

Over in Illinois, the ancient town of Albany was another great winter harbor for the wise men of the steering-wheel. At their pet resort they fixed up a large,
square, shallow wooden box, half filled with ashes. On
this they would map the river, using little sticks placed
end to end a few inches apart to indicate the banks.
Then with other sticks they would draw in the ashes the
steamboat channel at some hard-knot place and give
their different ideas as to the course that should be
steered. With seven or eight hundred miles of always
shifting channel to choose from, it will be seen that the
supply of this material was ample.

Other rivermen in the place played billiards, talked
about the news, or told stories. The little group of pilots
hung over its box of ashes. I used to know a chess-play-
ers' club in New York where men spent their days under
a similar enchantment. But never was another game
equal to this in the variety of its chances or the spell
of its attraction, and I think no chess-player ever lived
in his chess-board.

But, proud and haughty metropolitan, if you have
any notion of favoring with piteous thoughts the poor
souls condemned to pass a winter in an isolated river
town, you can turn off your grief at the fountainhead.
Life in Le Claire in the winter was anything but boresome; we had as much fun out of existence as anybody
going. The Le Claire Debating Society met every week
and furnished a first-class entertainment. Old Billy
Fowler ran a singing school and gave concerts by his
pupils. About every other week one or another of the
four churches would be engineering some kind of a

show, a donation party, or a supper or other frivolity. The snow came early and stayed late and helped things out with sleighing parties, and still better; for the long slopes of the bluffs made great places to slide downhill, and we could scoot far out upon the ice in the river, making a slide more than half a mile long and at the beginning steep like the roof of a house; and the girls had the reddest cheeks you ever saw—absolutely! Skating was an inexhaustible joy, plain and fancy; sometimes we had to clear the snow off first, and sometimes you could skate to Davenport on perfectly clean smooth ice. Old Dr. White took the "Atlantic Monthly" and held sessions at his house at night until it had been read aloud to us from cover to cover. Hospitality was unbounded; so was gossip. No, there was always something doing in a river town in winter, and as for retail business, the rivermen always came home with money in both pockets. Stephen Hanks said they started every winter with tenderloin steak and ended it with liver and onions.

Steamboat captains (when they were not also pilots) sometimes had a way of disparaging the general intelligence of the pilot brotherhood. Their argument was that the pilot must carry so much in his head that pertained to his peculiar business, so vast an array of facts about bars, crossings, and soundings, that there was not room for other lumber; hence, pilots did not know what was going on in the world and did not care, not having the time. Doubtless this was so in some cases, but my own observation among them, which was fairly extensive, never quite bore out the detraction. The pilots I knew were men of good minds. Many were also captains, and some were captains, engineers, and pilots all at once, carrying licenses in all branches of the trade—a fact that surely does not argue for limited intellectual powers. I have found in the records instances where pilots left the pilot-house to take charge of engines; and engines on a Mississippi River steamboat, with the water likely to foam and the doctor to choke, did not exactly represent a holiday excursion. Stephen B. Hanks, Walter Blair, E. E. Heerman, George Winans, and many others were expert pilots and expert masters. George B. Merrick in the course of his life filled every place on a steamboat from watchman to captain. He was at different times striker, clerk, mate, engineer, pilot, and master; and meanwhile in the winter seasons, learned the printer's trade, set type on a newspaper and wrote its editorials. He could command the pen powerful or graceful, as might be desired. With other things he wrote the standard river book of the ages, it seems to me, that comprehensive work entitled "Old Times on the Upper Mississippi"; also one called "Steamboats and Steamboat Men." That card catalogue of his included every steamboat that ever stemmed the upper river and what became of her, clear back to the old *Virginia*. He was also a good business man and first-class accountant. He finished by becoming an honored member of the staff of the University of Wisconsin, and I submit that few men in this age have shown a greater versatility.

This reminds me of the time the parson swore.

One of the men of the early days that left an enduring dent in river annals was Asa Barlow Green. He was born in Warren, Vermont, in 1826, and with only a common school education started West to hunt for a career. I may say with confidence that he found it. First he studied for the ministry, was admitted to the Baptist church, and ordained a minister therein. Then he studied law, settled in Washington County, Minnesota, became popular, was elected to small offices, then to be sheriff, then to be probate judge. About 1853, the lumber business being in the swift ascendant, and the river trade with it, the reverend judge abandoned Washington County and sought the river, where he rose rapidly from watchman to captain. This was but summer-time employment. His real business was something else. As soon as navigation closed he betook himself to the pineries, where he spent the winter going from one logging camp to another, preaching and holding services among the wild men. It was a labor that by all accounts was sorely needed, but he is the only person I have heard of that persisted in it. Men have even said that he made converts in these unpromising precincts, but I prefer to keep my narrative aloof from the imaginative. There is no question that he was self-constituted missionary to the loggers and that for many winters he devoted himself to this work.

With the going out of the ice he would be back again on a steamboat's roof. Side by side on his state-room wall he kept framed his master's license and his ordination papers.

By reputation he was a first-class preacher. As to that I do not know, but there seems to be no doubt that he was a first-class captain. He ran for years out of Eau Claire and was admired by the public and respected by his crew, which is saying much. He had saved a little money and in 1858 he bought a half interest in the stern-wheel packet *Equator*, which had been built five years before on the Ohio and had run several seasons on the Minnesota. The Reverend Judge Captain Green began to run the *Equator* as a tri-weekly packet between Prescott on the Mississippi and Taylor's Falls on the St. Croix. John Lay was chief engineer and George Merrick was cub pilot, under somebody else.

All that season the *Equator* made her trips on time, so that her regularity astonished everybody, being an innovation. She made money and the preacher-captain added to his worldly store.

The next season she resumed the same run. On May 26, 1859, she was taking an excursion from Hastings and Prescott to Stillwater. It was a beautiful day, warm and clear, and the excursion was a great success until treacherous Lake St. Clair was reached, that celebrated trouble maker for steamboats. Of a sudden a storm gathered and broke—a tornado, it was afterward called. "It might not have been a real tornado," writes George Merrick, "but so far as the *Equator* was concerned it answered every purpose." She began to roll and knock about alarmingly in those heavy swells I have before mentioned as seeming to arise by magic and to tower like hills.

Charles Jewell, the pilot, headed her up for the larboard shore to get under the lee of the bluff. This was wise and would have been salvation but for one thing. Just as the *Equator* was swinging toward safety, still a quarter of a mile away, the eccentric rod on the larboard engine snapped and the wheel stopped.

Instantly the boat fell off into the trough of the waves, which broke clean over the lower deck and poured into the hatches. In the cabin the tables had been set for dinner; the sudden heel to leeward sent all the tables and all they carried crashing into one confused heap. The strain in the seaway was so great that seams six inches wide opened in the sides of the cabin and it looked as if the whole superstructure would be smashed to pieces.

Among the excursionists wild-eyed panic reigned. People living along the river, it should be explained, had no experience with billows. Explosions they could understand, and collisions perfectly; but to have a steamboat pitching and tossing about like a cork was to them a violation of the laws of Nature. The screams of the women and the shouts of the men made maddening tumult. Some passengers seized life-preservers, tying on two or three apiece; some tore off the shutters of the cabin and prepared to launch themselves into the water.

The coolest man on board was the parson-captain. He took Pilot Jewell away from the wheel and sent him below to quiet the passengers, while he himself went to the engine-room to see what could be done. One other person on board was conspicuously self-possessed— Mrs. John Lay, wife of the engineer. She knew all about steamboats and engines, and knew as well as anybody that the break in the *Equator's* gear was beyond all helping and the ship was doomed, but she went about with a smiling countenance and a cheery voice, reassuring everybody. She was the engineer's wife, she announced, and she knew there was no danger. All would be well if they would only keep still and wait.

Among the passengers was a sawmill owner from Prescott, old, rich, mean, and universally detested in his town because he was a miser. I will call him Mr. D., not having another name for him. He now crawled to the companionway, got to the top deck or roof, and, creeping to the captain, embraced his knees.

"Oh, save me, Captain!" he shrieked. "Save me! I will give you a thousand dollars if you will save me!"

This was the time the parson fell from grace.

"Let go of me and get below, you ——— ——— ——— cowardly old ——— ——— ——— ——— ——— ," he roared, and he lifted his foot and kicked the palpitating bundle before him across the deck and down the companionway. Full, round, competent, mouth-filling oaths he swore, exactly like any man common and unregenerate.

Young George Merrick was at the wheel and heard all this. He had wisdom enough to see that his job **was** to try to hold the *Equator* head up to the wind, but he knew also that nothing could save her, for she was driving straight toward the other shore—and by a sad oversight they had left both anchors in the mud at Prescott!

Meantime, Mrs. Lay by incessant efforts was restoring some kind of order among the women and children, and Pilot Jewell with a club in hand and a few well chosen words was causing the men to behave. Mr. Jewell's methods were simple. He threatened the male cowards until they listened to reason, and then tore from them the life-preservers they had monopolized, for there were not enough to go around and he wanted them for the women.

About half-past twelve she struck the beach at Clermont. By marvelous good luck it happened to be a long shelf of sand, when it might as easily have been bluff or rock from which no one could escape. As she touched, she swung broadside to the waves and began at once to break up. The chimneys fell overboard, the pilot-house and cabin went next, there was nothing left but the hull. Marshaled by the preacher-captain, the men were lined up for rescue work. They must wade ashore and each carry a woman or a child. In this way everybody got to safety, the men being drenched and soaked. On shore they made a fire and with wreckage and boughs raised some kind of shelter.

The last man to leave the wreck was the captain-parson; he stayed to get all the mail sacks off and the boat's papers. Then he came ashore, ruined. All he had in the world was invested in that boat, and she carried no insurance.

At the same time that the *Equator* started up the lake that day, the largest log raft that had ever been launched on the St. Croix entered it, bound down. There were more than a million feet of logs in that raft. It

was not far from the *Equator* when the gale struck it
and tore it into fragments. All the rest of that summer
the eastern shore of the lake was lined with pieces of
it, and for a long time afterward steamboats passing
through must keep a sharp lookout for such of its logs
as were still floating.

It was the parson-captain's last appearance on the
river. That winter he was in the logging camps as usual.
Then the Civil War broke out, he enlisted as chaplain
of the Thirtieth Wisconsin, served with distinction
throughout the war, was mustered out in June, 1865,
and like Bob Eden headed for the rural spaces, becoming pastor of a church in a small western town, and
serving it until he died. I cannot but think it odd that
there should have been two such stories and George
Merrick a figure in each.

An exact report of that address to the skinflint was
circulated in Prescott and added greatly to the captain-
parson's popularity. People said they wished he would
come there to live so they could elect him to Congress.

I have often wondered what became of the crew on
that million-foot raft. I suppose they got to shore, for
there is no record of their drowning, but it must have
been a perilous time when the platform they stood upon
dissolved under their feet and they were cast into those
prodigious waves.

Lake St. Croix is almost at the end of the St. Croix
River before it enters the Mississippi. It is smaller than
Lake Pepin, which is twenty-eight miles long and from
three to five miles wide. Take it on a calm day and nothing seems less formidable. Yet for steamboats these two
lakes have been wicked places. The reasons why in these
comparatively small limits they can roll up so boisterous a sea and why their weather should be subject
to fits of total depravity have never been satisfactorily
explained. Sawyer's Bend, a famous reach above St.

Louis, is supposed to hold the record for steamboat disasters. Up to 1894 seventy had been lost in its insane whirlpools and on its treacherous bars. I have never seen a compilation of the steamboat and raft fatalities of Lake Pepin, but I should imagine offhand that its total would not be much below that of Sawyer's Bend.

All the winter day the tide of river talk flowed on wherever rivermen were gathered. An illimitable lore about a world that is passed and gone forever circulated in these precincts. I have managed to collect, mostly from George Merrick, partly from my own memories, a little of the jetsam. Famous old boats, and their immortalized triumphs in racing, famous old rivermen, famous old feats of piloting—for example, Bill Tibbals and the *Key City*.

Next to *Grey Eagle*, the old *Key City* was the grandest steamboat that ever climbed a bar, and there were eminent authorities that held her to have shaded the favorite. For years in the good old times she traveled up and down the upper Mississippi, never was beaten in a race, and never declined the chance of one, either. Incidentally, she was known as the best handler that ever went afloat.

"You could thread the eye of a needle with that boat," said one of the old-timers.

"You bet you could," said West Rambo. "Why, you could move that wheel with your eyelash."

Every up trip she used to make the run from Dubuque to Cassville, twenty-eight miles, in two hours, "just loafing along and looking at the scenery," said the old-timer. Once she steamed from Dunleith to St. Paul, 295 miles,[2] in 24 hours 29 minutes and made thirteen landings on the way.

[2] So it was then by the channel followed. Government charts now make it 265 miles.

A - Rafting on the Mississip'

She has also a certain though unacknowledged place in literature.

Readers of Mark Twain may recall the story he tells in Chapter XXIV of "Life on the Mississippi," about Bob Styles and the *Cyclone*. Mr. Styles has been condemning an untruthful man with whom he piously declined to associate. Then he says:

"That *Cyclone* was a rattler to go, and the sweetest thing to steer that ever walked the waters. Set her amidships in a big river, and just let her go; it was all you had to do. She would hold herself on a star all night, if you let her alone. You couldn't ever feel her rudder. It wasn't any more labor to steer her than it is to count the Republican vote in a South Carolina election. One morning, just at daybreak, the last trip she ever made, they took her rudder aboard to mend it; I didn't know anything about it; I backed her out from the woodyard and went a weaving down the river all serene. When I had gone about twenty-three miles and made four horribly crooked crossings—"

"Without any rudder?"

"Yes—old Captain Tom appeared on the roof and began to find fault with me for running such a dark night—"

"Such a dark night? Why, you said—"

And so on. To a landsman the notion of running a steamboat twenty-three miles without a rudder would seem to be grotesque enough to constitute excellent humor, but to a riverman there is nothing preposterous about it; it has been done more than once, conspicuously by Bill Tibbals and the old *Key City*.

One day she was coming down above Trempealeau in a fog and hit something that tore off the rudder. They stopped and fished it up and got it aboard but could not hang it again, because some of the irons had been broken out. Bill Tibbals was chief pilot. The Old Man (captain) said to him:

254

"Can you run without a rudder?"

"You bet I can," said Tibbals. "Start her right out."

They backed out of Trempealeau, straightened her down the river, and before long they saw the chimneys of the *Northern Belle*, another crack boat of the packet class. So they took after her and passed her at her best clip. Next they sighted La Crosse, where they had a landing to make, and it was one of the worst on the Mississippi, but the *Key City* negotiated it with ease. When they were through handling their freight at La Crosse, they backed out again and went on as far as Brownsville, forty miles from Trempealeau, where they stopped and put the rudder on her and went ahead.

On this occasion the *Key City* ran forty miles, passed a rival steamboat, threaded two crooked sloughs, made several nasty crossings and two landings, without any more rudder on her than there is on a church.

As she was going down-stream, part of each landing consisted of the delicate maneuver of rounding-to. That is to say, she came down below the landing, swept around in a semicircle, and landed, bow up—without a rudder.

At this landsmen will gape as at something impossible, but it actually happened. The feat was wonderful enough to be talked of many years, and is still, I think, wherever old pilots get together. It is not so mysterious as it may seem and was much less dangerous than Stephen Hanks's achievement of running in a fog. Landsmen overlook the fact that the two wheels of the *Key City* had independent engines. Tibbals steered her with the wheels, and Bob Styles could have steered the *Cyclone* the same way, if there had been such a steamboat. Instead of engine bells Tibbals used the speaking-tube.

"More on your labboard! Stop the stabboard! Go ahead on it! Ease off that labboard!" and the thing was

done. It was not just as easy as it is for a city council
to grant a franchise, but it could be done by a smart
pilot.

I have always believed that Twain got his humor
story of Bob Styles and the *Cyclone* from the true
story of Bill Tibbals and the *Key City*. One reason for
that notion is that the two stories begin in the same
way. "The old *Key City* was the sweetest thing to
steer that ever was," said the old-timer whenever he
warmed up to the Tibbals incident, and in that shape
it went the whole length of the Mississippi, St. Anthony
to the jetties.

Tibbals was celebrated for many achievements.

A good pilot could usually make allowance for the
always shifting channels of the river and get through
the most difficult places, but sometimes the best were
fooled by some new freak or insidious device of waters
possessed by the devil. If there was one stretch more
critical than another it was Coon Slough, where seemed
to reign the head fiend of all these transformations, and
if there was one part of Coon Slough that was worse
than another it was down at the lower end, where lay
the wrecks of two famous steamboats whose stories had
been told so often in pilot-houses that the very bell
ropes knew them.

One was the *Nominee*. In the fall of 1854 she hit a
submerged snag and sank at this ill-omened spot. Two
years later, October 23, 1856, the *Lady Franklin,*
one of the steamers still besung for beauty, was coming
down the slough, struck the same snag and went to the
bottom. Tibbals was one of the pilots.

"Before breaking the snag down," says Captain Tibbals, "she listed so badly that her chimneys went overboard. I had finished my breakfast and just after I
left the table I felt the boat strike. I ran to the side and
saw she was sinking rapidly, then forward and told

Captain Kennedy, then down through the cabin and notified the passengers to get upon the roof, the women aft and the men forward." It seems that the only stairway from the boiler deck to the roof was on the larboard side aft and unusable. Tibbals got to the roof and called down to the women to reach up their hands, one at a time, and he would pull them up to safety. The first pair of hands that was reached to him belonged to a young and delicate woman from Stillwater. Tibbals landed her up on the roof. Instantly, without a word or whimper, she kneeled and reached down her hands to help the next. With her on one side and Tibbals on the other they pulled to safety every woman and child on board.

Other officers herded the men. They were taken off by the *Falls City*.

These two wrecks lay there in hiding, side by side, and every pilot knew that they were fishing for his boat and that the current set toward them to help them fish. After almost forty years they landed something. The steamboat *Reindeer*, one of the best of the rafters, coming down with a huge log raft, struck those wrecks and sank at once.

Then the Government concluded to remove the wrecks. It picked for the job one of its most expert employees. He was Bill Tibbals.

In the Civil War, the upper Mississippi pilot did conspicuous service and shared in the warm indorsement Lincoln gave to his guild. In 1884 he suddenly appeared again in the white light of great events and this time far away. The British Government was preparing its Nile expedition to relieve Gordon at Khartum. It must have the best river pilots in the world, and it sent to the upper Mississippi for them. Captains Aaron Raymond Russell, John Segers, Jerry Weber, and Andrew A. Robinson were the men chosen. Aaron

A - R a f t i n g o n t h e M i s s i s s i p '

Russell kept a diary which is still extant. It contains some highly diverting entries. On one occasion when he was taking the steamer through the convolutions of the Nile, appeared on the scene a British major that was possessed of two illusions: (1) that he had garnered all extant knowledge concerning the operating of steamboats in mud-bottomed rivers; and (2) that he had a mission to instruct Uncle Aaron in these mysteries. The conference seems to have been brief but animated, and by Uncle Aaron carried on in selected words of unilateral significance. At its close the major had lost his illusions, but must have felt compensated in an increased knowledge of the resources of language.

He now withdrew in wrath, promising a court-martial for the American. The honor of the British army had been affronted.

Uncle Aaron put his head out of the pilot-house window.

"Come a-running with that court-martial," he called after the departing major. "Remember that the sooner the quicker."

Next candidate was a colonel.

The Nile was at an extremely low stage and navigation grew always more difficult, but the expedition continued to advance. At last they came to a place full of trouble and the colonel announced that he knew better than anybody else how that part should be run and would take charge.

"All right," said Aaron Russell; "in that case, I go ashore."

Which he did, and choosing a good spot sat down to see what would happen next.

The colonel had a bright idea. The river being so shallow, the thing to do was to lighten the boat. So he drew the fires and ran the water out of the boiler. He seems to have overlooked the fact that in steam navigation steam is requisite. He now got out a line and with soldiers and yelling Arabs attempted to pull the boat up-stream. Instead, she broke away, was swept down the rapids, lost much that had been gained with toilsome effort, and came near to wreck. Then they sent a boat, begged Uncle Aaron to come back and take charge, and the colonel retired from inland navigation.

The river continued to fall and the difficulties to increase. A day or two later they came to a place beyond which the native guides said it was impossible to proceed and the military commander wanted to stop and do the rest by land. Captain Russell protested earnestly.

"Where did this boat start out for?" he said. "Old Dongola, wasn't it? Well, then, it's going through to Old Dongola."

"But you can't," said the commandant. "It's impossible. There's no water."

"Can't?" said Uncle Aaron. "Where did you get that word? We don't use it on the Mississippi." And he took a field-glass and went ashore.

So then here is the test whether my poor tributes to these extraordinary men were, as you have thought, no doubt, prejudice, exaggeration, or fantasy. Here was one suddenly set down upon the other side of the world, on a river he had never seen before and knew nothing about, confronted with a piece of piloting that all local experts and other authorities said was impossible. And what did he do?

With his field-glass he went up a little elevation and studied the river ahead of him. There in that muddy, unknown, inscrutable stream he read where down at the bottom, hidden from other sight, lay the trough of the Nile, as a thousand times he had discerned the hidden trough at the bottom of the Mississippi.

Then he went back to the pilot-house, rang to go ahead, and guided that steamboat to and fro, around and about, on the dizzy maze of the course as he had perceived it.

Inch by inch they fought their way up the shallow current around cataracts, up rapids, over bars. Finally they came to a place full of boulders and with not more than a cupful of water trickling around them. Guides, the commandant, and the other officers agreed that this surely was the end and expected Captain Russell to join with them in conceding defeat. Did he?

Not he. "Give me the men I want and I'll get you through all right," said this confident person.

"Take them all—take the whole detachment," said the commandant. "But I don't know what you can do with them."

Uncle Aaron knew. He hadn't in vain studied with Tom Doughty the Red River campaign. He took the troops thus placed under his command, built a dam back of the steamer, raised the water, and went ahead.

They reached Old Dongola all right and landed the expedition where it was wanted. Captain Russell was rewarded with much money, two medals, letters of gratitude from high commanding officers, and the puzzled admiration of the staff. He had dented the upper Mississippi pilot into history with a mark that is likely to endure.

The British did not forget him and his skill. The next year they gave him command of the British government steamer *Alberta* in the great expedition against Louis Riel, when an aroused empire put forth its might to suppress the uprising of 216 half-armed and half-fed Indians in Manitoba.

But to come back to the Mississippi. Its perils were often discussed at the billiard-room amphitryon: for example, snags; also overhanging trees, which are snags in the making.

Many large trees grew along the river banks and on the islands, and the river was incessantly digging at their roots. Then at any time they might fall into the channel and obstruct it or lean over it so that they could snatch off the chimneys or bang in the upper works. When this happened in a narrow channel, as at the head of a slough, for instance, the consequences might be grave. A pilot could tell a hundred miles below what depth of water he would find on Paint Rock bar, but no human ingenuity could tell when a tree was going to fall into the channel.

This reminds me of Cap' Heerman's wedding day.

E. E. Heerman was one of the pilot kings of my time, equally good at handling rafts or packets, and celebrated from Sauk Rapids to St. Louis. He was another of the tribe of lightning pilots and as competent a master, for he could operate as either.

In 1856 he concluded that it was about time for him to marry the young lady he had been courting so long, and as she was persuaded to similar views the wedding day was fixed for November 5. Captain Heerman was then living at Beef Slough, at the mouth of the Chippewa River, the greatest of all the raft-making plants. There he built a house and furnished it for his bride. She lived with her parents six miles above Hastings, on the other side of the Mississippi. Not alone with her parents: she had six brothers and sisters, the brothers being noted for stalwart build and much development of the biceps.

The furnishing of his new house took longer than Captain Heerman had expected, and November 1 arrived before he was quite ready for it. A steamboat was due to leave Beef Slough for Hastings and St. Paul

on the night of November 3 or morning of November
4, which would do excellently for him and land him in
Hastings twenty-four hours before the wedding. It
was to be in the evening at the home of the bride's
parents.

The captain had ordered a wedding suit of choice
design, and this he packed into a valise with a new
collar and tie, and hied him to the steamboat-landing
on the evening of November 3. All that night he waited
but no boat arrived. As the morning of the fourth
began to wear away, the captain realized that the situation was becoming delicate. There being no telephone
in those days and no telegraph, communication was by
mail and not much of that.

It seemed to him that if he could get across the
slough to the main shore of the Mississippi he would
have a better chance to snare a steamboat. Beef Slough,
you will remember, is an estuary at the mouth of the
Chippewa, and divided from the Mississippi by an arm
of the land.

He now set out to walk around the slough, carrying
the valise with the precious wedding suit, and hoping
that maybe he might find a skiff and row across. A
vicious northwest wind was blowing.

He found a skiff, after some tramping, but it was
old and manifestly leaky and there was no bailer, not
even a clam-shell.

Still, the emergency was pressing and he took the
risk. Half-way across, the skiff began to fill with water.
The wind, against which he was rowing, held him back.
He put forth all his strength and was within a few feet
of the other shore, when the thing sank under him.

He saved the wedding suit unharmed and got it and
himself to shore.

Then he had a long walk through the woods in his
wet clothes. At the steamboat-landing, sure enough,

here came the old stern-wheeler *Flora* rumbling up the channel.

Heerman signaled her to stop. The mate, whom he could see plainly, only shook his head and pointed to windward. Heerman, for the first time in his life, lost his aplomb. The last chance to get to his own wedding was slipping before him. He danced up and down and shouted like a maniac, but the mate only shook his head with a smile. Just then the captain of the *Flora*, Washington Fairman, came out of the cabin and glanced toward shore. There he recognized his old friend Captain Heerman, and perceived what the trouble was.

"I can't land here," he shouted. "Go up to that big tree that has fallen into the river, crawl out on it, and we will try to pick you up."

A great elm, newly fallen, lay with its branches half in the water, half in the air.

Clinging with one hand to the valise and its dear freightage, Heerman crept from limb to limb until he hung as far out as he dared to go. The *Flora* came up and bumped so hard against the limb that the shock all but threw him into the water. Seeing that it was impossible to get him in that position, Captain Fairman ordered a deck-hand to run out a plank.

Meantime, the *Flora* was drifting astern. The plank was run out and Heerman crept toward the outer edge of it, but just then the deck-hand must swing it farther aft, and as it swung, Heerman slipped but managed to catch the plank with his hands, one wrist being thrust through the valise handle.

In this sad shape they pulled him aboard, and he looked at his watch. It was four o'clock on the afternoon of his wedding day and he at Beef Slough and his bride six miles above Hastings. Still, if the *Flora* would pick up her heels he might make Hastings by nine o'clock, hire a buggy, and skip over those six miles so as not to arrive quite too late. So he consulted the engineer about the advisability of hanging an anvil on the safety-valve.

The old *Flora* did not pick up her heels that night. On the contrary, it seemed to the nerve-racked Heerman that the old girl had gone spavined. Until midnight he sat disconsolate, watching the dim shores. Then he dropped to sleep. At nine o'clock the next morning they woke him up. He was at Hastings.

Valise in hand and fear in his heart, he walked the six miles to the farm-house of Mr. William Hanna, father of his bride that was to have been and was not.

When he arrived, his worst fears were realized. The father turned upon him a lowering gaze and would not speak to him; the stalwart brothers made unpleasant remarks about the duty of giving skulkers a proper hiding, and his affianced bride, locked in an upper room, absolutely refused to see him on any account. It appeared that the night before, all the neighborhood had gathered for the wedding, the clergyman was on hand, the wedding-cake of the best, the supper provided, and two expert fiddlers brought from Hastings to play "Buffalo Gals." Everything was ready except the bridegroom—and he never came. When the fact was apparent, Miss Hanna must be taken to her room in a state of hysterics and the company had slowly dispersed, making comments.

In this situation, Captain Heerman happily bethought himself that Mrs. Hanna was a kind, motherly soul and would probably sympathize with him. He asked for her, poured forth his tale of sorrows, and secured her help as ambassadress to the indignant bride. In the end the embassy was successful. Miss Hanna received the knight-errant again into favor and the wedding was fixed for November 10. To make sure, the captain anchored himself meanwhile to the spot.

They were not yet through with this chapter of adventure. From Hastings they took passage homeward on the steamer *City Belle*. The season was closing, ice was already in the river, and a short distance above one steamer was frozen in. On the way down Lake Pepin the *City Belle* encountered so much ice that her hull was worn almost through and the seams were opening. Constant calking from within was necessary to keep afloat. When all the oakum on board had been used for this purpose, the commander ordered the bedspreads to be cut up. It was a bitter cold night, the boat was unheated, and without bed-covers the passengers had to rise and dress to keep warm.

But about overhanging trees, they were a great nuisance. Suppose the channel to clip along close to the shore, as it often did, you might come suddenly around a bend and be into one before you knew it. I have a record somewhere of one of the best rafting boats on the river that was going up after a raft and swept like this under a newly fallen tree. Her upper works were cut off as if with a huge knife.

Chapter XVI

WHEN THE *JULIA* HIT THE BRIDGE

IF imminent danger, plucking always at his elbow, produced in the packet pilot a peculiar temper of cool command and a ready capital of resource, much more were these traits developed in a pilot of a rafting steamer, whose responsibilities were so much greater and whose perils more insistent. Of course, there were among them varying temperaments, as with the rest of us, but I think no instances are recorded of a rafting pilot that lost his head in any emergency, however sudden and sharp. No matter what it might be, it was something he had already discounted in his cold-storaged apprehensions. In a pinching place a pilot might emit profanity as water pours from a hose nozzle, but he always knew what he wanted to do.

This reminds me of the time I came near to wreck the *St. Croix.*

It was on my part a piece of gross stupidity the memory of which was long afterward a rankling wound in my self-esteem. First, I must explain that I was born by the riverside and grew up in the river's atmosphere. Some of my kin were noted rivermen, and besides, I had another claim upon the guild. My grandfather, the tailor-preacher, was widely known, greatly beloved for good works, and as much wondered at as the man that lived like the birds and often had about as much to eat. For these reasons being tolerated, and by right of nature being impishly persistent, I was all over the place whenever a boat was tied up at the Van Sant yards or a new boat was built there. I knew them all, the *J. W. Van Sant, D. A. McDonald, James Means, Le Claire Belle, Brother Jonathan, Hartford*, like the front yard at home, and was often taken to ride on them by amazingly good-natured and patient rivermen, who taught me river lore and pilot stuff and filled my young mind with a rosy dream that some day I might be a pilot and bask on the summit of earthly glory.

I was even once allowed (under supervision) to hold the wheel on the *Bill Henderson*.

Mr. William Henderson, for whom this swift and beautiful packet was named, was celebrated as the ablest bartender on the whole Mississippi, upper or lower, white or black. Indeed, the trump of his fame was of no circumscribed orbit but was sounded for miles up and down the Missouri and Ohio. It is recorded that intending travelers postponed their journeyings for days, and some said for weeks, that they might voyage upon a boat where he officiated at the bar, a reputation that seems to have been won with deserving. I have seen a description of Mr. Henderson's mint-julep, calculated (in these times) to bring tears to sympathetic eyes. It was defined as combining the elixir of spring with the glory of roses and the delicious coolness of a moon-lightened night. But it seems to have been his cocktails that truly touched all hearts to joy, all tongues to praise. My friend the batty poet of whom I have spoken made on this subject a copy of verses that are best forgotten, but I remember well his statement that when he had partaken of one Henderson cocktail he felt all the cares of earth dropping from him like a garment, and with two he soared the skies and heard celestial voices singing marvelous harmonies to an accompaniment of golden lutes of a thousand strings. This seems too good to be true, but I cite it for what it may be worth.

Mr. Henderson was not only master of a recondite art, but according to contemporaneous accounts he had a way with him. Whenever a tourist saw his broad and benevolent countenance arising from behind a pyramid of glasses, that tourist knew he was journeying with a friend.

At the zenith of his greatness the packet line in which he worked built a new and gorgeous sternwheeler, declared to be the best craft of her kind so far designed on the western rivers. Naturally, when the question of naming this beauty came up all minds turned at once to the designer of the marvelous mintjulep and the artist of the dreamy cocktail. Should it be said that in the new empire art was of slight esteem? Never, agreed the owners of the line, and with loud acclaim the new boat was christened *Bill Henderson* and under this name for many summers plowed the waters of the Mississippi.

Some years later my desk-mate in school and chief coparcener in crime was August Schricker, whose father, Lorenzo Schricker, owned the raft boat *St. Croix*. Young Schricker was as crazy about the river as I was, which is saying much, and the natural result was that many holidays we spent on and around the *St. Croix*. As she had at that time no passenger license, it was necessary to ship us as some form of supercargo or the like, and in that capacity I learned to run the "nigger" (donkey-engine), help fill the boiler, get in the way when the lines were being run and make some feint at "learning the river," the exercise preliminary to being a pilot.

When the *Julia* Hit the Bridge

In the summer of 1877, I think it was, we were coming down with a big log raft for the Schricker & Mueller mill at Davenport. As usual, we split at Le Claire to go over the Rapids. One of our pilots was a singularly reserved and reticent man that we called "Pete," although we knew that was not his name. He was good-natured and kindly, but seemed always to have little to say and that uttered in a voice not much above a whisper; a habit, I may say, not common in the tribe. He was on watch as we came down the tail end of the Rapids toward the Davenport bridge.

The custom was in running the bridge to point the raft between two bridge piers near the Iowa shore, then cast off when it seemed to be headed safely, sweep the steamer around, dart through the opened draw of the bridge and catch the raft below.

As the Schricker & Mueller mill was only a mile from the bridge, and the draw-span was far over on the other side of the river, the exact moment at which to let go and begin to turn and run for the draw was a matter of nicest judgment; also of weighty importance. The raft when caught again must be swung inside the Schricker & Mueller boom. If it missed that, good-night!—for one of the disadvantages about the rafting business is that you cannot tow rafts up-stream. If a raft missed the boom, the only chance was to sell it to some mill down the river, and being now bargain-counter goods it must be sold at a loss, perhaps as far away as Alton.

I had been out that morning on some fool errand to the bow of the raft and was coming leisurely back, when I was aware that the mate on the forecastle was shouting at me, and glancing up at the pilot-house I saw Pete beckoning. I looked at the bridge and it seemed so far away that there was plenty of time. Without hastening my pace I came back to the boat, and the instant I climbed over the bow they let go the lines and Pete began to make the turn.

The time was early summer and the river was high, with a booming current. It was quickly evident that the *St. Croix* had waited too long. By the time Pete had her partly turned around, the current had swept her down sidewise upon the bridge.

The height of it above the water was such that if we struck, it would shave off the pilot-house first and then the chimneys, and careen the boat so that she would instantly fill and sink where she was.

The engines were working as hard as it seemed to me possible for any machine to labor, but for all that we were being driven downward inch by inch. Now the up-stream edge of the bridge structure was over our wheel, now almost over the deck-house. On the bridge a row of lengthened solemn faces watched the fight. For me, I stood petrified with horror, for the boat was about to be wrecked and all for my fault. And then Pete the pilot, usually so quiet of speech, leaned over the speaking-tube and made a remark to the engineer below. He said:

"———— ———— ———— ———— ————, **** ——— ***** .... ——— ????? !!!!!!"

That was all and not in any louder tone than a man could hear a mile and a half away against a strong wind.

It carried home, for the great wheel was now spinning around with inconceivable rapidity and the whole boat shook. I do not know where good old George, the engineer, got the steam, but he got it, and just as I had given up all for lost, she yielded to the pressure and made headway up-stream.

We got around through the draw and caught the raft in the nick of time. Half a minute more and it would have been too late.

When the *Julia* Hit the Bridge

It was about half an hour before I recovered something like possession of my reasoning faculties, and then I began to wonder why that lightning blast had been discharged upon the engineer and not upon me, who had earned it. When I was able to steer my trembling legs into the pilot-house, Pete merely glanced at me and said in his usual way:

"It is better we don't wait so long before we cast off."

The bridges were always a peril. Usually, any raft must be split to get through any one of them, and to do this, float one half of the raft in safety through one span, with the steamboat to take the other half through the draw-span, and then unite the two halves was not child's play in a current that ran about five miles an hour through the bridge and was alive with cross-currents. The task became still worse when rafts ceased to be plaited together with the birch boughs and staples and were just masses of loose logs held with the brails. Tautening the brails after a bridge-split was heart-breaking work.

Snags, of course, we had always with us. The Government, after about 1870, provided a regular service of snag-pulling steamboats that lessened this evil but did not abolish it. A full-grown snag seemed ingeniously designed to work ruin. It was the trunk of a tree that had fallen into the stream, floated until it found the best spot for its vile purposes, and then embedded itself in the mud, with one long stout branch sticking up under the surface where it could run through the hull of a steamboat. Of course, if this prong were exposed or came too near the surface, the pilot would see it or the ripple it made, and save his boat. So the snag kept the prong well out of sight but just near enough to make sure of piercing the hull. It is odd, this evidence of perversity in inanimate nature. More attention should be paid to it. The pilots all thought so. "They're getting schemier and schemier," said Uncle Joe, referring to the snags; "yes, sir, schemier and schemier." (*Clang* on the "nigger" bell.)

Sometimes a pilot could detect an invisible snag by the peculiar "break" it made on the surface of the water, different from the "break" of a reef or a new bar. But at night or with the sunset in his eyes, what was he to do? Besides, it is well known that a snag is always hunting up new lodgings. As soon as you are sure that one is in a certain place, it will be somewhere else, but always with that prong up waiting evilly for steamboats.

In the earlier days, the boiler, as I have indicated, was a source of danger the pilot could not affect. He could weave around bars and miss snags (sometimes), but it seems that only Providence could keep him from going up in the air with the texas and pilot-house. Still another difficulty that pertained more strictly to our end of the boat was what pilots held to be the unaccountable habit of some steamboats to run away. This was the pilot's term for it; what they meant was that sometimes a steamboat would refuse to answer her helm and dart off suddenly and crazily to larboard or starboard. This apparent manifestation of an irrational and supernatural power often puzzled all observers: it looked as if wood and iron had taken on both intelligence and malignity. Some boats were notorious for this freak and were ill-omened in the trade as "bad handlers." A "good handler" never ran away. Other boats that were docile and of good conduct when loaded would shy and take to flight when empty or lightened above a certain line hard to discover. The physical explanation was to be found in the shallowness of the river and the shape of the steamboat hull, which must of necessity be flat; but there were times when undeniably the phenomenon would have brought grist to a grim-faced judge of Salem in the witchcraft days.

The old side-wheel steamer *Lone Star*, which had a single engine and both wheels on one shaft, had this shying habit, and once came near to sending for the author of these memoirs. I was coming up the river in my sail-boat, the *West Wind*. There was a strong breeze blowing straight up-stream and I was running before it. The *Lone Star* was coming along close behind me. The *West Wind* when running free tended to drag her rudder and was hard to handle, although a witch to go. The *Lone Star*, a little to larboard of me, kept getting closer and closer, but I thought nothing of that until I heard a warning shout and a peal of bells and looked up, and there she was right upon me like a shark. She had taken a sheer. I should have jibed if I had attempted to go to starboard, but to haul my wind and make to larboard was to risk being struck before I could get past her bow. I took a chance, went to larboard, and the *Lone Star's* guard passed over the *West Wind's* stern—but I won clear and escaped, shaking.

What this might mean to a pilot I can show by a single illustration from history.

It was on the night of May 14, 1859, near Lagrange, Missouri, a beautiful, clear night of the kind pilots love best; that is to say, star-lighted. The packet *Lucie May* was coming up heavily loaded with freight and a full passenger list; the packet *Cedar Rapids* was bound down. Passing signals were exchanged in due form, both boats to go to the left. The river was of a good stage, the channel wide, there was room enough and to spare. Just as the boats were passing in accordance with the signals, the *Cedar Rapids* turned and smashed the *Lucie May* forward of the paddle-box.

A - Rafting on the Mississip'

They rushed her for the shore and got her into shallow water before she sank. The passengers got off in their night-clothes, and losing everything else they had. Three deck-hands were drowned.

The accident seemed inexcusable, and Pilot A. M. Root, who was at the wheel of the *Cedar Rapids*, was arrested, brought up for examination, and promptly lost his license, with the promise of prosecution for manslaughter. For some years he was a ruined man. He continued to protest his innocence and to demand a rehearing, and at last he got it before a United States commissioner. Then he showed by the testimony of many pilots and rivermen that the *Cedar Rapids* was notorious as one of these obsessed boats, called in river speech, "brutes to handle." She was liable at any time to take a sheer, or to refuse to mind her rudder, or do any act of madness short of climbing the side of a house. Root said that she had one of these fits at the moment of the collision. She started to behave all right and then of a sudden, as she was passing, went mad, turned, and banged into the *Lucie May* before she could be stopped, although he promptly set her back on both wheels. On this showing he won his license back, but he might as easily have been out of a job the rest of his life.

It will sound highly incredible to landsmen, but sometimes rafts would seem to be possessed by a similar demon and fight down the ablest pilots. A conspicuous instance comes to mind now. The raft-boat *Julia* was going nimbly with a lumber raft twelve strings wide and thirty-two cribs long. Of course, they must split this to run Clinton bridge, and what makes the incident that followed so remarkable is that they had a bow boat to help them—that is, a steamboat placed sidewise across the bow of the raft to make the steering swift and safe. Both the pilots on the *Julia* were skilful and experienced men. Yet as they came down to the bridge the raft, despite the utmost efforts of the bow boat, went into the pier at the eastern end of the draw.

What followed was an interesting revelation of the power of these rafts when pushed by the river current. The bow boat hit the pier broadside on, the stern boat backing with all her steam, and yet the force of the raft lifted the bow boat out of the water until her wheel was level with the railroad tracks on the bridge— lifted it into that position and held it there, with her bow on the raft and her stern in the air.

To get the raft out of this absurd predicament was an extremely difficult task, and old George Winans himself, who owned both boats and was the dean of rivermen, had to take charge of it. But it was done, the raft was put together, the bow boat rescued and re-floated, and after a few days the outfit proceeded.

I doubt if these apparently magical feats of maneuvering and manipulating are to be recorded of any other navigation known to man.

Fire was at all times a deadly peril, and the loom of it was seldom absent from the careful pilot's thought. The western river boat having upper works like tinder and paper, when a fire once started in that flimsy structure it went with startling speed to destruction. Intense heat generated by all that blazing pine and paint would set anything else on fire that it came near. A fire that started on the St. Louis levee burned twenty-six steamboats before it was stopped. Fire on a rafting steamer, while it meant less peril to life than a fire on a packet, might mean far more disastrous consequences to property, for after the great oars had been abandoned there was nothing to steer the raft with but the steamboat, and if she were disabled the raft would go to irretrievable pieces, while its fragments might block the channel and pull down a string of other disasters.

The burning of the packet *S. S. Merrill,* one of the handsomest steamboats of the old Northwestern Line, was a story the pilots liked to tell, because it supported their habitual view of the landsman passenger, which was always good-naturedly contemptuous. It happened September 18, 1872. The *Merrill* was a new boat; I think this was but her third trip. She was coming up the river loaded to the guards, and had made a landing at Warsaw, Illinois, just before the supper hour. Two citizens of Warsaw, standing on the levee watching the loading and unloading, suddenly saw a whiff of smoke arising from the texas. They gave the alarm and the crew ran pell-mell for the roof.

Fate was all against the *Merrill* that day. The first attempt was with the patent fire-extinguishers with which she was liberally provided. They would not work. The fire-hose was run upon the hurricane-deck, and then it was discovered that the fire-pump would not work, either.

There was a fire-engine at Warsaw and it was brought to the scene at the first alarm. The firemen ran it down the levee under the lee of the burning boat. A strong wind was blowing. Before they could get a stream started the intense heat of the fire drove them away. On the levee close by, awaiting shipment, was a pile of baled hay. It took fire and blazed fiercely. Next was a large warehouse filled with goods. Its roof began to smoke. A band of citizens formed a bucket line and by drenching the roof saved the warehouse when the prospect was that it and all the other buildings on the levee would be burned.

But I started to tell about the passengers. They were at no time in the least danger; they had only to walk ashore to be safe. Many of them coolly devoted themselves to the fight against the flames, while others helped the crew to carry the boat's belongings ashore. But some were not so self-possessed. A local account of the disaster says:

> The scenes on the burning boat showed how wild men become under excitement. One tried to take down the chandeliers in the *Merrill's* cabin and failing in this grabbed a chair and smashed them to atoms. The table was just being set for supper, and some enthusiastic individuals, determined to save all they could, caught hold of the table cloth, pulled every dish off to the floor, demolished the table furnishings and then threw the cloth into the river.

The pilots were disposed to chuckle mildly over that paragraph.

Property to the amount of $125,000 burned in that fire, a sum that seems little to us but was staggering in those days. The *Merrill* alone represented a loss of $60,000.

The most famous fire disaster on the river was the burning of the *Ocean Spray*, and what made it of so great interest forever to all rivermen and especially to the tribe of pilots was the manner of it. She was burned while racing.

Racing was the summit of life and joy to real rivermen. Tradition has had much to say of a humorous or derisive nature about the custom of boats in a race to burn lard, fat hams, or anything else in the cargo that would make hot fires. There was nothing humorous about the fact, which was common, and often costly to the steamboat company when the irate shipper came in with his bill. On this occasion the *Ocean Spray* was carrying a deck-load of turpentine. In the excitement of the race the firemen broke open a barrel of turpentine and carried the fluid in tin dippers to throw it into the roaring furnace, leaving a trail of drops on the deck, for they went in haste. As one opened the fire-box door to heave in another dipperful, a flame darted out and caught the turpentine trail, then flashed by this path to the barrel and set it on fire.

The mate ordered it thrown overboard. Two deck-hands seized and upset it. Then the boat was destroyed.

"That's what comes of racing," sighed Papa Wisdom, in the person of Tom Doughty, waggling his head and gray beard.

"It's you for preaching," said Dana Dorrance the Rapids pilot. "If you were dead and buried and somebody should say 'Here she comes!' above your grave, you'd climb out to look for grate-bars to tie on the safety-valve."

A solemn nod of approval went around the circle in the billiard saloon, and soon afterward Captain Lancaster began his gripping illustrated lecture entitled "How to Run Cat Fish Bar When There's Only Three Feet on Prescott."

Chapter XVII

THE STEERING WHEEL GUILD

THE racing instinct was ineradicable in these people, if they were really of the river. Owners, underwriters, and elderly opinion (at a distance) were all against it, but it persisted virtually unchecked by good counsel as by imperative orders. Let two raft boats deliver rafts and start up the river about the same time; all the underwriters between Dubuque and kingdom come could not have prevented a race. The weight on the safety-valve had now been riveted to the beam, so there was no shifting of it; but nobody could prevent some handy article of a substantial character being hung where it would do the most good. Strict injunctions were issued against firing up for extra steam, and they were obeyed—in form. When an engineer saw behind him the smoke of an approaching steamboat, he was faithful to his employers and never gave orders to the firemen to heat her up. He only loafed forward in a casual way and said to one of the firemen:

"Jim, do you know what boat that is that is coming up after us?"

"Search me," says Jim. "I don't know."

"Well, neither do I," says the chief, "and the queer thing is, I don't want to know," and walks aft, whistling.

Or if the smoke was in front it would be:

"Jack, what's that boat ahead of us, up there?"

"I don't know, chief."

"Well, by Gosh, I wish I knew!"

About ten minutes later the steam had strangely risen from 150 to 165 pounds and the wheel behind was digging up the bottom of the river. No racing—that was the rule. But of course it was a fact in nature nobody would deny that one boat could travel faster than another.

But the people along the shore, they had no objections or pious scruples about steamboat racing. They thought racing was what steamboats existed for, and hoped to see them fulfil their destiny. All the exploits of all the famous fast boats of river history, the *Shotwell*, the *Eclipse*, the *J. M. Allen*, the *Key City*, the *Hawkeye State*, were known to everybody in Le Claire, better than other items of human knowledge more essential, if the truth is to be told. Let some one make an error, however slight, in stating the immortal run of the *Hawkeye State* from St. Louis to St. Paul in two days, twenty hours, and thirteen minutes and see what scorn would fall upon his blundering head.

I remember well the commotion that shook our citizens when the report was received that the *Annie Johnston* had beaten the *Phil Sheridan*. Townspeople that had seen both assured me that the excitement caused by the fall of Richmond was by comparison nothing. The *Phil Sheridan*, the pride and wonder of the river, the swiftest thing that ever floated there, the unsurpassed beauty of creation, with the picture of the Battle of Winchester on its paddle-boxes and its pilot-house dome neatly painted in blue with gilt stars— and now beaten by the *Annie Johnston*, that long, lean stern-wheeler—if the earth had opened and swallowed the Methodist meeting-house, men could not have been

more amazed. It was in the fall of 1869. The *Johnston* had been coaling about four in the afternoon
at Port Byron, when the *Sheridan* went by and the
Johnston had impudently taken out after her. By a
kind of electric telepathy, all the town knew there was
a race on and had crowded down to the shore to see it.
So far as most persons could see, it was neck and neck
when the two boats passed out of sight in the neighborhood of Princeton.

The next day came the devastating news that the
Johnston had won to Dubuque by seven minutes.

There was not lacking those that had clearly discerned as the race started that the *Johnston* was making
the better time, nor those that had always said that she
was the faster boat. Down at Waldo Parkhurst's grocery the debate got so hot that good old Mr. Parkhurst
had to interfere. The side-wheeler *Phil Sheridan*
beaten by the stern-wheeler *Annie Johnston!*—cre-
dulity itself would balk at that, said some. Yet here was
the report. For twenty-four hours the battle raged.
At last came trustworthy information that the dire
news was untrue. It was another boat and not the
Johnston that had arrived in Dubuque, the gilded laurels of the River's Pride were still undimmed, and a sigh
of relief went up from all Le Claire. Order in the heav-
ens had not been reversed. All was still well in the
world.

As to raft boats, their racing was done when they
were returning to the rafting works for a new tow.
Yet I have one record of a race with rafts that sounds
like a classic.

Andrew Larkin came to the river from Norway in
1873 and found employment as a deck-hand, greener
than grass, on the rafter *Champion* at $22 a month.
He was not much more than a boy. Nine years later
he had learned the pilot's difficult art, become known

as one of its expert masters, and was captain of one of the largest and best boats on the river, the steamer *Louisville.*

Owned by the same company was the *Menomenee,* of almost the same size and power, captained by Stephen B. Withrow, of Larkin's age, who had come along with him from the forecastle to the roof.

In May, 1883, it happened that these boats lay side by side at Read's Landing waiting for rafts to tow. On May 4 each got its raft, each raft was of lumber, fourteen strings or about two hundred feet wide and a little more than five hundred feet long— roughly speaking, about two million feet of lumber, bound for St. Louis, more than six hundred miles away. There had long been rivalry between the two captains. Huge, clumsy rafts as contestant units in a race seemed absurd, but they entered upon it and raced the whole 620 miles, day and night without stopping, through ten bridges and over two rapids that must be double-tripped. For one to pass the other in the channel was impossible. The race hung upon whether the stern boat could diminish the lead the first boat had when she left Read's. Sometimes she did this and sometimes the *Louisville* held her own. Sometimes the *Louisville* gained on the *Menomenee.* But the two were in sight of each other, day and night, and when they went into St. Louis in the opinion of all observers the distance between the tows was exactly the same as when the race began—a dead heat.

That same year Captain Withrow with the same *Menomenee* did a piece of raft work that won him another round of applause. He started from Read's Landing with a lumber raft 192 feet wide and 576 feet long, bound for Alton, Illinois. Lumber rafts were slower to push than log rafts, because the water running between the logs offered less resistance. but with a lumber raft you bucked its square front about two feet deep straight into all the water there was in the river. Alton is twenty-five miles above St. Louis. The *Menomenee* from the time it took this raft in tow never stopped once until she delivered the raft at Alton, six days and four hours from Read's—I think the best time ever made by a raft for that distance. It was on this occasion that Captain Dorrance, the Rapids pilot of Le Claire, performed a feat that has always puzzled me. He took the *Menomenee's* raft through Davenport bridge without stopping or double-tripping or splitting. He slid it between two piers that were hardly more than two hundred feet apart, so that for a length of 576 feet he had about eight feet on each side to spare in a place daft with cross-currents and exposed to the wind. He slid it through and never touched a thing, and all the pilots saluted him as a wizard at his trade. Unless he possessed some means of bewitching inanimate nature, I do not know how he turned the trick.

George Winans afterward was of the opinion that this record trip of the *Menomenee* had been exceeded by the rafter *City of Winona*, which took a raft from Beef Slough to Hannibal in six days and one hour. Hannibal is 112 miles above Alton, so that the *City of Winona's* performance, though good, was not equal to the *Menomenee's*. It is interesting to note that the fastest trip ever made by a floating raft was about 1869 by a raft commanded by Thomas Forbush, which ran from Read's Landing to St. Louis in nine days and two hours. If the *Menomenee* had run to St. Louis, her time would have been about four days and eight hours, so that she traveled approximately twice as fast as Forbush's floating raft.

The efforts of the West Point engineers to improve navigation on the Mississippi were frequently the subject of our ribald jest, but not always, for they had

their apologists. One night in the pilot-house of the
St. Croix, I had spoken some frivolity about these worthy men and promptly suffered rebuke from Uncle Joe,
the pilot.

"No, sir," said he with emphasis, while he glanced
ahead into the inky darkness, "folks hadn't ought to
talk in that way about the Government. It isn't right.
It's the Government that sends these men out here to
tell us what to do and how to run steamboats and things,
isn't it? Well, then, a man ought to feel that the Government knows what it's about and have a thankful
mind, and so long as he don't follow any of their instructions, I don't see what harm's done. These men
know their business, I guess. I'll bet they do, every time.
Why, just look at it reasonably. How many lights are
there between Cairo and Pig Eye's bar? Three hundred
and fifty-nine, says you. All right. Now you just try
it. You take three hundred and fifty-nine crossing
lights, and say you weren't out of college and didn't
have expert training in these things, and you tried to
put them in position, hit or miss, maybe with your eyes
blindfolded. You'd put some of them right, wouldn't
you? You bet you would. You just naturally couldn't
help yourself; you'd get some of them right as sure as
shooting. But I tell you now, to set three hundred and
fifty-nine crossing lights and set every one of them
wrong—no common man could do that. It stands to
reason he couldn't. A man's got to go to college to
know how to do that. No, sir, I'm against all this loose
talk about government engineers. Men that have
learned how to scatter three hundred and fifty-nine
lights along nine hundred miles of river and get them
all wrong are entitled to respectful treatment."

This reminds me of the Hennepin Canal.

About every two years, as nearly as I can estimate,
some gentleman arises in the halls of Congress to de-

nounce this body of water, pointing with scorn to the fact that whereas it cost the Government some millions to construct and a considerable item to maintain, the total traffic upon it is confined to three skiffs and a motor launch.

None of the denouncing gentlemen has ever taken the pains to discover why there is no traffic on the Hennepin Canal, although that might seem to be an admirable preliminary to any uptipping of the vials of wrath.

The Hennepin Canal was conceived by disinterested citizens as a means to unite the Great Lakes with the upper Mississippi and so have direct water transit from the grain-fields of the Northwest to the Atlantic seaboard.

At that time the Illinois and Michigan Canal extended from Chicago to the Illinois River. The Hennepin project merely aimed to supply the missing link from the Illinois River to the upper Mississippi.

A convention held in Davenport in 1867 warmly indorsed it and set it upon its feet to go.

More than twenty years of struggle followed. The proposed canal would parallel the Chicago, Rock Island & Pacific Railroad, which put forth all its might to prevent the threatened competition.

As an interesting reminder of a condition largely bygone in our affairs, I will tell an incident. The center of the movement for the canal was at Davenport, and one of its active promoters was a man named Nutting, who was a hardware merchant. One day Mr. Nutting came to my father and said:

"You will have to strike my name from the canal committee and expect no more assistance from me. I'm through."

"Why?" asked my father, much disturbed, for Nutting had been a tower of strength.

"For this good reason. I got my freight bill this

285

morning and found that the rate had been doubled on all my shipments. I went hotfoot to the agent, supposing that there had been some mistake. 'No mistake,' says the agent. 'The rate you used to have was the rate we make to our friends. The rate on your bill is the rate we are going to charge all persons that try to injure our business by backing this canal.' "

He was speaking truth. All the promoters of the canal that had any freight accounts were mulcted in the same way. My father need not have been and probably was not in the least astonished. The same agency had once cut off his coal supply on similar grounds.

The fight for the canal went on and developed a singular fact. Upon the coöperation of the army engineers the project first depended, and they were always against it. The strangest part of this was that the canal, if constructed and navigable, would be of great importance to the Rock Island arsenal, the largest in the Government's possession. Once when the engineers had been with difficulty argued into approving of the plan, it was by accident discovered that they had changed the proposed route to a region where construction would have been all but impossible. This was circumvented just in time.

Thirty-five years after the inauguration of the project, the bill passed Congress and the work began. Great rejoicing in the upper Mississippi River country. A long fight had been won for a great improvement.

When the work was done the discovery was made that it was no improvement at all. The locks had been made so short that no steamboat could get through them.

To make sure that the canal should be a failure, the railroads, aided by a Chicago newspaper, succeeded in inducing the State of Illinois to dismantle and abandon the Illinois and Michigan Canal, the eastern link of the waterway.

And that is why the Hennepin, which cost millions to build and an annual appropriation to maintain, is navigated only by three skiffs and a motor launch.

Good old Uncle Joe thought it was necessary for a man to go to college to learn to do such things. My own observation has been otherwise.

Every year about a thousand American travelers abroad, beholding the methods by which Europe transports its heavy freight so cheaply and easily by water, reflect upon our disused inland waterways, the greatest natural system on earth, and marvel that they are not navigated. Any one that will read with attention certain chapters of our history can surmise why.

But Uncle Joe has led me somewhat off my theme, which was what seemed to me the peculiar traits of rivermen.

All men that win their bread by their own efforts are more or less subject to the guild spirit, or if they have their bread and things provided for them, to the spirit of class; but the tie that bound pilots together was more than either of these. All rivermen, if they were susceptible to anything, were in at least a degree under the sway of a kind of freemasonry, gallant and debonair, and pilots beyond the others. I suspect pilots knew what pilots went through and felt that nobody else knew it or could know it, and so felt vaguely drawn toward one another. At least, there seemed to be a bond of good-will among them (most curious to note in a world of chilled-steel materialism) and therewith about as little of jealousy as may be in human emulations. When they grew old, this brotherly feeling was often shown in quite affecting ways. The comradery among them was simple, naïve, genuine; and I think there was no employment in the world where there was a better feeling of democracy.

Mr. Summers, who made a trip once on the sturdy rafter *Mountain Belle*, was much impressed with this fact. He noticed that officers and crew ate together in the main cabin, the firemen at the same table with the pilots, mate, and captain. It happened that the captain and the mate had fought in the Civil War on the Union side and two firemen had fought on the Confederate side, and all four had been engaged in the Battle of Lookout Mountain. Now they all sat down cheek by jowl at the same board. Surely, in no other country under the sun could such a thing happen. The rule was that the fare should be uniform throughout. Mr. Summers adds that when Captain Lancaster would come to his dinner or supper he would look over the officers' table and then go over and look at the crew's table and then summon the cook.

"What's the reason there are no green peas on the men's table?" he would demand.

"Well, Captain," says Mike the cook, apologetically, "you see, there wasn't enough to go around, so I put them on your table."

"Then put what there is on the men's table," says the captain.

This sounds imaginative, I know, and perhaps improbable, but it is quite true. On the lower river, conditions were different, particularly between engineers and firemen. The reason was that in rafting, after the coming of the steamboat, the crew was intelligent and interested, and on the lower river the infernal race feeling always had some play. Often on these boats in the New Orleans trade they had no regular staff of firemen and had to drive roustabouts to the task.

"That was how we got the name of being tough," wrote an old engineer long after he had retired from the river. "I or my second never went to the firehole for steam that some nigger wasn't hurt. They would let the steam down to get fired, but the only way they got fired was by knocking them out, and then we had to drive in others to take their place. We had to be tough. And I didn't have any license, either. I steamboated when they had no whistles. The pilot would tap the big bell, and many a time I have had to go dead slow until he could hear the other boat's bell. When the wind was blowing it was hard to hear. I knew how to fire, and I always had steam if there was anything on the boat that would burn."

Even on the northern river, if we speak of packets, until the end of the business the roustabout and that ruddy human volcano, the mate, ran more or less true to tradition's form, although in justice I ought to say that the mate was never as withering as he sounded.

Once when I was on the packet *Clinton* upward bound we stopped at Port Byron to take on coal. The mate was superintending the operation and uttering remarks in the vernacular. I was sitting on the roof, watching, and beside me happened to be a tourist from New York. Two of the negro roustabouts carrying a coal-box started to cake-walk while crossing the fore-castle and spilled about a peck of coal. Instantly the volcano broke forth.

"There," said the tourist, leaning back with a satis-fied sigh, "I've heard it. All my life I've been told about the Mississippi mate's wonderful swearing, and I hardly dared to hope it was true, but it is, and I've heard it."

A native that stood behind us listened to this with disgust.

"Huh! Call that swearin'?" said he. "Huh! Well, you just oughter hear ol' Cap' Moulton cut loose—ol' Uncle Ike Moulton of La Crosse. If he'd been here he'd a-given you something worth while, I tell you. Why, he'd a-just stood there and blasted them niggers until there wouldn't been anything you could see of them but two handfuls of burned bones. That ain't no real swearin' what that mate done. I can do's good's that m'self."

Captain Isaac H. Moulton of La Crosse, he meant; one of the most popular commanders on the river. It was true that he could swear on occasion and adorned his profanity with care and knowledge, having explored many tongues for it, including the Scandinavian and Pottawatamie; but there never was any malice in his blasting speech, and he had other traits that in the minds of the judicious overshadowed all faults.

He was the best dancer on the Mississippi and would rather dance than eat.

On every boat that he commanded he must have something that would make music, if it were only a mouth organ, and having it he must dance to it. So must other folks; there was nothing selfish about Uncle Ike. Every night he would organize a dancing party in the cabin—and lead it himself. If there were any passengers that were disposed to be shy and hang back from the joys he had prepared, he hunted them out of their corners and carried them out into the middle of the floor and made them dance. Tradition said that he could dance any kind of a dance ever known to man, red, white, black, or saffron, but his favorite at all times was the Virginia reel. He has had more than two hundred people lined up in his cabin, dancing this forgotten revel, which it was said he could dance better than the man that invented it. He was more than six feet in height, straight as an Indian, trimly built, and as light on his feet as a feather. For many years he led the grand march at the annual Charity Ball at La Crosse, and people went there only to see him perform this ceremony, which he did with a dignity and grace

RAFT BOATS IN A RACE

*The "Moline" (left) has been waiting for the "Silver Crescent" (right) and now turns on full steam. Exterior indi-
cations are of a "hot" engineer on each boat.*

that were deemed unapproachable in any other town on the river, big or little. It was an institution, an annual event; people dated their recollections from the first time they saw Cap' Moulton lead the grand march.

Once when he was no longer young he arranged a quadrille at one of these balls, and the three other men in it were well-known and important lumbermen and, like himself, from the Maine woods. As the dance was well under way, Captain Moulton suddenly called out to his three compatriots:

"Say, you fellows, let's give these kids here some real dancing," and cut a step that he had learned in his boyhood. The others among the woodsmen responded with joy, and in five minutes all the rest of the dancers and all the bystanders had gathered to watch with breathless interest an exhibition of dancing the like of which they had neither seen nor dreamed of.

On upper and lower rivers there was always a feud smoldering (or flaming) between the pilot-house and the engine-room, a fact that cements the navigation of the Mississippi with steam traffic the world over. It is one of the mysteries of human life that are unsolved and universal. Sometimes the engine-room talked back, but the law made the pilot supreme and for once was wise therein. This reminds me of Captain Jerry Turner, another impressive figure of the rafting cycle, who at ninety-one was still a prominent and active citizen of Lansing, Iowa.

Captain Turner between rafting trips, or through the long winters, was fond of solid reading, and with history and biography plowed avidly the somewhat barren fields of geology. One cloudy summer night he was coming up to Beef Slough Island, feeling glad that he was so near the end of the upward trip and singing "While Shepherds Watched Their Flocks by Night," when of a sudden his heart stood still and his breath stopped. Before his eyes, he a sober, Christian man, sane and without hallucinations, the whole island, nearly a mile long, burst into blaze.

"It's a volcano," he gasped, and reached for a bell-pull and stopped where he was. To his mind the crust of the earth had broken through somewhere in the middle of the river and this was the terrifying result.

The chief engineer happened to be on duty that night, and when he had stopped the engines he looked out to see what was the matter. The next moment he was calling up the speaking-tube.

"What's that?" he asked in a trembling voice.

"I don't know," said Turner in a voice that shook as much as the engineer's, "unless it is a volcano."

They lay where they were in the river and presently above the tree-tops appeared the red and green chimney lights of a steamboat. Then Turner guessed what the phenomenon meant and rang to go ahead.

A quavering voice came up the speaking-tube, the voice of the chief down below.

"You're not fool enough to run into that thing, are you?"

Turner (stiffly) : "Your job is to stay down there and answer the bells."

Chief (sorrowfully and after a pause) : "Oh, well, all right—I can ride to hell as fast as you can."

It was an electric search-light, the first ever seen on the river. The packet *Gem City* was carrying it. Next year Captain Jerry had one on his raft-boat and said it was great.

Chapter XVIII

THE *MINNIETTA* IN A STORM

EVERY pilot was a weather sharp and knew more about clouds, winds, sunsets, and signs than the chief engineer of the forecast factory. He had to know, in a region where storms were as plentiful as blackberries and steamboats were built as light as straw. Early summer was the open season for wind-storms, whether cyclone or hurricane, and that made little difference. Sometimes a cyclone would come up so stealthily that it burst almost without warning, but in general a pilot knew from something in the atmosphere whenever a tantrum was at hand.

If to watch the weather was important to a packet pilot, it was vital to a raft pilot, because the packet (except in Lake Pepin) could get to shore somewhere, but a raft had no chance for its life if taken unawares in a hard blow.

I have told what happened at Camanche. There were other storms as violent wherein the loss of life was luckily much smaller. One of the worst for force broke over the Mississippi on July 4, 1872, about six o'clock in the evening, some miles below Keokuk. Captain E. H. Thomas, one of the elect among pilots, was coming up the river in a rafting-boat the name of which has escaped my memory. He saw the heavy black cloud

293

approaching and studied it with the eye of an expert. When he saw that the edge turned toward him was freaked with red, he knew what that meant and made for shore. There he was not content merely to moor, but tied up with extra lines and chains.

It was a straight wind, no whirligigs such as cyclones have, but a wind of tremendous power. With his engines going full speed ahead, Thomas found it doubtful if he could hold his lines. The trees were falling and crashing all about him, the air was full of boughs, leaves, haystacks, and wreckage, and the roof of a brick business block at Lagrange took wings, flew over him, and fell into the river.

The crew fled for their lives, threw themselves flat upon the ground, and held fast to shrubs and roots. Thomas, expecting the boat to be blown loose, wanted their help, and ordered the mate to crawl ashore and bring them back. They refused to budge. The end of the world was come, said they, and their fancy was to die on dry land.

Just after he had made the shore and before the storm broke, there came along the packet *Spread Eagle*, owned by old Captain Leyhe. He had trained his son to be a riverman and pilot, and now this youth, eighteen years old and the youngest pilot on the river, was at the *Eagle's* wheel. She had six hundred passengers and a heavy load of machinery.

As she passed, young Leyhe put his head out of the pilot-house window.

"Is it going to be much of a blow?" he yelled through his trumpeted hands.

"You bet it is," roared Thomas, "and you had better make in here and tie up."

The young man shook his head. "I'm going on to Lagrange," he said and slammed the window down.

The *Minnietta* in a Storm

From where he was lying, Thomas could see all that happened next. Lagrange was only a short distance ahead. The *Eagle* was still off the landing-place when the storm struck her. She was broadside to the wind and went over so far that the larboard wheel was out of water and spinning in the air, while the starboard was buried deep. Thomas forgot his own troubles to stand and stare miserably, for he expected to see the packet go over before his eyes and he helpless to save a life. Through all the murk he saw the *Eagle's* larboard chimney topple over at the breeching, he saw young Leyhe keeping himself with one hand from falling out of the pilot-house while with the other he whirled the wheel. He could even make out that the young pilot's head was bent now and then over the speaking-tube and he must be bawling orders to the engine-room. It was a battle fought by inches, Wind against Steam, blind, furious nature against the works and strength and skill of man. For a time neither gained, as tooth to tooth they strove. Then slowly, slowly, bit by bit, Thomas saw the *Eagle* maneuvered so that her bow won more and more into the wind. Then slowly she righted, the larboard wheel dropped until it reached the water, and she forced her way toward shore.

Then the larboard chimney, which all this time had been hanging by a stay, fell and crushed all the forward part of the upper works. And there in the midst of this wreckage, with the pilot-house surrounded by débris and shaking, stood young Leyhe, turning the wheel and bending over the speaking-tube. Not a life was lost, and the next day the *Spread Eagle*, with one chimney, started up the river under her own steam.

Years afterward Captain Thomas celebrated the boy pilot's feat as the most marvelous exhibition of nerve and skill he had ever seen.

The next day the river was so full of trees, lumber, logs, bits of raft, and wreckage that he had to lie where he was until the mess should drift past him.

This reminds me of the time Captain Heerman hid in the woods.

Captain E. E. Heerman it was, whose wedding day we have already chronicled in these annals and whose adventures and masterly skill held my boyish admiration fast. It was in July, 1874, that he had his own most satisfying experience with the fitful climate of the great golden Northwest. With his steamboat, *Minnietta*, he was towing a log raft from Beef Slough to Burlington. Thirteen strings he had; so of course when he reached Clinton bridge, that seven times accursed place, he had to split the tow, drop a half between two piers, and then with the *Minnietta* take the other half through the draw.

Just as they caught up with the floating half and were busy renewing the fastenings, somebody looked up, and there was a cyclone bearing straight down upon them, the veritable cyclone, black funnel, whirling cloud, torn edges, and the rest.

Captain Heerman ordered the two parts of the raft to be lashed together as hard as possible, and then thought about his little son, nine years old, who was making the trip with him.

Every raft now carried what were called the "snubbing works" or "checking works" devised by Captain Hanks and described in a former chapter. These made a kind of platform of logs securely fastened and bore the huge cleats with which the raft was moored. Captain Heerman told his son to run for the snubbing works, lie down, clasp a cleat with both hands, and hold on. He might be wet, but that part of the raft would hold together and he would be safe if he did not move. Heerman then darted for the pilot-house.

On the stairs he met the cub pilot running so fast he seemed to be falling bolt upright with his heels playing a tune on the steps. "I'm going for the raft!" he yelled as he shot past; "the old boat can't live in this storm!"

Heerman got to the deserted pilot-house.

When the storm had struck, the *Minnietta* heeled far over to larboard, so that he could hardly stand. The pilot-house door was stuck fast. He forced a window open, straddled the sill, and getting to the speaking-tube asked the engineer if he purposed to stand at his post.

"I'll stick all right," shouted the engineer, "but this boat's done for. The water's up to the sheet iron on the boiler and covers the ash pan."

"Well," said Heerman, coolly, "you hearten the fire-man, if you have one, and if you two will stand by, I will save the boat."

Meantime, the raft had gone to pieces—literally to pieces, as if it had been to a cyclop's mill and ground. A fragment of about forty logs was left intact where the snubbing works were, and on this frail refuge all the crew was gathered except the three brave men on the boat. By skilful manipulation and backing hard, Heerman got the stern around until it pointed into the wind, and so eased the pressure on the side, but even thus the boat and the checking works were driven headlong upon the shore. The little boy obeyed his father and clinging desperately to the cleat came through unhurt.

But the raft was now destroyed, and when the storm had passed, the crew, demoralized, disgusted, and wet to the skin, refused to go out to chase the logs, which were scattered over all that part of Illinois. A raft commander must have tact as well as courage. Captain Heerman did not urge the point, but ordered the cook to get the men a first-class dinner; chicken with gravy, and pie. When they had eaten they forgot the mutiny and went to work.

Eight days they spent hunting those logs. Some were in corn-fields, some were hidden in creeks, some were on islands, some were sailing serenely down the river and must be pursued in skiffs. Hundreds had been carried into the thickets along the river bank. To dislodge them it was necessary to work in the brush with cant-hooks and levers, and before the task was done captain and crew were naked. Not by way of metaphor: I mean literally clad for the most part in their innocence, if any, and not otherwise. Thorns, briars, and branches had torn their clothes to tatters. In the whole entourage was not the clothing to make for one man a complete suit.

It was a log raft, a rafting steamer. There were but five barrels on board all in use. The traditional recourse in such cases was out of the question. They put together enough shreds and patches to enable one of the crew to go into town without being arrested, and Heerman went with him through the woods until they came to the outskirts of an Illinois hamlet. There, wrapped in a sheet, the captain hid while his emissary went to buy clothes. It was not a large store, the stock was limited and allowed no choice. When he returned the trousers for the captain were so small he could not button them around his waist.

They went back to the boat, got the skiff, and pulled to Cordova, and again the captain hid while his deck-hand went into town. This time he brought out a pair of trousers the legs of which were so short there was a space of five inches between the bottoms of the trousers and the tops of the captain's shoes. In this fantastic garb he went himself into the town, and by diligent inquiry came by a suit of clothes he could wear, got a supply for the crew, and went upon his way rejoicing.

He delivered that raft at Burlington with only three logs missing, a feat in rafting comparable to beating an army of veterans with a company of recruits.

Captain Heerman, by the way, was a fair specimen of the true riverman, quick of wit, full of resources, capable, efficient, never daunted. For some years he was engaged in steamboating on the Chippewa River and made money at it. When the railroad was built along the shore of the river, his business went to its end, leaving his fleet on his hands. He felt that he could not afford to remodel the boats into rafters, so he looked about for a new field and believed he had found it in Devil's Lake, North Dakota. It was then lost in the desert drear and wild, with nothing in the way of a human habitation except Fort Totten, down at one end; but Heerman made a careful examination of the country around and believed it would some day be populous. From one of his steamboats, the *Minnie*, he took the machinery and boilers, sold the woodwork, and sent boilers and machinery as far toward Devil's Lake as there was then a railroad.

The rest he purposed to do by hauling with teams.

As he started, winter came on. It took him thirteen days with nine teams of horses to haul one boiler twenty miles through the deepest snowdrifts he had ever seen and with the coldest weather. He got that boiler through and went back for the rest. Before spring he had the hauling done and was building a new boat on the lake. When the railroad was built to the lake, the new *Minnie*, Captain Heerman, met the first train and all others and thereafter connected regularly for passengers and freight.

I offer but a few examples to show men and ways of a departed era. This same William Tibbals that steered the *Key City* without a rudder began as a cub pilot in 1854. Fifty years later he was still piloting, being chief on the packet *Arkansas*. Season after season for half a century he had steered rafts, towboats and packets, with rudders and without, day and night, in all kinds of weather, past all kinds of perils, and had virtually never an accident. In 1914, reviewing his life, he recalled that the only mishap he had encountered was in his early days when he was steering the old packet *Keokuk*. A boulder had slipped by night from the bluff at Chimney Rock and lay in the channel, where nobody knew of it. He came along in the *Keokuk*, keeping the channel, and hit this rock, three feet under the surface.

Three steamboats were required to pull the *Keokuk* away from the obstruction, but her hurt was patched by her own crew, and under her own steam she went to the boat-yard at Le Claire.

All kinds of men made up the pilot world, as elsewhere, but the majority of them made on me an impression of character and worth that could not have been imaginary. For one thing, every moment of a pilot's work demanded a clear head and the best condition of his faculties. Consequently, old Barleycorn, who laid low so many others of the pioneer period, had little to say to him. But I think there was something else. They came out of New England with some moral standard bred into their bones, or, as before suggested, there was in the beauty that surrounded them some touch to a chord in human nature not well understood, or their dangers and responsibilities made them reflective. There were good men among them and others not so good, but the average was high. The world had a disposition to view all rivermen as more or less of the Ancient Order of Rough Neck. In this the world was astray so far as the pilots were concerned; pilots and many a captain too. It is singular but true that whereas, for example, all Mississippi River men were believed, as I have noted, to have reached the attainable summit in profanity, both plain and embroidered, there were raft captains and others that made a prideful point of never using a profane word and never raising their voices. I knew some of these men. Captain Van Sant was one. I have seen them in exceedingly trying positions and they never lost their command upon their tongues nor their quiet manner of restraint.

Not all were thus. There was one captain (he had never been a pilot) that was celebrated for excitability. One day he was coming down with a lumber raft through Betsy Slough when the wind drove him into a tow head, and six cribs smashed up and got astray. He stood forward on the roof bawling directions that were hardly needed, for the crew was experienced and under the mate was rapidly repairing the damage. There was one hand especially, Old Mose he was called, that had been through so many smash-ups that he could have dealt with one in his sleep. As he tore over the raft to the place of damage Captain S. from the roof bawled incessant directions to him.

"Oh, go to hell!" said Mose, and kept on his way.

When the cribs had been replaced and the raft was under way, Captain S. sent for Mose to come up on the roof. Mose ascended, knowing well that he was about to be discharged.

"Well, Captain," said he on arrival before the presence, "what is it?"

"Mose," said the captain, "I want to kiss you. You are the only man in that smash-up that said anything that had any sense to it."

There was an odd amount of religious sentiment, first and last, among higher rank rivermen, standing out as a thing incongruous against a background so lawless as that of the old-time raft crew—incongruous, and perhaps to be deemed now out of the human drawing, and yet existing, as more records easily witness.

A-Rafting on the Mississip'

We have encountered Commodore Orrin Smith on this head. He was so strict a Sabbatarian that he would never allow one of his boats to turn a wheel on Sunday. When twelve o'clock Saturday night came they stopped wherever they might be and waited until twelve o'clock the next night. Once, coming down the river with his packet, the *Nominee,* she ran aground just before midnight Saturday. They worked with the spars until twelve o'clock struck, when they stopped and nothing more was done until a minute past midnight Monday morning. When Sunday was approaching, Smith would try to make a town or village where he could tie up and all hands could go to church. Or if there was a clergyman on board and he discovered the fact, he would have the clergyman hold services in the cabin.

Bill Tibbals was a passenger on the *Nominee* the time she hung on the bar over Sunday, and thereafter had no joy in the commodore's way of registering piety. But Captain William Holcombe of the packet *Olive Branch,* who was as strict about Sunday as Orrin Smith, rose to be lieutenant-governor of Minnesota, if that may count as argument. There was even a mate named Paynter, Thomas Paynter, long familiar on the old packet *Northern Light,* who when he died was obituaried as "a model Christian gentleman." And he a mate. No particulars are given. Let us hope for the best. At least we know that Captain Samuel Rider was thirty-four years on the upper Mississippi, Missouri, Ohio, Arkansas, White, and Red rivers, and when he died it was widely asserted that no man ever heard a profane word from his mouth, and he was under fire in the Civil War at that.

Captain H. Leyhe, the elder, of the *Spread Eagle,* the boat that fought out the great storm, was another strict Sabbatarian, and had other unusual ways. Ac-

302

cording to reports printed at that time, he would never allow gambling on his boats, nor the sale of whisky, and always held religious services on Sunday. If there were no clergyman on board, he would conduct the services himself.

He had a strange superstition that a colored preacher and a white horse at the same time on a steamboat made an infallible omen of disaster, and he never would allow the combination on a boat that he commanded. The colored preacher was all right by himself and the white horse was all right by itself, but the two together were more than fate could withstand. He said he had looked up the records and knew what he was talking about. In every great disaster on the Mississippi there had always been a colored preacher and a white horse on board, and for himself he would take no chances with any such portent. His other phobia was about rats. He would stop his boat almost anywhere to rout out all hands and hunt a rat.

Some of these incidents may serve to remind us of shifting social customs. Ruel Murphy of Athens, Missouri, paid a demurrage of $1,000 rather than have a shipment on the steamboat he had chartered leave port on a Sunday. Captain Granville W. Hill would never allow a clergyman traveling on his boat to pay fare. If the fare had been paid inadvertently, the captain would hunt up the passenger and return the amount.

This may well suggest the time Bill Davidson got religion.

Old Commodore Davidson, the truculent fighter, the hard-headed chief of many steamboat companies, whose name will be repeated as long as the Mississippi carries a steamboat—that is the man I mean.

The Davidsons were a remarkable family that seemed to have a passion for steamboating; all of them had it, but William F. even worse than the rest. When he came upon the scene there were two lines of steamboats on the upper Mississippi. He started a third, putting on vessels cheaply constructed with pine hulls and dubious enginery, but able to get from port to port and to cut rates, which was the first objective. Before long he had vanquished the weaker of his two rivals and taken possession of it. He then started after the other, the staid and powerful old Northern Line, the aristocrat of all river institutions, the stock of which had for years yielded lusciously in dividends—the grand old Northern Line, some of whose boats had paid for themselves in three trips or fewer.

A furious and historic struggle ensued, lasted for years, and caused to many stockholders an immedicable grief. The madness of competition seized upon the two managements; at one time they were carrying passengers from Galena to St. Paul for fifty cents, and freight for less than the cost of handling. It was the halcyon day for the poor traveler; whole populations went gallivanting to St. Louis or Keokuk that never had dreamed of adventuring more than five miles from Sauk Center or Jonesport. The grit of the stockholders and the stubbornness of the Davidsons were probably more wonderful than wise. At last, when for three seasons the owners of the Northern Line had been confronted with assessments in the place of once glorious dividends, they surrendered. Davidson took over their steamboats and for a time reigned supreme.

Not for long. A new power was arising in river affairs that was destined to make him aplenty of trouble in his own turn.

One of the romances of American business, that field neglected for good stories, is the ascent of Joseph Reynolds. With his two hands and an iron will for capital, he came to the West from Sullivan County, New York, and began life in a tannery. Before long he had a tan-

nery of his own; small, but workable. The shipments of
hides made to him seemed to lack distinction; they must
have something to indicate that he was alive and doing
business; so he took to having his first name decorated
with four straight marks: "Jo Reynolds," with a kind
of diamond around the "Jo." In a short time he was
known as Diamond Jo, a name with which the Mississippi rang for years.

He prospered at his tannery and enlarged his business contacts. He was shrewd, relentless, indomitable,
and tireless as a steel spring; the typical successful
business man of that period. When he went out after
trade he got it; shot it on the wing, no doubt. In a few
years he began to turn his attention to grain; the upper
Mississippi basin was then the great wheat-producing
region of the world, and Reynolds sent there after it.
In three seasons he became a conspicuous buyer and his
grain a great item in river traffic.

About that time, Davidson attained to steamboat
monopoly or nearly so.

Mr. Reynolds was of a masterful temperament. He
found, or thought he found, that the Davidson boats
were not promptly handling his grain, and sent in a
hot complaint. Commodore Davidson was not used to
complaints nor docile under criticism. He replied in
kind. Reynolds came out in person to look after his
interests. The two men met on the top of a grain barge
going down the river in a tow. It must have been an
encounter worth noting, for both were fluent of speech
and in command of ample vocabularies of the blistering
kind. Reynolds declared with passion that his wheat
had been held up; Davidson roared back that the statement was untrue; or words to that effect. At one time
it was confidently expected by the interested spectators
that the vehement controversy would end in blows, but
to a world already gray with disappointments was

added the shattering of this fond hope. Nothing was exchanged more wounding than language. At the wind-up, Davidson agreed, with no good grace, that thereafter the Reynolds wheat should be pushed through speedily and the two parted; not amicably.

Soon afterward Reynolds had a barge of wheat held for many days at some shipping point. He said that was enough, bought a steamboat, and began his own transporting.

This was the origin of the Diamond Jo Line of steamboats that for years ran in opposition to Commodore Davidson and eventually put him out of business. Diamond Jo cut Diamond Bill, and all that.

It was before these last developments that the commodore got religion. When it had permeated his system he went in for it with the same enthusiasm he had shown in butting other people's steamboats off the track. One of the manifestations of the new life was to refuse to allow his crack boat, the *Phil Sheridan*, the unbeaten, the swift-footed, to accept a challenge to race—a thing unheard of in river annals and enough to cast old-timers into a state of coma. Another was to hold prayer-meetings down on the boiler deck and have passengers, crew, and all hands in attendance.[1] At these gatherings he would preside in person and with vigor if not with unction. Governor Hoard of Wisconsin, who was an incurable story-teller, got hold of an incident at one of these redemptory gatherings and made the most of it, with trimmings. He said that in the commodore's petition to the throne of Grace he remembered the poor and prayed earnestly that provision might be made for them. At the word he seemed to imagine himself once

[1] Captain McMasters, in his "Sixty Years on the Upper Mississippi," says (p. 191) that it was when Davidson was consummating his last and worst business deal that he "was holding out-door revival meetings on the levee at St. Louis and he took his final departure from this world in all the odor of sanctity."

THE RAFT BOAT "NORTH STAR"

A typical rafter built by the Van Sants

THE BOOM TIMES OF RAFTING

READS LANDING IN THE OLD DAYS

The steamboats are waiting for rafts to tow. The time was just be-
fore the side-wheel raft boat was displaced by the stern-wheel.

more in his office and directing the practical affairs of his line.

"Provision—provisions," he said. "A side of beef, two carcasses of mutton, a barrel of flour, a barrel of pork, a barrel of salt, a barrel of pepper—hell, no; that's too much pepper."

Women as much as the men became fascinated with the river. At the sewing circles in Le Claire the women talked with full knowledge about boats and boating; they actually talked boats as much as clothes; I noticed that singular fact when I was a boy. It was more than a perfunctory interest in the business of their husbands; it was the spell paramount that the stream cast over us all. Suppose a Le Claire woman to marry and move to Colorado or New Mexico. Twenty years later at the mention of the river her face would lighten and her eyes take on the familiar look, so that I knew she saw in her mind the bluffs back of Port Byron and the noble sweep of current below.

It is a subject that has allured the fictionist—with peculiar results. I recall moving stories of women that were said to have piloted rafts and raft-boats and with derring-do to have saved all from wreck, but these were pure fantasy. We have records of two women that actually held pilots' licenses and did actual piloting—one on the Illinois and one on the White River in Arkansas. The nearest approach to the woman skipper of fancy is the case of Mrs. Ida Moore Lachmund of Clinton, Iowa.

She was born in Philadelphia and married there. When her husband came West to look for a career she came with him. They settled at Clinton, where Mr. Lachmund went to work for a great sawmill firm. He was thrifty and far-sighted. Before long he was planting his savings in steamboats. Then he took to going up the river with boats that he owned in part, and she accompanied him. That determined her fate. The charm

307

of the river laid hold upon her. Two years later she was
investing her own money in boats. By 1887 she was
partner in the ownership of the rafter *Nina;* to this she
added interests in the *Lily Turner, Gardie Eastman,*
and *Reindeer,* all raft-boats. Then she made of herself
a kind of towing company, took contracts for the de-
livery of logs, and carried them out so efficiently that
she won fame as well as dollars. In 1896 the raft-boat
Robert Dodds, one of the best on the river, was offered
for sale. Mrs. Lachmund went to see it, personally
inspected the hull and machinery, and decided that it
was a good purchase. She bought it, had it repaired
according to her own ideas, and began to run it.

For the next six years she operated it with distinguished success. Then the rafting business went into
a sad decline. Often she made the trip on the *Dodds*
from Clinton to the pineries and back, sometimes accompanied by her son, sometimes by a woman friend. When
she was on board she divided her time between the pilot-
house and the kitchen, and it is said that she was warmly
welcomed in both. She never took on the notion that she
knew the channel better than the pilot, and she always
improved the cooking.

The average life of a steamboat on the Mississippi
being five years, if by reason of strength and luck it
might be prolonged to six or seven, yet was the addition
usually when she was in a way to shake to pieces. The
Phil Sheridan was one exception. For about the space
of ten years she was the pride and wonder of the valley,
and was still in condition, for she had been built with a
conscience as well as with hammer and adze, when accident ended her days. She was hauled out at La Crosse
and being fixed up for the coming season, when the
ways broke down and in the crash the *Sheridan* received
her death-blow.

Others occasionally endured to a ripe age. The old

The *Minnietta* in a Storm

St. Croix, my old rafter, built in 1870, was one. She
lasted until 1894. Then she was going through Dubuque
bridge one day and hit a log. The ancient hull, that had
sustained many a shock, gave way at last and down she
went. Another venerated relic of my time was the *Silas
Wright*. She was built in 1866 and ran every season
until September 3, 1892. On that melancholy day she
was acting as bow boat to help a raft over the Le Claire
Rapids. There was a buoy in the channel that had been
placed there by one of the West Point graduates that
the Government allows to muss up the river. It had a
ring-bolt in it; God knows what for. I always thought
that place had troubles enough without the higher education horning in with more. Nobody noticed this new
contraption of the West Point mind, and the raft hit it
broadside on ·for the venerable *Silas*. The ring-bolt
pierced her respectable old side and she gave up the
fight then and there. The raft ran over her and ground
her to kindling-wood. Then they fished the machinery
out of the wreckage and put it into a new boat, the
R. J. Kendall. But the grandmother of all rafting boats
was the *Helen Mar*, built in 1872, and year in and year
out towing rafts about as regularly as the equinox ar-
rives. Many times she was sold and many times repaired,
but she seems never to have been sunk or to have hit
anything, a record memorable in so busy a craft. She
lasted until 1904, thirty-two years, when she perished
at La Crosse of senile debility, I think. All but her
engines. No doubt they were taken out and to this day
are turning over on some vessel, probably on a southern
river.

Because that is a curious feature of the business.
Steamboats wore out or were blown up or snagged or
burned or something, but steamboat machinery came
near to being immortal. A new steamboat seldom had
new machinery; as a rule, the engines were supplied

from some predecessor gone halt. The engines of the *Ida Fulton* were put into the rafter *Glenmont* and, when she wore out, into the *North Star*. Away down on the Arkansas River the steamboat *Guidon* was reported to have sunk. The watchful Captain Van Sant snapped somebody down there, bought the engines, put them into the *D. A. McDonald*, then into the *Silver Wave*, then into the *Vernie Mac*. So late as 1915 there was a towboat owned at Lyons, Iowa, that had engines old enough to be retired on a pension. They were originally constructed for the *G. B. Knapp*, built about 1866. When the *Knapp* passed out they were transferred to the rafter *Cleon*. When she was no more they went to the rafter *Jennie Hayes*, then to the pile-driver *Good Luck*, next landing upon the *Arthur S.*, and thence to be transferred to something else belike after these chronicles shall be but dust.

I think the sage old grandsires of the billiard saloon were fondest of recounting the Odyssey of the engines of the packet *Jo Daviess*, once the proud property of the ubiquitous Harris family, who built her. When they sold her, she ran three trips and sank. The engines were dug up and placed in the first *Reindeer*. She made three trips and sank. Then the engines were again resurrected and put into a second *Reindeer*. She made four trips and sank. Out of the wreck emerged the engines triumphant and went into a new boat called the *Colonel Clay*. She made two trips and sank. Their next adventuring was in the new steamer *Monroe*. She ran all that season, and the best judges were satisfied that the hoodoo was broken. The next season she burned. The engines were now taken out and placed in a mill at Elizabethtown, Pennsylvania, with a serene confidence that short of earthquake the mill could not sink, anyway. But it could burn, and did so the next year. The subsequent career of these machines is so far unrecorded. It would seem likely to reward the inquiring mind.

But none of these boiler biographies contains anything equaling the adventures of the mechanical remains of the old towboat *Otter*.

About 1855 there arrived at New York two Frenchmen that, not being impressed with the beauties of a dictatorship, had fallen foul of Napoleon III. After his pleasing habit, this eccentric duce had hunted them out of France and they had gone to join Victor Hugo in his exile in the Island of Jersey. It seems they found themselves inadjustable to premature burial, so they made their way via England to America. They had evidently informed themselves of the needs of the growing West whither they were steering, for they brought along with them a steam boiler and an engine. This slightly unusual baggage they transported to Henderson, Minnesota, where they set up a grist-mill and made money.

A few years later they decided to go into the steamboat business and built the towboat *Otter*, into which they put the boiler and engine with which they had landed, taking them out of the grist-mill. For years this craft operated prosperously on the Minnesota and then was sold to Captain Jacob Hindermann, who used her in making up rafts at the rafting works at West Newton. At the close of navigation in 1879, Captain Hindermann put his boat into winter quarters, and when the ice went out in the spring it settled the case of the *Otter*, which was torn to pieces and sank.

The famous boiler went to the bottom of the river, where it lay in the mud undisturbed and forgotten for thirty-six years. Then Captain Hindermann had it fished up and presented it to the Junior Pioneer Society of New Ulm, Minnesota. On Sunday, August 26, 1926, the gift was received with appropriate ceremony and a grand parade. The old boiler was carried on a

311

decorated wagon drawn by six gaily caparisoned horses. Upon it, as Tiberius bestrode his horse in an Appian Way triumph, rode Captain Hindermann himself, dressed in what the press described as "a marine suit," whatever that may be, with a white cap having a blue front inscribed in gold letters "Captain." Before him marched Hoffmeister's justly celebrated Silver Cornet Band, discoursing harmony—"as that famous band only is capable of entertaining," remarks the local newspaper.

Thus in solemn state the procession marched through the streets to the public park. There were speeches and songs and the band played and a pleasant afternoon was had by all. So we are assured. Then the old boiler was put in place as a permanent feature of the park landscape. New Ulm is probably alone among cities in the adoption of this style of adorning. It is said to be a German place. Never tell me. Nothing could be more thoroughly American than this performance.

Chapter XIX

MR. HILL, MEET CAPTAIN PLUCK

WE left Stephen Beck Hanks planting cherry-trees and watering his geraniums on his little farm at Albany, Illinois, convinced that he and the river were thenceforth twain. No man that ever held a wheel on the Mississippi was afterward content at anything else, though he might eat from gold plate of nightingales' tongues. Hanks had been holding the watering-pot and the hoe about long enough to be fairly uneasy in his soul, when along comes his brother-in-law, Captain Jenks, with a proposal.

The towing of rafts by stern-wheel steamboats had been demonstrated to be the right way, and the *J. W. Van Sant* had been followed by a score of similar craft, all busily at work. Captain Jenks had gone into the business and now came to offer Hanks a place on the new rafter *Brother Jonathan* at $1600 a year.

The watering-pot fell with a crash.

The *Jonathan* had wintered a raft at Cat Tail Slough, which is close below Clinton, and Hanks went up there to take boat and raft to St. Louis. He had never tried to steer a raft with a steamboat, and, since the great days of his successes as a floating pilot, river conditions had changed. For one thing, the old stream had been spanned by many bridges.

313

A - R a f t i n g   o n   t h e   M i s s i s s i p'

Now to get a raft through a bridge is an art by itself. The first bridge that confronted Stephen Hanks was Davenport, which he negotiated all right. Next was Burlington, where he came to grief. He miscalculated the force of the current that ran through the piers; experienced, skilful, hawk-eyed pilot as he was, he miscalculated it; struck the draw pier and smashed two strings of his raft, so that logs were all over that part of the Middle West. The men put the pieces together as well as they could and went on.

At Keokuk the intention was to split and take the two pieces separately through the bridge, for this was the way of safety. But when the time came for the division, the two pieces could not be wrenched apart or not so that they would keep away from each other. By some witchcraft, or some strange operation of the law of cohesion, as soon as they were cut apart they drifted together again. So much time was lost in this way that the raft was still virtually intact when it reached the bridge. There was not room enough for it to pass between the piers. It struck on both sides and once more the wide Mississippi was littered with its logs.

Another delay followed in which the fugitive fragments were rerafted and the expedition proceeded. At Quincy bridge the splitting was safely effected. Captain Jenks went ahead with one section and Hanks was to bring along the other with the steamboat. Hanks held to his piece a little too long and could not straighten up in time, so he hit this bridge also, making a score of three on one trip. Once more they must stop and pick up their logs from a wide area of water and shore. But Hanks was learning. The rest of the journey he managed successfully. He ran without mishap the bridges at Hannibal and Louisiana and never thereafter had serious trouble with these steamboat traps.

He was now a raft-steamer pilot as good as the best

GOVERNOR SAM VAN SANT, 1864, CO. A 9TH 111 CAVALRY

SAMUEL R. VAN SANT, WHEN HE WAS NOMINATED FOR GOVERNOR

and stuck to the work the rest of his career. The next season after he had learned what a well-placed bridge attending strictly to business can do for a raft, he was able to furnish some tuition about rafting to his partner and brother-in-law.

They had a contract to take a raft late in the season, a lumber raft from St. Paul to as near St. Louis as they could go before the ice should form. When they reached Cassville Slough, which is a narrow and crooked place, a fierce wind was blowing down-stream, and Hanks said it would be necessary to split the raft to run that slough in safety.

"Aw, nonsense," said Jenks; "it isn't necessary to split."

"It is," said Hanks.

"It isn't," said Jenks.

"It is," said Hanks.

"It isn't," said Jenks. "Not with a pilot that knows his business."

"If you think you're that kind you'd better grab a root on that wheel and start in," said Hanks.

"Well, I bet I can run that slough in one piece, anyway," said Jenks.

"No time like the present," said Hanks, and marched in dudgeon out of the pilot-house.

Hanks and Jenks; unequaled chance for comedy. The next passages of the act looked all the other way. Hanks walked out to the bow of the raft, feeling sure that before long he would be needed there. At the first bend in the slough, Jenks at the wheel hit the shore and knocked off one string. Hanks had lines out and rescued it. An island showed up in the middle of the channel, and Jenks leaned out of the pilot-house and yelled which side of it should he go.

"Go either side," shouted Hanks, "but don't try to go both, and anyway take the raft with you."

A-Rafting on the Mississip'

Brother-in-law seems to have tried to play fairly with the island. He hit it with the center of his bow and tore the raft wide open, about half going on one side and half on the other.

Once more Hanks was ready with his check-lines and secured the vagrant sections. Brother-in-law was still unconvinced that Providence had not designed him to be a great pilot. So they put the raft together, and as soon as they were able to travel again he wrecked it once more, this time on Hurricane Island. After that he was content to leave the job of steering rafts to other hands.

In 1877 Captain Hanks went to work for the Lambs, the great sawmill house of Clinton, and never was out of their employ thereafter until he thought the time had come for him to quit piloting.

The same odd readiness of resource and persistence against difficulties that had made him of mark in his packet experience helped him out of the tight places in his new way of life.

In the spring of 1878 the Lamb mills were without logs, and the owners and workers impatient to begin sawing. They had a raft in Lansing Bay where it had wintered, and they sent Hanks up in their steamer the *Lafayette Lamb* to get it. When he reached Lansing he found the raft still frozen fast in the ice and out of reach, the ice being two feet thick.

Here was an apparently impossible situation. Hanks sat down to think, and what he thought most of was the men at Clinton eager to get to work after the long winter. It seemed to him there must be a way to get that raft out. He went down to some men that had been cutting ice that winter and borrowed their saws and other tools. Then he sawed strips around the edge of the ice field in the bay. Next he drilled a hole through the ice, made a line fast to the middle of a small spar, and passed the spar through the hole. Then he carried the other end of the line to the *Lamb* and began to back slowly. The line tautened up and held and foot by foot he towed the ice-field out of the bay and set it adrift down the river.

Then he got to his raft, broke it loose, and steamed away for Clinton.

He continued to be master and first pilot of the *Artemas Lamb*, another of the Lamb fleet, until the fall of 1890, when, being arrived at the age of sixty-nine, he concluded that the time had come for him to retire, and he went back to his cherry-trees. The next spring, hardly had the ice gone out when he began to look longingly upon the river. As before, he found that the watering-pot and the life of ease in Dingley Dell were not what they were reputed. In plain terms, he was bored to death and forgot all about his years, for when an offer came to be second pilot on the *J. S. Keator*, a raft-boat from Moline, he jumped at it. Another man, after being master so long, might have balked at the demotion. Not Hanks; anything on the river was better than anything on shore. Once more he cast the garden rake over the house and made haste to get the wheel in his hand. The next year he took a similar position on the rafter *Joe Long*. It completed his fiftieth year of piloting, and his relatives and friends persuaded him to stop. But every year he left the cherry-trees long enough to make at least one trip to Stillwater and look at his beloved old river.

The other great figure in these annals, Captain Pluck, we left butting his way with head down against debts, and creditors, and misfortune.

Not for long. If ever a man's faith in himself, in his destiny, and his judgment was vindicated, it was here. In the face of a cloud of counselors coming with wisdom, he clung to his belief in the prairie and his calculations that the rafting business would grow and not decline. The steamboats that he built and operated made money; the ways of the Van Sant boat-yard were filled every winter, filled from the edge of the water to the edge of the street, every available space filled; packets, raft-boats, towboats. The packet company wintered there some of its gaudiest vessels, and Van Sant & Son repaired them with nobody to watch the work, check it, or connote the charges for it. When their bill was presented it was paid without question. Up and down the river, men said that John Wesley Van Sant, even in the midst of his harassing business troubles, would have as soon cut off his right hand as make a charge a cent above right. In the winter the firm got up by candle-light to go to work, and quit long after the evening whistle had blown. Every summer Captain Pluck served as master of one or another of the firm's boats, and knew his job if any man ever did. It was said of him that he could get more rafts down the river in less time and with less trouble than any other man on the roof. Everybody liked him; yet he made no compromises. When he was captain he was captain. Many a time I have sailed with him and watched him. He had a way of giving orders that I think would have put intelligent zeal into a crew of mummies, and there was nothing about logs, lumber, and rafts that he did not know, from the tree in the woods to the lath in the wall.

Gradually the horizon cleared for him. Only nine in ten of his townspeople were his creditors now; then only four in five. He paid Dave Carr and Rothmann the butcher and Jimmy Davenport the grocer. He paid the man that had come with the mortgage, and found that, counting interest, he had paid him twice. He paid the man that hastened to Beef Slough with the glad hand outstretched; he paid the notes at Ben Woodward's bank, and woke up one morning with the blissful thought that he owed not a cent in the world.

Still the business grew and expanded; J. W. Van Sant & Son added to their fleet until they had twenty rafters at work and had reached easily the first place in the industry. Then it became too great to be managed from Le Claire or Davenport, and in 1883 Captain Pluck moved to Winona, Minnesota, whence he could better direct operations in the making and towing of rafts. He had been there only a few years when he was persuaded to be alderman from his ward. Next a delegation of his new townsmen came to ask him to be a candidate for the legislature.

At this Captain Pluck shied. He had always voted the Republican ticket, but he knew little about politics and the career political never looked good to him. He was a riverman. Rivermen should stick to the river.

His petitioners pointed out that the district was Democratic, but that if he would run, because of his great popularity, he could wrest it from the hated foe. So then, he being a good Republican, what was his duty before God and man? They asked him. Should he let personal preferences silence his tongue and palsy his right arm when he could strike a blow for righteousness? He admitted that this was something different again, and at last consented to put sacred duty above ease of mind, confidently expecting to be snowed under.

Instead, he went in with a bang, took his turn at the state capitol and made a first-class legislator. The next election, without effort, he won again, and when he took his seat was astonished to find that he was slated to be speaker of the House, a position to which he was chosen under conditions unusual in American politics. He was elected unanimously, Republicans,

319

Democrats, and Populists all following his band-wagon.

Admiring friends pointed out that he was the logical candidate for governor.

By this time he had acquired a notion that it was almost as much fun to steer a political ship as it was to steer a steamboat, and he conceded that he would like to be governor if the nomination were tendered to him by the convention.

The nomination was not tendered. Somebody else got in ahead with the required number of delegates, of which Van Sant had 158. "I wasn't running for the nomination," he assured the convention in a humorous speech; "I was only walking."

Two years later he gave an exhibition of running that startled the old-timers, for he appeared in the convention with 401 delegates. They were not quite enough and another got the prize award. On this occasion he made a speech that should have a place in American political oratory, a perfectly plain, frank, good-natured speech, a riverman's speech, in which he said he was not ashamed of having tried for the nomination and not cast down because he had not won it; that two years later he would be trying again, and that, meantime, his post-office address was Winona, Minnesota.

That speech made his nomination inevitable by the next convention.

He went into the campaign with the strongest man in the State running against him—John Lind, universally respected, known as "Honest John," and advantaged with an excellent record as governor.

Not for days after the election was the result known. Then it was apparent that Captain Pluck had won by 2254 votes.

"The intelligent raftsman," he had been sneeringly called by opponents lofty of brow. He had shown that at least he was intelligent enough to upset all their calculations.

When he stood up to be inaugurated, instead of placing his right hand upon the Bible, as was customary on such occasions, he placed it upon the shoulder of John Wesley Van Sant, who had come up from Le Claire to witness the ceremony. That day was his ninety-first birthday. The old firm had carried on to the end.

Captain Pluck made a great governor, but first and last had a plenty of trouble. James J. Hill was then the political master of six Western States, Minnesota being the first province in his domain. His career had been such as a fictionist might balk at. From obscurity and near-penury he had been lifted without investment or exertion into great wealth and the control of some of the most important railroad properties of the United States. Sudden success and power had made him confident and a little arrogant. He had lately added to his railroad possessions the Northern Pacific and now started to consolidate it with his own original railroad and private mint, the Great Northern, famous in Wall Street for its delectable melon produce.

An opposition arose that visibly astonished and annoyed him. Persons said that as these railroads were parallel and competing lines the laws of the State of Minnesota and the constitutions of six States affected absolutely forbade their consolidation.

"What's the Constitution between friends?" once observed Timothy Justinian Campbell, long-time congressman from the Dry Dock district of New York. Mr. Hill seems to have had a like generous view of this antique document. He announced the consolidation, constitution or no constitution, in November, 1901, and was proceeding sunnily with his plans, when he encountered a stupefying report that the governor of the

Hill province of Minnesota was against the project and would even take steps to prevent it.

This seemed to the governor's friends so unusual that they doubted it. They were not allowed to rest long in hopeful uncertainty.

One night in Winona the governor wrote out a statement that settled the matter, a clear-cut statement to the effect that the merger, being against the law, would be carried out in Minnesota over his political dead body—or words to that effect. He then telephoned to "The Winona Republican" office to send up a reporter.

The reporter came and read the statement with gasps.

"Governor," he said gravely, "you are committing political suicide. This will be the end of your career. I beg of you, don't do it. Here, let me tear it up. Nobody will ever know of it."

"No," said the governor. "It goes."

"When you had such a brilliant prospect—it's a shame and a crime to do such a thing. Think of your townspeople. They have been proud of you and expect you to go up higher."

"Well," said the governor, "I'll tell you—take it to your office and I will think about it. Then I will call you up and let you know." Ten minutes after he had reached his office, Captain Pluck had him on the wire with the information that the statement was to go exactly as written and go at once.

Friends came in troops and battalions to save his political life, urging that with prompt first aid he could still be resuscitated.

"But it's against the law," said Captain Pluck, and brought out the statute.

It was next expounded to him that he was acting against his own interests. It lay in Mr. Hill's power to reëlect him, and, besides, there were greater honors than being governor of Minnesota—political honors. Not for many years had there been a Vice-President from a Western State. How about that?

"But it's against the law," said Captain Pluck.

The machine of his party now started out to make an end of this strange, unpractical person. They could not, for insuperable reasons, prevent his renomination, but they knew how to deal with him when election day should come, and on all sides arose the sound of the ready knife upon the grindstone.

On January 7, 1902, the governor directed the attorney-general of the State to bring action against the merger and sat by to see his own ruin.

When the campaign came on, ruin was what lowered at him from every thicket. Mr. Hill made no secret of his wrath. He even took the stump himself against this renegade. For instance, he arranged a gigantic meeting at Crookston, which is a railroad town, and, to be sure of an audience of size, he ran excursion trains from all directions. Twelve thousand persons gathered to hear him describe the perils that awaited Minnesota if this evil man should again be governor.

. "He is the enemy of law and order," said Mr. Hill. "He is the enemy of progress. He is the enemy of prosperity and stability. He is the enemy of business. He is the enemy of this nation. He is the enemy of every railroad man. He is your enemy. Not in fifty years will Minnesota recover from the blow if he should again be its governor."

"Hooray!" shouted the crowd, led by Mr. Hill's employees. It was plain that he had made a deep impression.

Governor Van Sant came along soon afterward and desired a chance to refute Mr. Hill. He was not allowed to hold a meeting in Crookston nor in the county wherein Crookston lay.

It was a dismal, dreary, up-hill fight. His friends turned against him, the press was unkind, the political organization was generally hostile. The logging and lumber interests fought him with all their resources. Men for whom he had for years towed logs and regarded as warm friends would have nothing to do with him.

One night he was to speak in an important town in the logging region. A prominent committeeman came by stealth to his room in the hotel and explained that he could not attend the meeting nor give him any countenance. The hall was about a quarter filled with a dispirited and apathetic audience.

On election day he went back to Winona, where all the experts knew he was defeated. The next morning they awoke to the fact that he had carried the State by nearly 60,000. In the logging town where he could not draw an audience, he ran two thousand votes ahead of his record in the previous election. At Crookston, where he was not allowed to speak, he carried the county by 1700; two years before, he had lost it by 1800.

The people cheered Mr. Hill and voted for Captain Pluck.

The fame of his success and his defiance of corporate wealth went about the country and awoke surprised attention with loud applause. With others that gave heed to it was one that found in it something useful to him in his business. Theodore Roosevelt was then President of the United States and hailed as himself an opponent of the financial autocracy. He ordered his attorney-general, Philander Knox, to begin in the federal courts a suit against the merger similar to that Governor Van Sant was urging in the state courts. More attention was now centered upon the Minnesota man, and in 1904 he was widely mentioned as the appropriate candidate for Vice-President—Roosevelt and Van

Mr. Hill, Meet Captain Pluck

Sant, it was felt, would be a great ticket to win with. At the Republican National Convention, because Minnesota was viewed as surely Republican and Indiana was doubtful, Charles Warren Fairbanks was named for the second place. By so narrow a margin did Captain Pluck escape a national office. I violate no confidence in saying that Mr. Hill shed not a tear.

The suit in the federal courts against the Hill merger was pressed to a momentous conclusion. The Supreme Court upheld the position that from the first Governor Van Sant had affirmed and the merger was off. The case made history and passed into everlasting precedent. Many other legal complications have been smoothed out by the one decision in this Northern Securities case.

At the close of Captain Pluck's second term he might easily have had a third. But he was so quaintly old-fashioned that he reverenced his Revolutionary traditions, and particularly the example of Washington. Besides, the old firm had been dissolved by death, the river traffic had come to its melancholy decline, he had accumulated in it a modest fortune, and he determined to pass the rest of his life in quiet and leisure except for work in behalf of the Civil War veterans, of whose national organization he had been the head.

His retirement was coincident with the close of the great epoch in which he had been such a commanding figure. There had come an end to rafts and rafting.

Chapter XX

THE END FROM THE BEGINNING

THERE is rafting of logs on the River Elbe in Germany; much rafting of logs. All day long the rafts there follow one another down the stream as once rafts used to crowd the Mississippi. There has been rafting on the River Elbe for a thousand years. So far as any one can see, there is likely to be rafting on the River Elbe for a thousand years to come; much rafting.

Rafting and lumbering on the Mississippi lasted seventy years and ended. With it ended a great, useful, profitable industry.

So, then, Germany, an old country, thickly populated, keeps on with its lumbering century after century, and the Mississippi Valley, sparsely inhabited, exhausts in seventy years its once magnificent forests. Why is this?

Germany has laws by which its timber supply is conserved. For every tree that is cut down a tree must be planted. In the United States we have been free to waste and despoil and bid the future take care of itself or go hang. According to a government report made in 1910, a half century from that time would see the exhaustion of the last of the timber supply in the United States, once so inconceivably rich. A half century will not see the exhaustion of the timber supply in Germany.

The End from the Beginning

If the law of Germany had been the law of the United States, there would be to-day a like supply in the United States. The next generation in the United States, importing timber at fancy prices, is likely to read with wonder of the spoliation of what should have been its inheritance. With wonder but without a rhapsodical joy.

Yet one may recall that when Gifford Pinchot asked serious attention to the wrong we were inflicting upon our children and others, he was told in round terms to mind his own business, and when he persisted was tagged as a pestilent crank. It would be interesting to know what verdict the year 1950 will pass upon his warnings.

But so long as we allowed the Mississippi lumber business to go on it was a colossal activity. From Minneapolis to St. Louis all day sounded the buzz of saws and the rattle of logs on the runways. The crest came with 1892, and then the whole thing began to dry up and blow away faster than it had come. Of a sudden we awoke to the fact that the supply of white pine Providence had so wisely bestowed upon us as a reward of merit was not inexhaustible but almost done for. One by one the mills began to be abandoned. The rafts grew fewer and fewer and were always constructed of smaller logs, until they came to be made up of material that twenty years before would have been scorned. The rafting steamers were sold into the lower river or the Ohio trade or were broken up for sidewalks.

Long before that time the railroads had all but strangled the packet business.

At last the great and wonderful river that had once bustled with traffic lay virtually deserted. At rare intervals an excursion steamer would wake the lonely echoes of the bluffs with an unaccustomed whistle, but mostly the broad stream flowed on, year in and year

327

out, unruffled by a steamboat prow. The Government
continued to spend money upon its improvement, much
money; more money than ever before. It put in wing
dams, some of them where they might be of use; it
chiseled rocks on the rapids; it patrolled the vacant
waters for snags that now would never have caught
anything. The 359 crossing lights between Cairo and
St. Paul were burned religiously every night, but even
if any of them had been in the right positions there
was nothing to steer by them. It had been a great
chapter in the nation's real history; also a gorgeous
riot in the nation's great and always merry game of
waste. It ceased with the destruction of the last of
the providential pine-trees.

The closing page of the narrative was marked with
a singular reversal of what had been the normal tides
of commerce as of national expansion. For about fifty
years lumber moved westward from the Mississippi
across the prairies, even to Denver; moved in a great
stream of traffic. I went back to the river country a
few years ago and found the lumber stream moving
from West to East. To learn that Muscatine, Clinton,
Davenport, Dubuque were now getting their lumber
supplies from Oregon was a shock comparable to the
upsetting of all fundamental faith in nature. On the
site of a great mill at Muscatine I found a yard that
dealt only in pine brought across the continent, from
Puget Sound or something like that, and the world
seemed all topsy-turvy as I looked at it.

I went to Le Claire. The old sawmill was gone. Of
the town that had bustled with activity, half was dissolved away, half an inert suburb. Still the river flowed
out of the mystery above the point into the mystery
below the bend, and the shape of the bluffs was un-
changed. But the old boat-yard that had been the scene
of Captain Pluck's great fight and had built so many

The End from the Beginning

proud vessels and played so great a part in business
—that was a waste of weeds and silent as the grave.

In one corner was an object that seemed familiar. I
made a way to it and found it a discarded pilot-house.
The name board still remained, and pushing the weeds
aside I traced the outlines of the name—*Le Claire
Belle!* Often I had stood in that pilot-house with Captain Jack McCaffery and looked out upon a procession
of rafts going down the river and a procession of rafting steamers ascending it for more, and this was the
end of that vision.

Not far away was a sign over a wood-yard. It read:
"Oregon Pine."

Fate has no sense of humor, maybe, but it certainly
shows at times an extravagant predilection for irony.

The last scene of all in this passage of history was
not without a touch of sentiment. Of rafts upon the
Mississippi, the final raft started upon its voyage in
August, 1915. It was of lumber, as the first had been;
of lumber gathered from remnants left at mills that
had ceased and given over. It was towed by the steamer
Ottumwa Belle, last of her tribe. As they neared Albany, Illinois, the captain bethought him that there
was living in that town a man that had a peculiar and
unequaled interest in this funeral procession, a man
that had played a notable part in the raft story and
borne great honors in river navigation.

He sent a yawl ashore and invited this man to come
and ride upon the final raft of the Mississippi. The
man came. He stood in the pilot-house of the *Ottumwa
Belle* and held the wheel. He looked out at the scenes
that had been so familiar to him, noted with the pilot's
eye where the channel had changed, foretold with the
pilot's sixth sense where it would make other changes.
He rode as far as Davenport and saw the bridge swung
for the last time on a raft-boat. He landed and had

a reception from old rivermen and citizens and was escorted back to Albany.

It was Stephen Beck Hanks.

He had ridden upon one of the first lumber rafts that descended the Mississippi; he had piloted the first log raft. He had seen the beginning, the culmination, and the end; the whole thing had passed in one man's lifetime.

He died on October 7, 1917, two days before he would have begun his ninety-sixth year.

Aged ninety-five—it was a rare old age. Not for rivermen. With all the other remarkable facts about these remarkable men, one is struck with their longevity and the stretching out of the years in which they retained their faculties and were active. Captain Samuel S. Hanks, a brother of Stephen, lived to be ninety-five. Sixty-six years he had been upon the river; of forty-five steamboats he had been master or pilot. Captain William R. Tibbals, whose exploits with the *Key City* I have recounted, was active at ninety-one and lived to be ninety-four. Captain George Winans, commodore among pilots, the first man to tow a raft with a steamer on the river proper, lived to be eighty-seven and was at work almost to the time of his death. Captain Aaron Raymond Russell, one of the pilots that the British Government took to the Nile, died at the age of eighty-nine. Captain Max Blanchard, a pilot of the *R. E. Lee* in her immortal race with the *Natchez*, was sixty years on the river and lived to be eighty-seven. On March 28, 1916, Captain J. R. Williams of Warsaw attained to his one hundredth birthday, but passed out before he reached his one hundred and first. Captain E. E. Heerman of the *Minnietta* and of many other steamers, the man of so many strange adventures on his wedding day, celebrated his ninety-fourth birthday on April 18, 1928. Captain Oscar F. Knapp died at the age of

THE GREAT DOUBLE RAFT

*Three million feet of pine logs towed by the "J. W. Van Sant" with
the "Lydia Van Sant" for bow boat*

eighty-nine, Captain Augustus R. Ruley at eighty-seven, Captain E. W. Durant, who became a prosperous manufacturer, at eighty-seven, and Captain Edwin T. Root at eighty-four. In 1928 Captain Jerry M. Turner, whose encounter with the first search-light I have told, was ninety-two and still hale. He had traveled on the Mississippi more than 500,000 miles, and a third of his piloting had been done at night.

Captain Charles T. Hinde died in California, March 10, 1915, aged eighty-three. Captain Marcellus Stevens died in Downsville, Wisconsin, July 6, 1918, aged eighty-two.

Captain Daniel Smith Harris of the *Grey Eagle* and many other boats lived to be eighty-six.

Chief Engineer S. S. Fuller, of a family renowned in steamboat engineering, died at Minneapolis, November 15, 1925, aged eighty-three. His brother-in-law, Captain John T. Howard, veteran riverman, died at Hastings, Minnesota, October 13, 1925, aged eighty-four.

Captain John Geary, long chief pilot of the great packet *Northern Light* and then of many other noted vessels, lived to be eighty-three.

Past his eightieth birthday, Captain Ben P. Taber, whose adventures in the Civil War interested many readers of "The Burlington Post," was actively engaged in business at Keokuk.

Captain Grant Prince Marsh, the great hero of the Missouri River, died at Bismarck, North Dakota, at the age of eighty-two. It was he that after the hard fighting in the Little Big Horn region, June, 1876, when Custer had been defeated, took the steamboat *Far West* down the Big Horn, Yellowstone, and Missouri rivers to Fort A. Lincoln, at Bismarck, nearly a thousand miles of strange and dangerous waterways, in fifty-four hours, and cast an imperishable glory over the noble art of piloting, for the *Far West* was loaded with wounded and he was saving their lives.

At a dinner of pioneer rivermen, St. Paul, 1916, appeared a rosy-cheeked and sprightly young fellow whom nobody knew.

"Are you looking for the rivermen's dinner?" asked Captain Fred Bill.

"Sure I am."

"But you're not an old riverman, are you?"

"Sure I am."

"When did you leave the river?"

"In 1856."

It was William Cairncross, whose remarkable adventures on the lower river and the frontier Captain Bill was afterward to publish. Cairncross was then aged eighty-seven.

Captain William Davis, an old raft pilot, died at North Superior, Wisconsin, October 22, 1918, aged 106 years.

In the history of packet navigation, no master's name is encountered more often than that of Captain Alexander Lamont. In July, 1917, he being then eighty-five, he piloted the steamer *Illinois*, belonging to the National Guard, from Alton up the Illinois River to Hardin and back, without the least difficulty, although he had not seen the Illinois for many years.

Captain Isaac H. Moulton, who danced so well and swore so competently, lived to be ninety. Horace Bixby, with whom Mark Twain was a cub, was still piloting at eighty-two. At eighty, William Ward, who did his first rafting in 1843, was in business at Winona Lake. William H. Glynn, who had been an engineer, died at Lansing, Iowa, April 1, 1926, aged ninety-three, leaving thirty-eight grandchildren, seventy-six great-grandchildren, and two great-great-grandchildren.

When he was eighty-four, Captain Pluck Van Sant

drove a pioneer wagon in a pageant through the streets of Minneapolis, and in Washington was consulting with the President and vigorously engineering veterans' pensions bills through Congress.

Every riverman will know that this list is incomplete and will be able to supplement it.

How does it happen, all this longevity in the trade?

I shall be told that the open-air life accounts for it; that and the careful walk, for of course all these octogenarians had steered away from the hot and rebellious liquor trap and could never have wooed the means of debility. But to my mind there was something more.

It was the gift of the river; with this she rewarded her devotees. Not mystically—reasonably. One and all having the love of her in his heart, to the end of his days had her for a vital interest. Life never grew stale or weary for him. To watch the river and talk about the river and dream about the river and recall old scenes on the river and old stories about the river and snap up every line of news about the river and tell again his days and ways of love for the river—it was enough. Men wear out first in their spirits. No riverman's spirit flagged so long as he could remember the river.

But we were speaking of Stephen Beck Hanks.

Among the changes that had passed before his eyes was a great increase in the size of the rafts and consequently in the difficulties of navigation and the responsibilities of pilots. When he began, a raft three hundred feet long was deemed of a good bulk. I will give some records of the later days to afford a comparison.

The smart steamer *F. C. A. Denckman,* a raft-boat in the Weyerhaeuser & Denckman interests, brought from West Newton to Rock Island a raft 1625 feet long and 275 feet wide. Captain Otis McGinley was in charge. When he stood in the pilot-house the bow of his raft was almost a third of a mile away. The handling of such a body of logs around the curves and over the crossings of the Mississippi, in daylight and in dark, is, to my mind, as great a triumph of man's technical skill as the history of all navigation affords.

Captain Orrin Smith of Le Claire commanded the bow boat on this occasion. It was his father, Captain John E. Smith, one of the great men of the old days, that invented the bow boat.

With his celebrated *Saturn*, Commodore George Winans, in 1901, towed from Stillwater a lumber raft of sixteen strings, forty-four cribs long. Allowing for the space between the cribs, this would mean a raft 1450 feet long and 270 feet wide.

In these records Captain Pluck and his associates had full part. Among log rafts still clacked about in river towns was one of theirs. The first *J. W. Van Sant* had gone the way of mortal handiwork and the firm built another; also a bow boat named for Captain Pluck's mother, *Lydia Van Sant*. These, with Captain George Twombley of Le Claire in charge, brought down a double-decker log raft that was 1400 feet long and 276 feet wide. It was in fact two rafts, one upon the other, the lower raft having the logs lengthwise of the stream and the upper with logs at right angles to the lower.

In 1907 the steamer *E. Rutledge*, Captain William Whisler, brought to Rock Island a raft 1430 feet long and 285 feet wide. Captain Robert N. Cassidy, another historic figure in these pursuits, is said to have brought down a raft that was more than 1700 feet long, but I have not found a record of it.

It would be perilous to say that any one of these was the largest raft ever floated upon the Mississippi, because that would be to touch a question still hotly disputed, but assuredly they are among the largest. In one way the *Saturn's* was the chief, because, while it was not so long as the *Denckman's*, it contained more lumber. In the *Saturn's* raft were 704 cribs, each 32 by 16 feet and containing twenty-six courses of boards, or 13,312 feet in each crib. This would give an apparent total of 9,371,648 feet. But it is necessary to make deductions for the space about the grub-pins. Allowing 10 per cent. for this, we have 8,434,284 feet as the contents of the raft itself. Most of it was consigned to a firm in Lyons, Iowa, and nearly every crib of this consignment carried from 3000 to 5000 feet of stock boards, piled on top as deck-loading. It is safe to say, therefore, that this raft contained more than 9,000,000 feet of lumber. About nine hundred freight-cars would have been required to transport this amount. The raft occupied more than six acres of space and must have made in its voyage something like two hundred crossings, without mentioning bars, tow heads, and bridges that it must negotiate.

Commodore Winans, who performed this feat, kept a record of 975,000,000,000 feet of lumber that he transported in rafts. He had been in the business some time before he began his record, so that it is safe to say this one man steered down the Mississippi more than a billion feet of lumber.

Or again, as to the size of the business that thus waxed and waned in one man's lifetime, let me quote a few figures.

We have seen that the pine-woods that contributed their logs and lumber to the Mississippi were in five regions, being the basins of the Wisconsin, the Black, the Chippewa, the St. Croix and the upper Mississippi above the Falls of St. Anthony.

We will take the region of the St. Croix as an example. In a paper prepared by an expert for the Minnesota State Historical Society,[1] the cut of logs for rafting purposes, whether as logs or lumber, was given year by year from 1837 to 1898 inclusive. I run down the list and select sample years:

Year	Logs cut, feet	Year	Logs Cut, feet
1837-1838	300,000	1870	165,000,000
1840	1,500,000	1875	121,389,720
1845	15,000,000	1880	214,444,000
1850	75,000,000	1885	225,520,800
1855 135,000,000		1890	452,360,890
1860 150,000,000		1895	353,062,850
1865 130,000,000		1898	344,728,217

The total output for the whole period was 10,050,-303,207 feet. To this we must add 7,359,000,000 feet of lumber manufactured in the St. Croix region and shipped out by rail. This gives as the total output of the region in fifty-one years, seventeen billion feet.

But even these figures are much short of the reality, for they cover the cut until only the year 1899.

In 1904 Captain Edward W. Durant, a well-known authority, estimated the total cut of the St. Croix region that floated through Lake St. Croix from 1837 to 1903 inclusive at 15,083,781,000 feet. Adding 7,800,000,000 feet as the amount cut and shipped out by rail, the total to 1903 is about twenty-three billion feet, a record without a fellow in the history of the world outside of the United States.

In the upper Mississippi region, that is to say above St. Anthony's Falls, logging began late, and up to 1848 the total cut was no more than 2,000,000 feet. How it grew thereafter is to be seen in this little table.[2]

[1] Vol. IX.
[2] "History of Pioneer Lumbering on the Upper Mississippi and Its Tributaries," by Daniel Stanchfield.

The End from the Beginning

Period	Total Cut in Feet
1848 to 1850	12,000,000
1851 to 1860	315,373,561
1861 to 1870	817,840,410
1871 to 1880	1,813,425,027
1881 to 1890	3,428,596,480
1891 to 1899	4,482,444,728
Total	10,869,632,106

Statistics are lacking for the Chippewa, the Wisconsin, and the Black. There is reason to believe that together these regions contributed as much as either the St. Croix or the upper Mississippi; perhaps more. Even if we assume the aggregate to be approximately that of the upper Mississippi, we have a total of more than forty billion feet, a sum before which the imagination staggers, equal to about eight million miles, or enough to make a lumber chain thirty-three times between the earth and the moon.

Virtually all of this was once the property of the people of the United States.

In the literature of waste, this is the Iliad.

The forests are gone and will not come back, but the river remains and offers to man, as before, help for his practical needs and consolation for his spirit. Some day these people will awake to the other and less understandable waste that lies in the transporting of heavy commodities upon costly, artificial, and perishable highways, while the cheap, natural, everlasting highway goes unused past the front door. Some day, also, these people, turning their eyes at last to their own possessions, will rediscover the wealth of the beauty that belongs to this incomparable and neglected stream and may deem it better than all the other wealth that their fathers wasted.

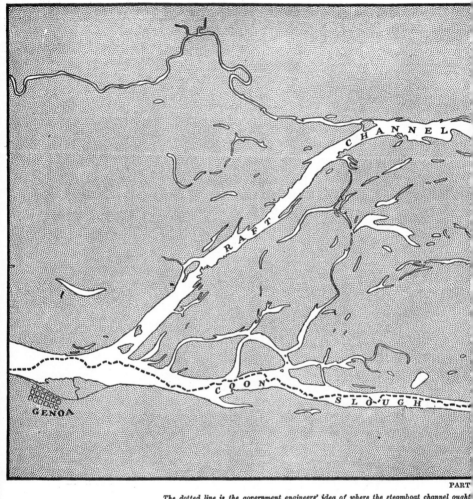

Labels within the map: CHANNEL, RAFT, COON, SLOUGH, GENOA

The dotted line is the government engineers' idea of where the steamboat channel ought

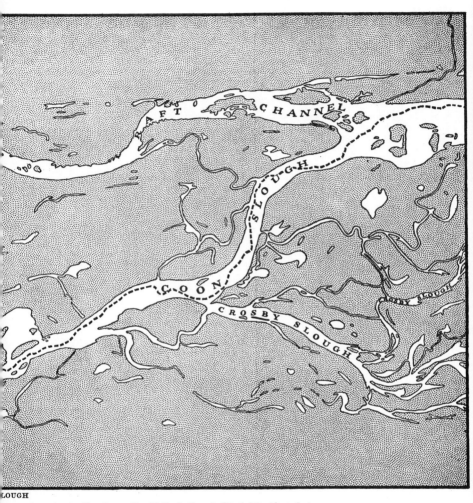

Appendix A

UPPER MISSISSIPPI RIVER DISTANCES

Compiled from the government surveys. It is to be noted that the Government measures distances along the middle of the channel and in consequence its figures are everywhere less than the accepted figures of rivermen, who measure the distance traveled by a steamboat between two points.

FROM ST. LOUIS TO ST. PAUL

	Distance in miles from St. Louis		Distance in miles from St. Louis
Alton, Illinois	25	Camanche, Iowa	348
Hannibal, Missouri	137	Albany, Illinois	350
Keokuk, Iowa	194	Clinton, Iowa	355
Montrose, Iowa	206	Fulton, Illinois	357
Nauvoo, Illinois	206.6	Lyons, Iowa	357
Fort Madison, Iowa	215	Sabula, Iowa	373
Burlington, Iowa	237	Savannah, Illinois	375
Muscatine, Iowa	290	Bellevue, Iowa	395
Andalusia, Illinois	308	Gordon's Ferry, Iowa	405
Buffalo, Iowa	308	Dubuque, Iowa	419
Davenport, Iowa	317	Specht's Ferry, Iowa	432
Rock Island, Illinois	317	Cassville, Wisconsin	447
Moline, Illinois	321	Clayton, Iowa	466
Hampton, Illinois	327	McGregor, Iowa	475
Rapids City, Illinois	332	Prairie du Chien, Wisconsin	477
Port Byron, Illinois	333		
Le Claire, Iowa (Head of Rapids)	333	Harper's Ferry, Iowa	487
		Lansing, Iowa	505
Princeton, Iowa	338	De Soto, Wisconsin	509

341

Appendix A

Appendix B

A RAFTSMAN'S ORATORY

The celebrated speech of Captain Van Sant when defeated
for the Republican nomination for governor in 1898. From
H. P. Hall's book entitled "Observations," pp. 304 *et seq.*

After [the nominee] had made his acceptance speech, Van Sant,
who was present, was called upon to respond as one of the defeated candidates, and he did so in a most manly way. I quote what
he said as an object lesson. These were his words on that occasion:

"Mr. Chairman and Gentlemen of the Convention:
"As I sat on the platform listening to the speech of my successful
rival, the thought occurred to me that if it seemed 'funeral-like' to
him while waiting at the Windsor for the result of your deliberations,
just imagine my feelings! He won! I lost! I had hoped to return
to my home occupying a front seat on the band wagon; instead, I
go back in the hearse. Again, imagine my embarrassment! I prepared
a speech to deliver to this convention, but alas, it would not be appropriate for this occasion. Besides, I have been for six months talking
to the Republicans of Minnesota, and it does not seem to have done
much good. Why should I speak more. But, my friends and fellow-
workers in the vineyard of the Republican party, I want to say right
here and now that from a full heart I thank the four hundred true
and tried men who stood by me through thick and thin and to the
last, and have only the kindliest feeling toward those who opposed
my nomination. There was but one trouble—I did not have soldiers
enough. Let me assure you that there are no sore spots on me. I
most earnestly congratulate Mr. Eustis; he fairly won the nomination. Like him I, too, thought I heard a voice two years ago. I was
mistaken. He heard the call; it remains with us to make the election
sure. We are all Republicans, but no Republican will carry the flag
farther into the enemy's camp during the coming fall than I will
unless he have a stronger constitution or greater ability. This will
be a Republican year, a glorious year of sunshine; already the
warming glow of prosperity is assured. The promise of McKinley
and prosperity is a fact, and business conditions are so rapidly and
permanently improving that our country is destined soon to become
and remain the greatest on the face of the earth.
"Again I congratulate you, Mr. Eustis, not only upon your nomination but upon the glorious victory that awaits you in November;
and to the end that it may be as nearly unanimous as possible let

Appendix B

us all return to our homes and go zealously to work burying our hatchets, if we have any, so deeply that they will never again be resurrected. Personally, I am satisfied, and am ready for the conflict. I have been carefully taking account of my political assets; I find that all I have remaining is my post office address. If you desire my services in the coming campaign all you will have to do is to address me at Winona. I will fight just as hard as a private soldier and in the trenches as if your leader and in command. I believe in the grand old party, its success brings prosperity to all the people. No disappointments, however great, can cause me to sulk in my tent; I weigh two hundred pounds, and every ounce of it is for my party and its candidates.

"Gentlemen of the convention, in closing let me assure you that there is some compensation even in defeat. I shall go home to family and friends to rest and to quiet, while Mr. Eustis assumes the strenuous duties of campaign and office. The happier man I."

On this Mr. Hall makes the following comment:

This was as manly an acceptance of defeat as has ever occurred in the state, and I give space to what Governor Van Sant said in this book for the purpose of showing the younger politicians the wise way of accepting their defeats. Do not nurse a common boil and endeavor to enlarge it into a first-class carbuncle. Take for your lesson the manly course of Governor Van Sant on that occasion. A man cannot always win in politics, but if he allows defeat to sour and embitter him, he can always be a sorehead and never again come to the front. It was really Van Sant's speech at the time of his defeat which made him, later, governor of the state. He received at that time scores of pledges of support in the future. Pledges are not always honored, but in this case they were. As the result proved, his defeat for the nomination was the greatest victory which could have come to him. . . .

The defeat of Eustis made the pathway clear for a new deal in 1900. The Republican convention met in St. Paul on June 28th of that year, and then Van Sant was in his element. Scarcely any other candidate was talked of, and when it came to the selection of governor he was nominated by acclamation by a rising vote. His speech of two years previous had not been forgotten. A young man entering politics had better turn back and re-read this speech and take it to heart if he wishes to prosper in a political career. I regard it as a model method of accepting defeat.

Appendix C

THE RIVER BARD

HOME MADE POETRY ONCE POPULAR ON THE MISSISSIPPI

The author of this compilation that follows is unknown. It seems to have been circulated by recitation, after the manner of true folklore, but finally got into print. In 1927 it was resurrected by Mr. F. X. Ralphe of Hastings, Minnesota, who found it among old papers and sent it to "The Burlington Post." Old rivermen recognized it as a once popular ballad of nomenclature. All the names are of steamboats once well known on the river and most of them raft boats.

The *Fred Weyerhaeuser* and the *Frontenac*,
The *F. C. A. Denckmann* and the *Bella Mac*,
The *Menomenee* and *Louisville*,
The *R. J. Wheeler* and *Jessie Bill*,
The *Robert Semple* and the *Golden Gate*,
The *C. J. Caffery* and the *Sucker State*.

The *Charlotte Boeckler* and the *Silver Wave*,
The *John H. Douglas* and *J. K. Graves*,
The *Isaac Staples* and the *Helen Mar*,
The *Henrietta* and the *North Star*,
The *David Bronson* and *Nettie Durant*,
The *Kit Carson* and *J. W. Van Sant*.

The *Chauncey Lamb* and the *Evansville*,
The *Blue Lodge* and the *Minnie Will*,
The *Saturn* and the *Satellite*,
The *Le Claire Belle* and the *Silas Wright*,
The *Artemas Lamb* and the *Pauline*,
The *Douglas Boardman* and *Kate Keen*.

The *I. E. Staples* and the *Mark Bradley*,
The *J. G. Chapman* and the *Julia Hadley*,
The *Mollie Whitmore* and *C. K. Peck*,
The *Robert Dodds* and *Borealis Rex*,
The *Pete Kerns* and the *Wild Boy*,
The *Lilly Turner* and the *St. Croix*.

345

Appendix C

The *A. T. Jenks* and *Bart Linehan,*
The *C. W. Cowles* and *Brother Jonathan,*
The *Pete Wilson* and *Anna Girdon,*
The *Inverness* and the *L. W. Barden,*
The *Nellie Thomas* and the *Enterprise,*
The *Park Painter* and *Hiram Price.*

The *Dan Hines* and the *City of Winona,*
The *Helen Schulenburg* and *Natrona,*
The *Flying Eagle* and the *Moline,*
The *E. Ruthledge* and *Josephine,*
The *Taber* and the *Irene D,*
The *D. A. McDonald* and *Jessie B.*

The *Gardie Eastman* and the *Vernie Swain,*
The *James Malbon* and the *L. W. Crane*
The *Sam Atlee* and *William White,*
The *Lumberman* and the *Penn Wright,*
The *Stillwater* and the *Volunteer,*
The *James Fisk Jr.* and the *Reindeer.*

The *Thistle* and the *Mountain Bell,*
The *Little Eagle* and the *Gazelle,*
The *Mollie Mohler* and the *James Means,*
The *Silver Crescent* and the *Muscatine,*
The *Jim Watson* and the *Last Chance,*
The *Kate Waters* and the *Ed. Durant,*
The *Dan Thayer* and the *Flora Clark,*
The *Robert Ross* and the *J. G. Park,*
The *Eclipse* and *J. W. Mills,*
The *J. S. Keator* and the *J. J. Hill,*
The *Lady Grace* and the *Abner Gile,*
The *Johnnie Schmoker* and the *Georgie Lysle,*
The *Lafayette Lamb* and the *Clyde,*
The *B. Hershey* and the *Time and Tide.*

Index

Afton, see *Effie Afton.*

Albany, Illinois, river town; place of settlement of the Hanks family, 80; as a winter harbor for pilots, 245; the "ash-can pilots" of, 245.

Amulet, the, Mississippi packet, caught in the ice in Lake Pepin and rescued by Hanks, 110-111.

Annie Girdon, the, side-wheel raft boat, 157.

Annie Johnston, the, race with *Phil Sheridan,* 280-281.

Anthony Wayne, the, Minnesota River packet, makes a record with Hanks as pilot, 116.

Bad Axe, battle of, 18.

"Banditti of the Prairies," the, operations and alleged extent of, 163-170; partly exposed and broken up by Edward Bonney, 164-173; murder Colonel George Davenport, 167.

Bean pot, the, in the lumber camp, 51-52.

Bill Henderson, the, Mississippi packet, origin of its name, 268.

Bill Nye, adventures and observations in a lumber camp, 53-54.

Birch, ——, arrested by Edward Bonney for the murder of Miller and Liecey, 170-171; escape, 172.

Blackhawk, Indian chief, career and death, 14-18.

Blackhawk War, origin, 13-17; battle of Stillman's Run, 17; battle of Bad Axe, 18; end of the war, 18; results in settlement of Mississippi basin, 19.

Black River raftsmen, the terror they inspired, 4-10.

Blakely, Captain Russell, master of the *Dr. Franklin No. 2,* 120; experience with the Rollingstone colonists, 120-127.

Boiler explosions on early steamboats, a record of, 29; on the *Princess,* 30-31; on the *Geneva,* 31; on the *James Malbon,* 31; on the *Lansing,* 31.

Bonney, Edward, detective, takes up the Miller and Liecey murders, 164-165; arrests the three Hodges, 165; takes them to Iowa for identification, 166; hanging of Stephen and William Hodges, 166; murder of Col. George Davenport, July 4, 1845, 167; undertakes to run down murderers, 168; encounters Granville Young on the *War Eagle,* 168-170; learns trail of the assassins, 170; arrests Fox, Birch, John and Aaron Long as the murderers, 170-171; escape of Fox, 171; trial and hanging of John and Aaron Long and Granville Young, 171; escape of Birch, 172; charges against Bonney, 172; the picture on the *Lamartine,* 172-173.

"Buffalo Gals," raftsmen's song, alleged history of, 211; attempt to improve, 217, 219.

Burlington, city of, 213.

Camanche, Iowa, scene of the great cyclone of 1860, 143-144.

"Captain Pluck," origin of title, 237-238.

Cassville, Wisconsin, decayed city of the upper river, 122-123.

347

Index

Chicago-St. Louis rivalry for the Mississippi basin trade, 64-65, 70-72.

City Belle, the Mississippi packet, in last phase of story of Cap' Heerman's wedding day, 264.

Clinton, Iowa, city of, 231, 242.

Clinton bridge, error in its construction, 100-101; hit by the *Julia's* raft, 274-275.

Clinton, the, Mississippi packet, narrow escape of, 225-226.

Coon Slough, Hanks's raft in, 88-89; *Nominee, Lady Franklin,* and *Reindeer* sunk in, 256-257.

"Corn-Fed Girl," the, story of, 217-219.

"Crabs" as a means of controlling rafts, 158.

Crime in the Mississippi Valley in early days, 163-164.

Cyclone, see Camanche.

D. A. McDonald, the rafting steamboat built by the Van Sants, 227; explosion on, 228; raising of the wreck of, 229-230; sunk at Keokuk bridge and again raised by S. R. Van Sant, 236-238; city council objects to her landing at Keokuk, 237.

Darragh, J. W., Mississippi River captain, his record of steamboat disasters, 29.

Davenport bridge, attempts to have it legally abolished, 65, 70-72; attempt to destroy by fire, 65; Captain Merrick's opinion of, 73-74; causes the wreck of the *Grey Eagle*, 74-78; one method of running it in safety, 101; raft traffic through in 1873, 238; Rapids Pilot Dorrance's work at, 283.

Davenport, city of, 19.

Davenport, Colonel George, early pioneer, 22; his career, 167; his villa, 167; pilots the *Virginia* over the Le Claire Rapids, 167;

murdered by the "Banditti of the Prairies," 167.

Davidson, Commodore W. F., noted riverman, thinks the *Mc-Donald* wrecked beyond rescue, 236; when he got religion, 303, 306-307; his controversy with Joseph Reynolds, 305-306.

Davis, John B., early Mississippi captain, attempts to transport his vessel to Big Stone Lake, 28-29.

Democracy on the river, 288.

Des Moines River, early navigation on, 22, 25-28.

Diamond Jo line, origin of, 305-306.

Disasters, steamboat, see Darragh, J. W.

Dr. Franklin No. 2, race with the *Nominee,* 117-120; brings part of the Rollingstone expedition, 120-128; sunk in collision with the *Galena* in Maquoketa Slough, 129.

Dorrance, Captain Dana, takes *Menomenee's* raft through Davenport bridge without stopping, 283.

Doughty, Thomas, chief engineer, birth and education, 148; comes to Le Claire, 148; a "hot" engineer, 149; enlists in the national army, Civil War, 149; invents the periscope, 150; it saves the U.S.S. *Osage* and wins a great victory, 150-151; studies the rafting problem and builds the *Le Claire*, first sternwheel raft boat, 151, 155-157; failure of the *Le Claire*, 156-157.

Drenning, Thomas G., Mississippi pilot, the "Jim Bludso" of the burning *Galena*, 138-139.

Dubuque, city of, 19, 21, 34; growth of, 213; advantages of, 242.

Dubuque, Julien, early French pioneer, 12.

348

Index

Index

Index

Index

Index

rance's feat at Davenport bridge, 283; fraternal feeling among pilots, 287-288; pilots as weather prognosticators, 293.

Pinchot, Gifford, efforts to conserve national resources, 327.

Pine, the primeval forests of, 20; filched from public, 40-49; land-grant swindle, 41-42; theft of timber, 42; the "timber cruiser," 43-44; false entries, 45-47; George Henry Warren's discoveries concerning these frauds, 46-48; terrorizing tactics at auction sales, 48-49; change in the character of the workers, 50; a typical lumber camp, 50-51.

"Pock Marked Lynch," leader of the riot on the *Dubuque*, 201, 203-204.

Prairie du Chien, city of, 89.

Prairie State, the, Mississippi packet, burning of with the *Kentucky No. 2*, 182.

Princess, the, boiler explosion on, 30-31.

Profanity on the river, 289-290.

Racing, Tom Doughty on, 278; fixed instinct in all rivermen, 279; how prohibition of was evaded, 279-280; the *Grey Eagle* versus the *Hannibal City*, 75; the *Grey Eagle* versus the *Itasca*, 76; the *Dr. Franklin No. 2* versus the *Nominee*, 117-120; the *War Eagle* versus the *Galena*, 134-135; the *Phil Sheridan* versus the *Annie Johnston*, 280-281; the *Louisville* versus the *Menomenee*, 281-282.

Raft, floating, record trip of, 283.

Raft, log, the making of one, 78-79; first to be towed down the Mississippi, 152-155; early experiences in towing, 184-187.

Rafting, growth of business illustrated, 238.

Rafts, lumber, the method of making them, 81-82; notably large, 334-335.

Raftsmen, old style, 104-105; ill-will between them and steamboatmen, 136-137; amusements ashore, 189-191; disappearance of the old type of, 199; their songs, 206-210; parasites that preyed upon, 213-217.

Railroad land grants, swindle of, 41-42.

Read's Landing, Mississippi town, deserted city of the upper river, 121; scene of battlings between raftsmen and steamboatmen, 193-195.

Red Wing, city of, 83; once great wheat market, 222.

Reindeer, the, Mississippi raft boat, wrecked on the wrecks of the *Nominee* and *Lady Franklin*, 257.

Reynolds, Joseph ("Diamond Jo"), early history, 304-305; his quarrel with Commodore Davidson, 305-306; starts the Diamond Jo packet line, 306.

Riot on the *Galena*, quelled by Hanks, 136; historic riot on the *Dubuque*, 200-204.

Rivermen, their fondness for the river, 239-241; instances of remarkable longevity among, 330-332.

Robert, Captain Louis, early pioneer and steamboatman, tied up by a strike at Galena, 37; early history, 85; adventures in the New Ulm massacre, 85-86.

Rock Island, city of, how the *Fortune* sailed over its site in 1840, 33; growth of, 213.

Rock River, early navigation on, 21, 23.

Rockingham, Iowa, extinct city, 120-121.

Rollingstone, tragic history of, 120-128.

Index

Index

Index

CHARLES EDWARD RUSSELL (1860–1941) was born in Davenport, Iowa. He was one of the most prominent journalists of the muckraking era and is perhaps best known for his scathing exposés of the beef and tobacco trusts. He also wrote of the racial and industrial conditions in the South for the *New York Herald*, an experience that led him to civil rights activism. In 1909 he cofounded the National Association for the Advancement of Colored People (NAACP). He was a member of the Socialist Party and a candidate for governor of New York in 1910 and 1912. The author of twenty-seven books, he won the Pulitzer Prize for biography in 1927 for *The American Orchestra and Theodore Thomas*.